BRITAIN by BRITRAIL
How to Tour Britain by Train '

Help Us Keep This Guide Up to Date

Every effort has been made by the authors and editors to make this guide as accurate and useful as possible. However, many things can change after a guide is published—establishments close, phone numbers change, facilities come under new management, etc.

We would love to hear from you concerning your experiences with this guide and how you feel it could be made better and be kept up to date. While we may not be able to respond to all comments and suggestions, we'll take them to heart and we'll also make certain to share them with the authors. Please send your comments and suggestions to the following address:

The Globe Pequot Press
Reader Response/Editorial Department
P.O. Box 833
Old Saybrook, CT 06475

Or you may e-mail us at:

editorial@globe-pequot.com

Thanks for your input, and happy travels!

BRITAIN by BRITRAIL
How to Tour Britain by Train

Nineteenth Edition

written by
LaVerne Ferguson

edited by
Stephanie Bell

The Globe Pequot Press

Old Saybrook, Connecticut

The author and the publisher gratefully acknowledge the kind permission of the *Great Britain Passenger Railway Timetable,* of Eurostar Passenger Service and its Web site, and of the *Deutsche Bahn Kursbuch* to use their resources in the compilation of the timetables in this text. The rail maps on pp. vi-vii and all ferry schedules are reproduced courtesy of the *Thomas Cook European Timetable.*

Cover photo: courtesy of Intercity
Cover design: Laura Augustine
Inset photo: © Charlie Westerman/Liaison International
Text and map design: Paul Costello

ISSN: 1081-1117
ISBN: 0-7627-0313-X

Manufactured in the United States of America
Nineteenth Edition/First Printing

DEDICATION

This book is dedicated to the memory of my late husband and dearest friend, George Wright Ferguson.

George was coauthor of *Britain by BritRail* and *Europe by Eurail* and was instrumental in educating the public about how to maximize the economy, convenience, and pure enjoyment of rail travel in Britain and contintental Europe.

In the travel industry, he was known as "Mr. Eurail." The staff of Rail Pass Express, Inc., and I pledge to continue George's legacy and passion for train travel by providing the most current rail information combined with the best customer service.

Rail nomad and adventurer, great educator and friend, we all miss you!

Larne
Coleraine
Portrush
Antrim
BELFAST
LONDONDERRY
Newry
Dundalk
Drogheda
Dun Laoghaire
DUBLIN
Wicklow
Bray
Wexford
Rosslare
Kilkenny
Waterford
Donegal
Enniskillen
Carrick on Shannon
Longford
Mullingar
Ballybrophy
Thurles
Cahir
Ballina
Sligo
Claremorris
Athlone
Portarlington
Roscrea
Limerick Junction
Mallow
CORK
Westport
Galway
Tralee
Killarney

Kirkwall
Stromness
Thurso
Scrabster
Wick
Helmsdale
Georgemas Junction
Lairg
Dingwall
Inverness
Garve
Kyle of Lochalsh
Invergordon
Nairn
Elgin
Keith
Dyce
ABERDEEN
Arbroath
Montrose
DUNDEE
Aviemore
Pitlochry
Perth
Stirling
Kirkcaldy
EDINBURGH
Berwick
NEWCASTLE
Sunderland
Hartlepool
Middlesbrough
Whitby
Durham
Darlington
Galashiels
Hexham
Appleby
Penrith
Keswick
Carlisle
Ambleside
Windermere
Whitehaven
Workington
Stornoway
Uig
Ullapool
Lochmaddy
Lochboisdale
Tarbert
Mallaig
Fort William
Crianlarich
Oban
Kilchoan
Port Askaig
Port Ellen
Tiree
Kennacraig
Claonaig
Lochranza
Brodick
Largs
Ardrossan
GLASGOW
Kilmarnock
Ayr
Girvan
Cairnryan
Stranraer
Dumfries
Portrush
Coleraine
Antrim
Londonderry
BELFAST

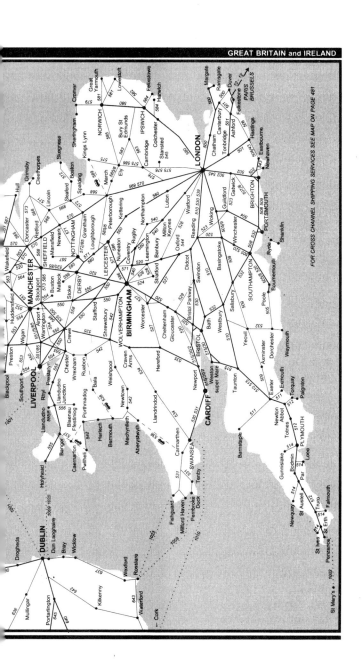

FOR CROSS CHANNEL SHIPPING SERVICES SEE MAP ON PAGE 481

Contents

The *Britain by BritRail* Team

LaVerne Ferguson and her late husband and business partner, George, first co-authored this unique and comprehensive guide to touring Britain by train in 1984. Unfortunately, in 1993 George's illnesses prevented him from participating further. Sadly, he passed away in November 1997 and was buried with full military honors at Arlington National Cemetery in Washington, D.C. George, a gentleman who had a great passion for trains and an even greater commitment to passing on the joy of riding the rails to fellow travelers, is missed not only by us at Ferguson Rail Publications and Rail Pass Express, Inc. but also by many friends and acquaintances around the world. He is irreplaceable.

Before leaving the team, George—globally and affectionately known as "Mr. Eurail"—wanted to ensure that accurate British and European rail travel information would continue to be available to tourists. LaVerne has maintained his legacy by providing the best rail travel information, products, and guidebooks to the independent traveler.

LaVerne's technical writing and editorial background, her academic education in English, world history, and communications, and her experience in research and development for an international research institute add considerable substance to her twenty-two years of traveling the rails in Britain and throughout Europe. She also custom-designed European tour packages and itineraries for individuals and groups. Calling Columbus, Ohio, her home—but Europe her "backyard"—LaVerne had dreamed of traveling the world since discovering, in third-grade geography class, that there was so much to see, learn, and do. She pursued her goals through higher education at The Ohio State University, and by living in and traveling throughout Europe.

LaVerne is director of the international research/writing teams of Ferguson Rail Publications, Inc. and Rail Pass Express, Inc. She is dedicated to staying on track with the latest rail information and continuing to update the successful guidebooks—*Britain by BritRail* (now in its nineteenth edition) and *Europe by Eurail* (now in its twenty-third edition). She also is President and CEO of Rail Pass Express, Inc., the Columbus, Ohio–based company begun by the Fergusons in 1986.

Rail Pass Express, Inc. has now blossomed into one of the largest consumer-focused European rail sales outlets in the world. The well-trained (pun intended) and well-traveled staff at Rail Pass Express, Inc. provides informational resources and rail-travel products necessary to pursue the itineraries and concepts as outlined in the Ferguson guidebooks, *Britain by BritRail* and *Europe by Eurail*.

The Team

LaVerne's team of international researchers and all employees of Rail Pass Express, Inc. share her devotion to and enthusiasm for the exciting world of European train travel—its comfort, speed, and continuous adventure.

Britain by BritRail's team is devoted to producing a comprehensive, practical, yet friendly guidebook to touring Britain by train. As proven by its continuing best-selling status, Ferguson's popular Base City–Day Excursion™ concept really works.

• **Stephanie Bell**, Editor, employs her excellent editorial and research skills on the Ferguson guidebooks and maintains an extensive European rail research library. A multifaceted graduate of Fine Arts from Ohio Wesleyan University with an extensive publicity and creative background, Stephanie also contributes her valuable abilities to the Marketing Department of Rail Pass Express, Inc.

• **Karen Cherdron,** Administrative Assistant, is the vital link between the British and European railroads and our customers. Key in accurate information and product flow, she plays an integral customer relations and overall business operations role. Karen has also traveled extensively throughout Britain and Europe—we are grateful she calls Columbus home.

• **Sheila Clowes,** Training Supervisor, is originally from London,

England. She is credited for maintaining the highest-quality customer-service standards of the company's representatives. Sheila was instrumental in investigating and updating key changes in rail-station facilities and operations in Britain. She also assists in expanding the British resource library of Rail Pass Express, Inc. We are proud to call her our "Resident Expert" on all things British.

• **Mary DiThomas**, Director, and **Susan Hidegkuti**, Assistant Director, of the Rail Pass Express EuropeanVacation Tours & Groups offices in Bloomington, Indiana, and Columbus, Ohio (visit the new Web site at http://www.europeanvacation.com or call 888–TOUR 404), have blessed us with their enthusiasm, knowledge, and comprehensive experience of the travel industry. Mary also supplies valuable itinerary development and planning strategies for the books and analyzes the British rail network infrastructures' impact on the travel industry for *Britain by BritRail.*

• **Mary Kish** is General Manager and Director of Operations for Rail Pass Express, Inc. and Ferguson Rail Publications, Inc. Her managerial excellence and ingenious business acuity keep everyone on the right track and moving in the right direction. Mary runs a tight ship—perhaps because of her Navy background. We happen to think she is an angel in disguise.

• **Matthew Palma**, an invaluable strategist and business planner, is the International Business Coordinator for Rail Pass Express, Inc. and Ferguson Rail Publications, Inc. A graduate of The Ohio State University in Communications and Business Administration, Matthew has played a major role in streamlining operational systems and procedures and has been a wonderful asset to the company for years.

• **Kevin Siegmann**, a graduate of The Ohio State University's top-ranked Industrial Design Program, is Graphics/Systems Designer. He designs and maintains our award-winning Web site, http://www.railpass.com, which contains *Britain by BritRail* and *Europe by Eurail* information for its online readers, an extensive British and European rail-related database, and a *secure* online ordering system for rail travel products. Kevin is an integral part of the creativity center of the Marketing Department and overall operations. We wish we could clone him!

• **Ellie Byrnes**, **Emily Elsom**, and **William Stafford** are our royal rail information experts at the Point-to-Point and Reservations Office. They meticulously decipher complicated timetables in order to choose the best and most convenient trains for *Britain by BritRail* day excursions and rail connections between base cities. Our clients enjoy their travel trek and globetrotting stories while planning itineraries and making train reservations. Call (614) 793–7650.

Other rail customer service specialists include **Colleen Beader, Laura Biemel, Paula Britton, Courtney Crane, Jennifer Halloway, Donna Heap, Erin Robinson, Jack Rothenbuehler, Sonal Shah, Brian Sherwood, Jerry Theodoropoulos,** and **Debbie Wanstrath-Norwich.**

A special note of thanks goes to the former Assistant General Manager, **Emma McComis,** for her assistance, experience, and style during the high season.

Researchers for *Britain by BritRail* include **H. Milton Peek,** who was instrumental in updating rail schedules and some of the day excursions. Milton also helps with the Café on www.railpass.com and has played a much appreciated role in both books.

Other researchers include **Major Robert Bean,** a true train enthusiast and continental Europe rail expert as well, and **Joseph C. Kosinski** (also known as "Joe Cool"), who shed a whole new light on London and Edinburgh.

A special thanks goes to our many friends in the tourist offices, and travel partner professionals throughout the British community, including **Raymond Mathias,** Wales Marketing USA; **Paul Barrett** and **Cheryl Milsom,** Cardiff Marketing, Ltd., **Robert K. Titley,** British Tourist Authority; and Heinz Wesner, **Barbara Schmidt,** and **Chlöe Winiesdorffer** of DER Travel Services.

We always enjoy hearing from our readers. Please send your comments and suggestions directly to LaVerne Ferguson at Rail Pass Express, Inc., 2737 Sawbury Boulevard, Columbus, OH 43235-4583, USA; or via e-mail at ferguson@britainbybritrail.com.

Train schedules, fares, and prices appearing in this edition are updated to press time. They are, however, for planning purposes only and are subject to change by the railways. We cannot be held responsible for their accuracy.

In the Beginning

"My heart is warm with the friends I make, /And better friends I'll not be knowing; /Yet there isn't a train I wouldn't take/ No matter where it's going."

—Edna St. Vincent Millay

Like thousands of other discerning visitors, you are about to learn that the British rail system offers a truly delightful way of traveling throughout the length and breadth of Europe's only English-speaking nation—Britain. So welcome aboard *Britain by BritRail!* You are embarking on a unique and rewarding traveling experience.

Train travel is an anomaly for most Americans. Millions of Americans have either forgotten or have never had the opportunity to learn what travel by train can be like. The Europeans' outlook on train travel is different. They need trains for transport; thus, they have created trains with the simplest and yet most extravagant amenities of their cultures. In so doing, they provide fast, economical, and often elegant modes of transportation.

Britain is a rather compact nation. It's about two-thirds the size of California or approximately one-third larger than the New England area of Maine, Vermont, New Hampshire, Massachusetts, Rhode Island, and Connecticut—the North American area to which Britain has contributed much of her heritage since Colonial days.

This nineteenth edition of *Britain by BritRail* encompasses rail travel in England, Scotland, and Wales. Northern Ireland is a part of Great Britain, but its railways are operated by a separate company that does not accept the BritRail Pass. It does, however, accept the BritRail Pass + Ireland, which combines England, Scotland, Wales, Northern Ireland, and the Republic of Ireland. Northern Ireland and the Republic of Ireland will be included in *Britain by BritRail 2000*. Since the Republic of Ireland is one of the seventeen Eurail (European rail system) countries, please consult our sister publication, *Europe by Eurail: How to Tour Europe by Train* or our Web site http://www.europebyeurail.com.

London is a tourist magnet, but despite what other writers say, London is not Britain. Britain has some of the most beautiful countryside in the world. Its mountains may not be a match in size to the Alps, and its seas are not azure blue like the Mediterranean, but what it might lack in spectacular scenery is offset by a magical quality of green so peaceful and picturesque that, in a mere glance, the visitor becomes aware that what he or she sees is history. A visit to Britain that does not include at least a few days in the countryside is unthinkable.

The difference between traveling along Britain's congested highways and riding on British InterCity trains must be experienced to be believed. By rail, it is a smooth, relaxing journey uninterrupted by traffic lights and traffic jams. Rent-a-car visitors are usually too involved with starboard steering and keeping a close watch on the car in front to appreciate much more about Britain than the fact that the road signs are in English.

In Britain, you'll find more than 15,000 trains traveling to more than 2,500 destinations daily. The service is so frequent that if you miss a train, chances are you won't have to wait more than a half hour to an hour for another. The British frequently seize such an opportunity to nip into a nearby pub for a quick pint and a game of darts. So follow the adage "When in Rome, do as the Romans do." It applies equally well in Britain, which inherited some of Rome's customs, too!

Aboard a British train, the driver (that's what the British call their train engineers) takes care of all the driving while you sip on a beverage, enjoy an uninterrupted view of the countryside, and stretch out in a comfortable seat. You can even respond to "nature's call" at your own option rather than sweating out making it to the closest petrol (gas) station—many are closed on weekends and holidays!

Few places in Britain cannot be reached by train. By employing the base cities of London, England; Edinburgh or Glasgow in Scotland; or Cardiff in Wales, the splendor of Windsor Castle in England, Inverness and the legendary Loch Ness Monster in Scotland, or the natural beauty of Swansea Bay in Wales are all but an easy, comfortable train ride away.

How to Use *Britain by BritRail*

Britain by BritRail is a train travel guidebook written to provide detailed train-related information to its readers in a direct, pragmatic manner. *Britain by BritRail* does not include comprehensive hotel listings, but quaint bed-and-breakfasts or personally selected hotels convenient to rail services may be mentioned. Our primary purpose, insofar as accommodations are concerned, is to point out the most convenient tourist information center or hotel booking (reservations) facility and how to get there.

Restaurants are treated in the same manner. We appreciate good food, along with the service that complements it. With few exceptions, however, the choice of what to eat and where to find it remains the option of the reader perusing the wealth of excellent publications catering to this most worthy pursuit. We do, however, include some of our own personal recommendations.

Britain by BritRail, like its sister publication, *Europe by Eurail,* is devoted to the visitor who goes to Britain expecting that its train services will provide the necessary transportation for a holiday that is different. We have gone ahead of you, probed what can be done, and solved the problems of doing it long before you arrive. We personally experience every city and day excursion and our researchers pledge to constantly recheck, revise, and help to expand subsequent editions. This is accomplished by personal visits and through our British and European network of correspondents in the areas described.

Britain by BritRail presents a concept for comfortable, unhurried travel by train in Britain. By utilizing the economy of a BritRail Pass, along with the innovative, fully described Base City–Day Excursion™ method, you can really see Britain at its best—by train.

Britain by BritRail is the perfect traveling companion for visitors using the BritRail Pass. This book helps to introduce and establish the reader in the base cities of London, Edinburgh, Glasgow, and Cardiff. Establish yourself in affordable, comfortable accommodations. Then, when you have finished your sightseeing and shopping in the base city, let *Britain by BritRail* guide you to its recommended day excursions. For the most part, these interesting places are based on train schedules and geographic locations that assure your return each night to the same hotel room. With a BritRail Pass and a current copy of *Britain by BritRail*, you become your own tour guide and avoid the constant packing and unpacking that accompanies most bus tours attempting to cover the same territory. *You* call the shots, not the tour bus driver.

Britons and their continental cousins have employed rail services for "holiday-making" on the British Isles for decades. Train travel is too fast for any possible chance of boredom setting in, yet it is leisurely enough to enjoy fully the constantly changing scene of hills and hamlets, farms and forests, countrysides and cities—everything that forms Britain's fascinating landscape.

Should you pause to ponder why, for example, an English gentleman would leave his motorcar at home when he's "off on holiday," you will find the answer very quickly when your train parallels a major highway or flashes across a bridge through the center of a British city. The super-highways—right down to the ancient, narrow streets—are packed with vehicles, all proceeding at a much slower pace than you and your train.

In the chapters describing the base cities and day excursions, *Britain by BritRail* meets you upon arrival at the base-city airport or train station and then leads you step-by-step to those essential facilities such as tourist infor-mation sources, currency exchanges, and hotel accommodations.

Britain by BritRail provides an overall picture of each destination. Each day-excursion section begins with the distance and average train time for the trip, along with the tourist information office location and hours of operation. Explicit directions on how to get from the train station to the city tourist information office are also located right at your fingertips, at the beginning of each day excursion.

Readers requiring advance information regarding the base cities of London, Edinburgh, Glasgow, and Cardiff should contact the closest British Tourist Authority office listed in the Appendix of this edition, or visit the BTA Web site on the Internet at http://www.visitbritain.com. Another great site to try is http://www.england.com.

To avoid reader frustration, *Britain by BritRail* compiles addresses of information sources and useful telephone numbers in the Appendix.

Train schedules between the base cities of London, Edinburgh, Glasgow, and Cardiff are included at the end of each base-city description. This particular information should prove helpful when you are initially planning your BritRail trip.

Train schedules for the day-excursion trips out of the base cities are also provided in the text describing each day excursion. With a few exceptions for overnight excursions, we chose trains departing from the base cities on morning schedules and trains returning from the day excursions usually in the late afternoon or early evening.

Please remember that the timetables and schedules appearing in this edition are provided for planning purposes only. Every care has been taken to make the timetables and schedules correct. The information is checked with authoritative sources up to press time. *Britain by BritRail* and/or its publisher cannot, however, be held responsible for the consequences of either changes or inadvertent inaccuracies. Current rail schedules are posted in all British rail stations, and timetables from the base cities to each day-excursion point are available for the asking in the base-city train stations. Please consult them, or visit the point-to-point pages of http://www.railpass.com, or get rail schedule information from http://www.railtrack.co.uk.

Planning a BritRail Trip

A plan is often defined as "a program of action." Plans vary in detail and complexity, according to the nature of the user. We have observed two general types of rail travelers: one conservative, the other adventurous. One traveler may require a detailed, hour-by-hour-schedule for a day's activities; another may merely plan to get up in the morning and see what happens.

One of the first questions to answer when planning a trip is "When can I go and how much time can I spend there?" In Britain, April through October are the most popular months for tourists and for many events; during the Christmas and New Year's holidays, London literally sparkles. When planning your trip, take British Bank Holidays into consideration since banks, postal services, and most shops and many attractions are closed, plus some transportation services are reduced. Bank Holidays include New Year's Day, Good Friday, Easter Sunday, Easter Monday, May Day, Late Spring Holiday, Late Summer Holiday, Christmas Eve, Christmas Day, and Boxing Day. (See the "Trivia" section in the Appendix for specific 1999 dates.)

Whether you admit it or not, everyone has a problem budgeting vacation time. It's human nature to try to see as much as possible in as little time as possible. This "sightseers' syndrome" could be dangerous to your vacation. Avoid it by planning an itinerary that allows ample free time. Also, vary the day excursions by going on a short one following a particularly long outing away from the base city. Press too hard by trying to see and do too much on your vacation and you will return home looking as if you desperately need another one.

How long should your BritRail tour be? There are many factors bearing on such a determination, the most important being the individual. How much annual vacation time do you have? How do you use it—all at one time or in two or more segments? BritRail Passes can accommodate just about anyone's personal needs, with passes ranging from eight days to one month of travel and flexible passes ranging from four to fifteen days of travel in one month (two months for youth). BritRail Passes permit travel on all scheduled British trains.

Even if you don't have two weeks or more for that grand tour of Britain, travel magazines and the travel sections of the Sunday newspapers are usually loaded with one-week bargain fares to almost anywhere, the British Isles and mainland Europe included. By coupling our Base City–Day Excursion™ mode of easy travel with a four-day BritRail Flexipass you can maximize the time that you do have to spend in Britain.

Once you know how much time you have for your BritRail trip, the next step is to develop a clear idea of where you want to go in Britain, what you want to see, and what you want to do. Develop your objectives well before your departure date. We disagree with those who believe that anticipation of travel is more rewarding than its realization. But we do agree that the planning phase can also be a fun part of your trip. Properly done, this "homework" will pay substantial dividends when your travel actually begins.

To get things started, write to or telephone the British Tourist Authority at (800) 462–2748 for information. (BTA office addresses in North America are listed in the Appendix.) Be specific. In your request, indicate when you will be going, where you wish to go within Britain, and what in particular you would like to see. If you have any special interests or hobbies, be sure to mention them in your request. By spelling out your information needs, you will obtain better responses.

Don't overlook the Internet and your local library as valuable information sources. Travelers who have computers and access to the Internet can do an incredible amount of research and planning in the comfort of their own homes or offices. The great "information highway" is at your disposal.

You may want to start with some basic Web sites about Britain in general and then do subject-specific searches. For example, to obtain general information on Britain, start with the British Tourist Authority's (BTA) Web site: http://www.visitbritain.com. Other sources of information may be found in the Appendix of this edition.

If you want to know more about British rail travel and BritRail Passes, call (800) 722–7151, or write to Rail Pass Express, Inc., 2737 Sawbury Boulevard, Columbus, OH 43235, or check out the Web site at http://www.britainbybritrail.com for British rail information.

Seek out friends and neighbors who have been to Britain. No doubt you'll find their experiences flavored by their own likes and dislikes. Nevertheless, any and all information you can gather prior to your trip will eventually find its place in your memory bank. Surprisingly enough, you'll find yourself recalling many of these fragments of information during your own journey.

Now comes the decisive phase of your trip planning—constructing an itinerary. The moment of truth is at hand! Your only limitations during this portion of the planning phase are the lack of more than twenty-four hours in a day and the fact that the week contains only seven days.

For Internet users, we have found that downloading the personal travel planner EuroData to be extremely easy, understandable, and beneficial. Go to http://www.railpass.com, then scroll down to "Planning Your Trip" and click on EuroData. The Windows-based software program is simple to download. Changes are quickly and easily updated as you finalize travel plans with the help of icons for air, rail, and lodging, plus maps. Print when finished (even includes any notes you may have made) and there you have it, instant itinerary!

Or draw a blank calendar-style form covering a period from at least one week prior to your departure to a few days following your return. Make extra copies of the form—you'll need them. (Perfection is a long time coming in this project!) Begin to block your itinerary into the calendar form, being mindful that the itinerary can be changed, but the number of days in a week remains fixed at all times. Possibly by the third time through the exercise, you'll begin to "see the light at the end of the tunnel." It's only human to try to cram too many activities into a day, but it's better to discover your planning errors before starting your trip rather than in the middle of it.

With your itinerary in a calendar format, you can determine your housing requirements, seat and sleeper reservations, and the other facets of your forthcoming trip. The days blocked out in advance of your departure can show your "countdown" items, such as stopping the newspaper, having mail held at the post office, and so on. Make several copies of your completed itinerary and leave some behind for the folks with whom you want to stay in touch. Above all, take copies of your itinerary with you—you'll refer to them frequently.

If there have been any break-ins in your neighborhood, you should take steps to assure that it doesn't happen to you while you are gone. Alert the neighbors to keep a watchful eye for suspicious people and their activities. Many professional thieves have been known to park in a driveway in broad daylight with a moving van. The police should be advised regarding your absence. Also check with the insurance agency that writes your homeowners policy. Ask the same question they ask in those television commercials: "Am I covered?" You may need additional coverage during your absence. One final caution: Don't announce your forthcoming vacation plans in the newspapers. Many thieves can read, too. Save the social column for your return.

U.S. citizens are required to have a passport to be admitted into Britain; a visa is not necessary. If you do not have a passport or if yours has expired, write immediately to one of the U.S. passport offices listed in the Appendix. Allow a minimum of one month to obtain your passport. There are ways to expedite the process, but be safe by planning ahead and making this the first order of business when you've decided to make your trip abroad.

Travel Economy

"Know before you go," the slogan of the U.S. Customs Service concerning what you may return with, also applies to the financial aspects of vacation planning. The fluctuation of the dollar's purchasing power in Europe over the past few years has left a lot of us wondering whether or not we could afford a vacation on the other side of the Atlantic. It is sometimes difficult to determine what effect Europe's inflation will have on your dollars once you're there.

Advance planning and purchasing most of your vacation needs in advance (particularly transportation) in American dollars are probably the most effective ways to combat inflation and price fluctuations. Buy as much of your vacation needs as you can before you go and plan to limit your out-of-pocket costs paid in foreign currency to a minimum. In this way, you are protected against fluctuating currency values.

The idea of doing things that were previously thought impossible—like filling a Ford Escort with $50 worth of gas—emphasizes train travel in Europe as the best means of effectively stabilizing your travel dollars. Prepayment plans, such as the BritRail Pass, are ideal. Not only do you purchase the pass with American dollars prior to departure, but the BritRail Pass also provides the most inexpensive way to travel in Britain— the quickest, too!

Most travel agents still have a penchant for wanting to sell a "fly-drive" program to clients who want to vacation in Britain. But, in general, car rentals have one basic fault—the price you see is not the price you pay; it always seems to be higher. As a rule of thumb, add to the quoted price another 20 percent for personal accident insurance, collision insurance, and taxes. After that, consider fuel costs at about three times that of fuel in the United States. And don't forget about the 17.5 percent value-added tax (VAT). Then order an economical BritRail Pass by calling BritRail's sales outlet, Railpass Express, Inc., at (800) 722-7151 (secured online ordering address: http://www.britainbybritrail.com).

Accommodations usually account for the greatest share of a traveler's budget. Low-cost air fares and transportation bargains like the BritRail Pass can get the traveler to and around the British Isles, but the real bite out of the buck comes when the visitor opens his wallet to pay for a night's lodging. Attractively priced accommodations packages are being offered by some tour operators, but too few suit the needs of individual itineraries, as is the case for travelers on a BritRail vacation. With advance planning and advance payment, however, you can realize significant savings if you are willing to put forth the extra time and effort to do your home-work. Visit http://www.europeanvacation.com.

Well ahead of your intended departure date—preferably two months in advance, but no less than six weeks—write to one of the British Tourist Authority (BTA) offices listed in the Appendix of this edition and request information regarding lodging (including the bed-and-breakfasts) in the areas you intend to visit during your BritRail journey. You may make reservations, or "bookings," as the British call them, in a variety of ways.

Call (888) TOUR–404 to make hotel bookings, or arrange hotel accommodations by mail or fax with central booking offices. The best assurance that you will have a room waiting upon arrival is to make an advance deposit directly to the hotel, then take care of the balance with the hotel's cashier when checking out. And always ask the hotel to confirm the room rate when you check in. This will avoid delays and possible financial embarrassment when leaving.

One final bit of advice on reducing the cost of accommodations in Britain: Use your BritRail Pass. Too many of us overlook the fact that the BritRail Pass can actually provide exceptional savings in housing costs by permitting you to stay outside the base city's center, where hotel rooms, pensions, bed-and-breakfasts, and the like are far less expensive than their in-town counterparts.

London particularly lends itself to such a suburban arrangement because there are many areas outside the city's center that are readily accessible by rail. Anytime downtown accommodations become difficult to find, or too demanding on the budget, tell the housing people you have a BritRail Pass and can easily stay in the suburbs.

Staying in London's northern or western suburbs has other advantages too. From many of the suburban stations, you can board a fast InterCity train for a day excursion without ever going into a London terminus. You can return to the suburbs in the evening, too, without becoming involved in London's rush hours.

Watford Junction, 16 miles from London's Euston Station, is one of the stations in London's suburbs that offers excellent InterCity connections to such day-excursion points as Birmingham and Coventry, as well as the base city of Glasgow. Most InterCity departures from Euston Station on weekday mornings pick up at Watford Junction sixteen minutes later. On weekday evenings, most InterCity trains set down at Watford Junction twenty minutes ahead of their arrival times in Euston Station.

Going to St. Albans, Perth, or the base cities of Edinburgh and Cardiff, we recommend transferring to King's Cross or Paddington from Euston to continue the trip.

Other rail points in London suburbs are Luton, for direct rail connections to Nottingham and Sheffield; Stevenage, along the main line to Edinburgh via York; and Slough or Reading, for connections to Bath as well as the Welsh cities of Cardiff and Swansea.

There are times when accommodations in the base cities are very limited. Edinburgh, during its annual Military Tattoo and Festival every August to September, is an excellent example. Lodgings in the suburbs, à la BritRail Pass, can be more economical and just as convenient as those in the base cities.

If you have your heart set on lodgings in London when inquiring as to availability, you will be asked the inevitable question, "What do you want to be near to?" Naturally, when you're traveling by rail, your response will be, "The rail station." You are in for a surprise: At last count, London had seventeen primary rail stations. Because these terminals rim the vast, sprawling city, a better site-selection statement would be to ask for a hotel nearby one of the major lines of the Underground (the "Tube").

How to Get There

Transatlantic air traffic is so frequent and varied today that no description of it—short of an entire book—could do it justice. Excursion fares are available in a multitudinous variety. Charter flights are available too, and they are still mostly money savers. But some excursion rates are less expensive than charters. It is not uncommon on a regularly scheduled airliner winging its way to Europe to find that every passenger in your row of seats paid a different fare for the same flight on the same schedule with the same service!

We refer readers to their travel agents for airline information. But there has been an erosion of such information in travel agencies, brought about in general by the proliferation of air fares. Travel agents face the almost impossible task of keeping tabs on the rapidly changing airline industry. If you've dealt with a reputable travel agency over the years, contact it for air-excursion-fare options. Or, at your leisure, you can call the various airlines' toll-free telephone numbers and ask them for suggestions and fare information. We have listed the toll-free numbers of a few airlines in the Appendix. Don't be disturbed if you receive a variety of responses. Sift them out until you find what you're looking for. Internet users can search online for those bargain fares. Long-distance calls can be made in the United States without charge when calling businesses that have toll-free numbers. Obtaining the proper toll-free number to call is easy: Dial (800) 555–1212 and tell the operator the name of the airline information office with which you wish to speak.

Regarding charter flights, inquire about them but investigate them thoroughly before making any final decisions. Here again, get your travel agent involved, even if it's only to obtain the tickets. Even some of the most reputable air-charter carriers still operate on a "Go–No Go" basis. This means that if enough passengers sign up for the flight, it will go as scheduled; if there are not enough passengers booked, the flight will be scrubbed.

BritRail Passes

A BritRail Pass is a ticket for unlimited train travel for a specified number of days in England, Scotland, and Wales. You don't have to purchase a Rail Pass to travel by train in Britain; having one, however, is very convenient and economical. For example, with a BritRail Pass , you do not have to purchase a ticket every time you want to make a trip somewhere by train. Just board any train that is going your way and travel whenever, wherever, and as often as you like throughout the period in which your BritRail Pass is valid.

BritRail Passes are not available in Britain and must be purchased in North America prior to departure. You may order directly from BritRail's U.S. sales agent, Rail Pass Express, Inc., at (800) 722–7151; secured online ordering is available at http://www.railpass.com. You may also purchase some of the passes through your local travel agent or from a British Tourist Authority office (see Appendix). A list of British and European rail passes and their corresponding prices is available in the Appendix. Expand your horizons—don't leave home without one!

Visitors to Britain should consider purchasing a BritRail Pass if they plan to travel primarily by train. To help you decide whether or not to purchase a BritRail Pass, we have included a selection of British one-way rail fares in the Appendix. The fares are listed in U.S. dollars. To obtain the rate for converting dollars into pounds, consult the financial section of your newspaper, currency exchange rates on the Internet, or the international department of your bank. Compare the individual fare rates with the cost of a BritRail Pass shown in the Appendix for your itinerary.

Keep in mind when comparing the point-to-point rail fares to the cost of the pass that convenience in travel has a value, too. Standing in line ("queuing") to purchase train tickets is an inconvenience that can be avoided. With a BritRail Pass, you need do this only once—when you validate your pass.

Even short-time visitors to the British Isles may find it advantageous to purchase a BritRail Pass in lieu of point-to-point tickets. For example, the cost of point-to-point tickets for a circuitous journey—like a quick dash out of London for a look around Edinburgh and Bath—exceeds the cost of an eight-day first-class or standard-class adult BritRail Classic Pass; the economy of the pass becomes immediately apparent. Also, consider that the London–Edinburgh–Bath–London circuit could be made comfortably in as little as three days, leaving five more days of unlimited rail travel available to the pass holder. Even if you could not extend your stay, you would still save money, in this case, by purchasing a BritRail Pass.

BritRail Passes are available for first- or standard-class rail travel. First-class seats are wider; consequently, first-class coaches are more spacious since they accommodate fewer passengers. BritRail's standard class, however, is also very comfortable. Some trains in Britain have entirely standard-class carriages. One thing in common to both classes is the view. Whether in first or standard class, you can lounge ensconced in comfort while watching the countryside glide by.

When traveling in Britain on certain peak days, holidays, or summer Saturdays, seat reservations are recommended. You may make them at any rail station or at the rail counters in Heathrow, Gatwick, and Manchester airports. Although you can make seat reservations in the United States after you purchase your BritRail Pass (two weeks prior to departure is recommended), it is more economical to make your reservations in Britain.

There are two basic types of passes to choose from: BritRail Classic Pass and BritRail Flexipass.

BritRail Classic Pass. The Classic Pass offers unlimited consecutive-day rail travel in England, Scotland, and Wales. Choose to travel for eight, fifteen, or twenty-two days or one month. The BritRail Senior Classic Pass (available to adults sixty years and over) offers a 15 percent discount off the first-class BritRail Adult Classic Pass. BritRail Youth Classic passes are available for those ages sixteen through twenty-five; youth passes, however, are available in standard class only.

BritRail Flexipass. This pass provides exactly what its name implies: flexibility. Travel on any four, eight, or fifteen days within a one-month validity period in either first or standard class. Unlike the Classic Pass, your travel days need not be consecutive, thus enabling you to stay in your favorite location for several days until you choose to continue your journey. A BritRail Senior Flexipass (age sixty and older) offers first-class rail travel at a 15 percent discount off the adult BritRail Flexipass price. A Youth Flexipass (ages sixteen through twenty-five) is available in standard class only for any four or eight days of travel in one month or any 15 days of travel within a two-month period and is offered at a 20 percent discount off the BritRail Adult Flexipass.

BritRail Family Pass. With BritRail, kids count, too. With the purchase of one Adult or Senior pass, one accompanying child (age five through fifteen) gets a pass of the same type and duration free. Passes for additional children may be purchased at a 50 percent discount off the regular adult pass price. Children under age five travel free. The BritRail Family Pass program is available with BritRail Classic, BritRail Flexipass, BritRail Party Pass, BritRail Senior, BritRail Pass + Car, and BritRail Pass + Ireland.

BritRail Party Pass. A discount of 50 percent is offered on passes to the third and fourth persons of groups with three or four passengers traveling together at all times. The BritRail Party Pass program applies to the BritRail Classic, BritRail Flexipass, and the BritRail Senior passes. All travelers must purchase exactly the same type of pass to qualify and must travel together at all times.

BritRail Pass + Car. Although Britain's compactness makes it convenient to take the train and see the sights, there are but a few nooks and crannies that cannot be reached by train. Those who want to combine the thrill of driving on the left-hand side of the road with rail travel can opt for the BritRail Pass + Car. Use the fast, comfortable British trains for the longer journeys and the freedom of a Hertz rental car to explore the beautiful British countryside.

First, purchase your BritRail Pass + Car voucher from (800) 722–7151 or http:/www.railpass.com. The price includes a BritRail Flexipass for unlimited rail travel (choice of first or standard class) for any four days within a one-month period and car rental vouchers for any two days within the same month. Then, at least seven days prior to departure, telephone Hertz toll-free at (800) 654–3001 to reserve your first car rental date. Be certain to state that you have already purchased a BritRail Pass + Car and mention the program code ITGERM. You should make these reservations as soon as possible, particularly if you want a car with an automatic transmission. For the remainder of your car rental reservations, Hertz has rental offices at rail stations throughout England, Scotland, and Wales.

Since your car rental vouchers may be used only during the validity period of your BritRail Flexipass, the most economical way of utilizing them is to arrange for a car to meet your train at a day-excursion point, do your exploring, and return the car to the same station before returning to your base city by train. Prebooked requests for a car to meet your train will be honored seven days a week.

Each car rental voucher includes a twenty-four-consecutive-hour rental with unlimited mileage, no drop-off charge, and government tax (VAT) of 17.5 percent. The renter is responsible for collision damage, personal accident insurance, and gas. Payment of these charges may be made by credit card or a deposit at the start of each rental period. Aside from gasoline, the other additional charges average about $11 (U.S.) per day. The BritRail Pass + Car option rates are based on two adults per car; the pass for a third or fourth person is offered at a reduced rate.

BritRail Pass + Ireland. For unlimited rail travel in England, Scotland, Wales, Northern Ireland, and Ireland, this is the pass for you. The price also includes one round-trip ferry service on the Stena Line (within the validity of your pass) between Holyhead and Dun Laoghaire, Fishguard and Rosslare, or Stranraer and Belfast via superferry, HSS (High Speed Sea Service) or Stena Lynx catamaran. The BritRail Pass + Ireland is available for any five or ten days of travel within a one-month period in either first or standard class (no senior or youth discounts; children under five travel free; one free child's pass, ages five through fifteen, with purchase of adult pass).

BritRail SouthEast Pass. Casual, short-term, or business visitors to Britain may benefit from this special flexible rail pass tucked in their pocket before leaving home. The SouthEast Pass offers unlimited rail travel throughout a large area of southern England for any three or four days out of an eight-day period or for any seven days within a fifteen-day period. Choose first- or standard-class rail travel; special children's rates are applicable.

Freedom of Scotland Travelpass. The Travelpass offers unlimited rail travel in Scotland on ScotRail's network, including travel to and from Berwick and Carlisle for any four days within an eight-day period or any eight or twelve days within a fifteen-day validity period. The pass includes transportation on most Caledonian MacBrayne ferries and Strathclyde ferries to the islands of Scotland; some discounts on P&O ferry routes are also offered. No discounts are available for children, youth, or seniors.

The Great British Heritage Pass. This pass provides entry to more than 500 of Britain's public and privately owned historic sites. **The London Visitor Travel Card** gives unlimited travel on London's red double-decker buses and the Underground (subway, or "Tube," as the Britons say); and the **BritRail Pass + Eurostar Discounted Rate** combines Britain with the Continent. Special rail tour packages are explained in the "Special Itineraries" section or call 888–TOUR–404.

A catalog detailing BritRail's many economically priced programs may be obtained free of charge by calling Rail Pass Express at (800) 722–7151.

Travel Tips

Planning Pays Off. Careful planning is key to every successful thing we do, and planning a rail vacation in Britain is no exception.

How Much to Take? Half the clothes and twice the money! Obviously, practical advice would be "as little as possible." We usually tend to pack everything we conceivably might use during a vacation, lug it everywhere, use it very little, and return home with longer arms. In these days of wash-and-wear fabrics (and deodorants), this is not necessary. A good rule of thumb is to take one medium-size suitcase with wheels and a shoulder bag. Hold to this rule and you will have a more comfortable trip. Regardless of how comfortable you expect the weather at your destination to be, pack a sweater. Brief cold spells in Britain are not uncommon. Stow a small pocket flashlight in your shoulder bag together with a collapsible umbrella or rain hat in the "unlikely event" that you may need them.

Bring a wash cloth if you normally use one; washcloths are not frequently found in European hotels. Take an electrical converter and adapter plugs for your electric appliances such as electrical razors and hair dryers. Travel-size dual-voltage hair dryers are convenient; you only need to switch the voltage to the European 220 and add the adapter plug for Britain.

If you must take expensive jewelry with you, take as well a copy of its insurance appraisal as proof of purchase to customs officials upon your return. Same for watches produced by foreign manufacturers. You may have bought that solid-gold Rolex in a Saint Louis pawnshop for a song, but the customs inspector may have you singing a different tune if you can't come up with the paperwork!

If you wear prescription eyeglasses or contact lenses, take a copy of your prescription. The same applies to prescription medications. Even if you only use over-the-counter drug products, we suggest taking an adequate supply of the item in its original container. Many such products are not available in Europe or are sold under a different label or packaging.

Samsonite, one of the major manufacturers of quality luggage, has published an interesting booklet on the subject of suitcases and travel. With the catchy title *Lightening the Travel Load—Travel Tips and Tricks*, it is crammed with helpful tips, everything from analyzing your luggage needs and the basic points of safeguarding it through packing for a trip. Helpful hints on carry-on luggage, how to tip, how to clear customs, and how to stay healthy while on your trip are also included. For a free copy, write to Samsonite Traveler Advisory Service, P.O. Box 39603, Denver, CO 80239. Include a self-addressed business envelope with postage affixed to cover up to two ounces first-class.

For rail travelers, we recommend the *Thomas Cook European Timetable*. It contains complete timetables covering every major rail route in Britain honoring the BritRail Pass. In the United States and Canada, copies of the *Thomas Cook European Timetable* can be purchased from Forsyth Travel Library, *Tel:* (800) 367–7984. In Britain, the timetable may be purchased at most Thomas Cook travel agencies and bureaux de change (money exchange offices). Rail schedules for Britain may be found online at http://www.railtrack.co.uk. Free schedules can also be obtained at any British rail station.

Cash, Cards, and Credentials. Don't carry more cash than you can afford to lose; use ATMs (automated teller machines) or carry traveler's checks. You will, of course, need both U.K. and U.S. cash to pay for tips, snacks, refreshments, and taxi fares at your arrival city. Distribute your currency around in pockets, briefcase, money clip, and money belt. A money belt is an ideal way to carry the larger notes.

ATMs offer the best exchange rate on foreign currencies, but if you plan to use them, do your homework first. Ask your bank for a list of ATM locations in Britain and whether or not your magnetic imprint needs to be modified to work in foreign ATMs. Be certain to know your PIN number and inquire if the bank will charge you per overseas cash withdrawal. Although U.S. banks levy surcharges for the luxury of using their machines, these charges do not extend to U.S.-issued cards at machines overseas. Remember, though, that a cash withdrawal on a credit card is like a "temporary miniloan," and there is an interest charge.

You can avoid interest charges by using a debit card (cash withdrawals and purchases are deducted from your checking account). You probably will still pay a fee of around $2.00 per withdrawal with a debit card. If you do carry traveler's checks, cash them at the branch-bank facilities located in or near railway stations and airports. Banks and official currency-exchange services are government supervised and are required to pay the official exchange rates. Hotels and stores seldom give you the full exchange value and often add substantial service fees.

Make a list of credit card, traveler's check, and airline ticket numbers that you plan to take. Leave a copy at home and pack one in your suitcase or carry-on bag. Credit cards are handy for paying the larger expenses such as hotels and restaurants. The charge is converted into dollars at the applicable exchange rate on the date the charge is posted.

Make two copies of your passport. Leave one copy at home and take the other one with you. Carry a certified copy of your birth certificate and a few extra passport photos. Taking the time to do this will save you days of delay on your trip if your passport is lost or stolen. If your passport is lost or stolen, report it to the local police and contact the nearest U.S. Embassy or Consulate.

Cameras and Film. If you plan to take a foreign-made camera with you that you purchased in the United States, take the sales slip with you. Otherwise, go to a U.S. Customs Office before leaving the country and have your equipment registered. Carry a copy of the sales slip or the registration form with your passport and keep a spare copy tucked away in the camera case or shoulder bag.

Despite what airport officials tell you, their electronic luggage-checking devices could fog your film. The best way to avoid it is to not have film in your camera when you go through airport security, and place unboxed film in clear plastic bags. Ask that your cameras and film be inspected by hand. Above all, do not pack film in your check-through luggage. Although special lead-lined bags are available at most camera stores, luggage is subjected to a high level of radiation, and the film may still be damaged.

The cost of color film in Britain includes processing and is usually more expensive than the same at home. Solution? Take all the film you'll need with you.

En Route Tips

With all the luxuries of flight that modern aircraft offer, there is still something about flying that makes it more demanding on your system than a similar amount of time spent at home or in the office. A transatlantic trip with a minimum of incidents and inconveniences is what we're after. Here are some suggestions that we've found helpful on our flights.

In-Flight Comfort. If you plan to catch some shut-eye en route, ask for a seat alongside a bulkhead. Bulkheads don't mind being leaned on, but passengers do. If you need more legroom, sit in an emergency exit row, but be prepared to accept the responsibility for being physically capable of standing and opening the exit hatch if necessary. Also, be sure your seat reclines. On some planes, the row of seats forward of the emergency exits does not recline. Opt for seats in the forward section of the airplane; passengers in the forward section generally experience less vibration and engine noise.

Wear loose clothing. Unfasten your shoes, but don't take them off. Your feet will swell following several hours of immobility. The best remedy is to walk the length of the aisle in the airplane every hour or so. Try deep knee bends. To reduce swelling, consider wearing elastic stockings.

Flying dehydrates your body. Drink lots of water and watch what you mix with it—alcohol dehydrates, too. Special meals for special diets are no problem with the airlines, but requests should be made at the same time as reservations.

Tax-Free Purchases. At press time, tax-free shopping in Europe is in serious jeopardy; it is scheduled to be abolished in June 1999. Every international airport currently has a "tax-free" shopping service. The routine is generally the same. You select your purchases, pay for them and add them to your carry-on luggage, find safe storage for them during the flight, and then haul them off the airplane. And there are variations. For example, at JFK in New York, you select the items from a sample or catalog. The items are then delivered "for your convenience" to your departure gate for pickup. The hazards of this system are many. If the delivery person gets things mixed up and fails to make the right gate at the right time, you'll be off into the wild blue yonder sans purchases. Or, if you are late passing the pickup point, sometimes an unknown "benefactor" tries to help by taking your purchases on board the plane ahead of you. Finding this so-called benefactor can prove to be difficult.

Solution? Buy your "booty" aboard the airplane while en route. Most international airlines carry aboard a good stock of tax-free items, which you may purchase from the cabin crew. It's always best to check at the airline counter, however, to be certain that this in-flight service will be available on your particular flight. "Tax free," by the way, is a misused term. Many items, with the exception of alcohol and tobacco, normally can be purchased cheaper in the arrival city.

Keep in mind that everything you purchase, "tax free" or otherwise, is subject to customs duty when returning home. Consequently, know your quotas and attempt to stay within them to avoid paying duty and the ensuing delays involved. Good luck with customs. Honesty is always the best policy!

Prior to Landing. Fill out all the customs forms your flight attendant gives to you and keep them with your passport and airline ticket. Keep this packet handy, but secure, until your credentials are required by the customs officials at the airport.

What to Do about Jet Lag

For North Americans, it takes an entire day to reach Britain by air and an entire day to return. Although the flying time aboard most jet airplanes ranges from seven to eight hours, airport to airport, it will be day two before you arrive in Britain. (Most eastbound transatlantic flights depart at night during day one and arrive the following morning, i.e., day two.) During the flight, you will be exposed to a cocktail hour, a dinner hour, a break for an after-dinner drink, followed by a full-length feature movie. In the morning, as the sun rises in the east over Britain, you'll be awakened for breakfast an hour or so before landing.

Add up the time consumed by all the scheduled events while en route, and you'll quickly conclude that your night spent in the sky over the Atlantic Ocean consisted of many things—except sleep. Even if you did manage to sleep during the entire trip instead of eating, drinking, and watching movies, your body and all its functions will be arriving in Britain a few hours after midnight by North American time. You will crave adjustment to the phenomenon known as "jet lag," which will try its best to interrupt your plans for a carefree vacation.

The following explanation of what jet lag is and some means to combat it should prove helpful to any traveler undergoing four or more hours of time change.

The human body has numerous rhythms; sleep is one of them. Even in a cave without sunlight, your body will still maintain a twenty-four-hour wake/sleep cycle. The heart rate falls to a very low ebb in the early hours of the morning, when you are usually asleep. Body temperature, which affects the mental processes, also drops during this time. Consequently, if an air traveler is transported rapidly to a time zone five or six hours ahead of that of the departure point, even though it may be eight or nine o'clock in the morning at the arrival point in local time, the traveler's body functions are at a low ebb. As a result, the traveler feels subpar, a feeling that can persist for as long as two or three days unless something corrects it.

To cope effectively with jet lag, start varying your normal sleep–eat–work pattern a week or so before your departure. If you are normally up by 7:00 A.M. and in bed around 11:00 P.M. or so, get up earlier and go to bed later for a few days. Then reverse the procedure by sleeping in a bit in the morning and going to bed ahead of your normal time. Vary your meal times, possibly putting off breakfast until lunch time. This will condition your body to begin accepting changes in routines. In turn, when the big transatlantic change comes, it won't be as much of a shock on your system.

To lessen the effects of jet lag en route, avoid excessive drinking and eating. After your arrival, exercise the first day by taking a vigorous walk, followed by a long nap. You should have set your watch to local time at your destination as you departed on your flight. By doing this, you subconsciously accelerate your adjustment to the new time zone. For example, how many times have you looked at your watch and then realized you were hungry? Rest on the day of your arrival, and begin doing everything you normally do back home according to the new local time.

Some seasoned transatlantic travelers take even stronger precautions to avoid jet lag. They follow the rule of "no coffee, tea, food, wine, beer, or liquor" on the day of the flight to Europe. They do, however, advocate lots of fruit juices, vegetable juices, and water (no carbonated drinks). This method follows the theory that your body clock will then go on hold, waiting for you to restart it with breakfast the day you arrive in Europe. Resist the temptations of the airlines up to the point of breakfast and try to get some sleep. Some current studies have shown the hormone melatonin to be useful in combatting jet lag, but as with any other over-the-counter drug, you should first consult your physician. And then there's the "light theory—using a blue light source behind your elevated knee caps. Regardless of which remedies you choose, respect jet lag by taking some precautions, and you'll enjoy your vacation.

Train Travel Tips

"What affects men sharply about a foreign nation," wrote G. K. Chesterton, "is not so much finding or not finding familiar things, it is rather not finding them in the familiar place."

Arriving in Britain for the first time, you may experience a confusion of terminology and learn too late that what you sought was really available throughout your visit. The problem may have merely been not knowing where to look or what to call the desired obect. The following information may enhance the pleasure of your BritRail adventures.

Handicapped Travel. First know that the British rail system is a leader in providing facilities in its stations and aboard its trains for the disabled and the handicapped. Rail travel therefore has become an increasingly chosen method of transportation and recreation for disabled persons. Many aids for the handicapped have been incorporated into rail station design. Trains are designed with wider doors for wheelchair access; some even have a removable seat to make room for a wheelchair. Ramp access to toilets, buffets, and other facilities is provided. Folding wheelchairs are also available at main stations so occupants can be transferred to a regular seat once aboard the train. Stationlink bus service is also offered by London Transport (*Tel:* 0171–918–3312) between train stations.

The railways of Britain are most eager to provide as comfortable a journey as possible for the disabled passenger. To do this, prior notice of intended travel plans helps both the traveler and the authorities.

Those readers who want to learn more about this innovative approach should write to the Royal Association for Disability and Rehabilitation, 25 Mortimer Street, London, W1N 8AB, England, for details. The association has published *A Guide to British Rail for the Physically Handicapped.*

In the United States, contact Mobility International USA, P.O. Box 10767, Eugene, OR 97440; (503–343–1284) for information about services and referrals to international affiliates. They also produce a book, *A World of Options for the '90s: A Guide to International Educational Exchange, Community Service and Travel for Persons with Disabilities.*

If you plan to travel in Britain with a handicapped person, call the National Rail Enquires at 011 44 (0345) 484–950; (0845) 605–0600 (Minicom) for information on the train company you will be using, or contact one of the British Tourist Agency (BTA) offices listed in the Appendix as soon as you establish your itinerary and begin making arrangements. The same applies to the airline you'll be using for your transatlantic flight. Provide them with all the details of your itinerary, the nature of the disability, and any other information that will help them help you, such as if a wheelchair is needed at departures and arrivals. Specifically, tell them about special diets, medications, and toilet and medical-attention requirements. With these details attended to, you can look forward to a pleasant journey.

Baggage Carts. Many otherwise able train visitors to Britain impose a severe disadvantage upon themselves by arriving with more luggage than three men and a small boy could possibly carry. Train porters are nearly an extinct species, and their demise was expedited by the luggage trolley— Britain's version of our baggage cart—an elusive device that, whatever your position on the train platform, haunts the extreme opposite end and requires insertion of £1.00 to use. Our number one tip to all train travelers is to "go lightly." At most, take one medium-sized suitcase with wheels, augmented by a modest shoulder bag. There still will be times when you will wish you could discard your suitcase.

If you have purchased a model with built-in wheels, it usually will follow at your heels like a well-trained dog as you apply minimum pulling power. Unlike a dog, the wheeled suitcase cannot climb stairs, so be prepared to lift it on and off the train.

Rather than relying upon the trolleys in the train stations, consider investing in your own baggage cart to take with you if your suitcase does not have built-in wheels. There are many types available.

When loading your luggage onto a baggage cart or station trolley, keep the load as narrow as possible. You may need to pass through rather narrow ticket barriers going to and coming from the trains. A Samsonite suitcase loaded sideways on a baggage cart or one of the station's trolleys will just clear, but a wardrobe case is trouble every time. The trolleys provided by the station should not be taken aboard the train, although we've seen it tried. Again, if you are taking your own cart with you, fold it before boarding. If you don't, you may spend an embarrassing ten minutes or so on the station platform extracting a hapless fellow traveler from it as your train eases out of the station without you.

Using the Lifts (Elevators). The greatest problem in using the train station's luggage trolleys (or your own baggage cart) is traversing the station hall to the platform area, because practically every station has stairs. You can overcome this problem by using the station's lift (elevator). This polite announcement is found posted in most British rail stations: "Lifts are available for passengers who have difficulty in using the stairs. Please contact station staff if assistance is required." In searching for a lift, don't always look for a modern, automatic-door elevator brightly lit with soft music playing. Instead, sometimes you will find the old-fashioned, double-door, manually operated freight elevator, large enough to hold a Mack truck and usually illuminated with a single, bare light bulb—but it works. As the sign says, station staff will assist you.

If you use lifts frequently, however, you will develop the knack of handling them all by yourself. One word of caution: Lifts will not operate until both barriers (usually a door and a gate) have been closed securely. Furthermore, the lift will be left inoperative if you fail to close the doors after you have used it. Be considerate of other passengers and the station staff by making certain that all doors are secure.

As a matter of interest, if your rail journey takes you to continental Europe, the use of rail-station lifts by passengers is usually forbidden.

Porter Services. Porter service is on the wane but still available in some train stations, particularly in the larger ones. We found Virgin train personnel provided the best service and assistance, particularly with luggage. The best way to locate a porter is to inquire at the "Left Luggage" (baggage storage) area or at the station's incoming taxi stand. Waterloo, Gatwick, and Liverpool stations have left luggage areas; other stations may offer luggage lockers, but many stations have stopped this service and even removed trash containers for security reasons.

If your luggage has been checked in at the station, there will be a handling charge, but the tip remains a personal item between you and the porter. We suggest £1.00 minimum as a reasonable gratuity. Most porters will take your bags to the train and place them aboard in the luggage racks over your seats. Porters are rather scarce on arrival platforms. If you must have assistance, approach the stationmaster's office or the train conductor prior to departure with the request that a porter be asked to meet your train upon arrival at your destination.

If you are transferring between base cities or changing hotels from one city to another, you can request the hall porter at the hotel you are leaving to arrange for the arriving hotel's hall porter to meet your train upon arrival. A small tip should arrange everything.

A Few More Train Tips. A few more train travel tips to make your trip more enjoyable:

• "Mind the gap!" when boarding and disembarking.
• Show your BritRail Pass, or ticket, upon request, and in the case of the rail pass, have your passport handy should the conductor like to see it.
• Don't place your feet on the seats of the train unless you have removed your shoes or have provided a protective covering for the seat.
• Place your luggage in the overhead racks provided for that purpose—not on the seats so that other passengers won't be able to crowd you.
• Observe the smoking/nonsmoking areas and rules. Rather stiff fines can be imposed for those smokers who violate the nonsmoking rules.
• Observe seat reservations. They are usually marked by a ticket inserted at the top of the seat. Even though it is apparent that a seat is unoccupied, if there are other passengers seated opposite, ask if the seat is open—it will avoid embarrassment later if the person holding the reservation happens to return.
• For dining-car reservations on long-distance trains, it is often best to arrange for them soon after boarding. Inquire with the guard (train conductor). If he or she cannot make them for you, a member of the dining-car crew will do so. Generally, they pass through the train prior

to the first seatings for that purpose. There are usually two seatings, so be prepared to select the one to your liking. You can also inquire about the menu at the same time. The second seating is scheduled so that the dining-car crew has time to tidy up before the train reaches its destination. Therefore, the first seating is preferred by many because it does not seem to be as rushed.

• If you plan an overnight journey on a sleeper, ask the attendant to explain how the equipment in your compartment operates. For example, newer sleeping cars have electric shades. A push of the button and they open; another push of the same button and they close. If you did not know the button's function, you just might try pushing the button while the train is standing in a station and you are not dressed for the occasion! It's proper to tip the attendant for his or her services; the proper time to do so is when the attendant serves breakfast.

Safety Tips

Picking pockets is an art that is practiced throughout Europe. Don't carry anything more valuable than a handkerchief in hip pockets. Money belts, holster wallets, or pouches that can be hidden are the safest way to carry cash and other valuables.

A concealable money belt or pouch is a good investment. Also, women should place the straps of their purses across their chests and carry the purses in front, not on the side with the straps only on the shoulder. Motorcycle thieves can grab the purse from your shoulder very easily. Men should modify the inside pocket of a coat or jacket with a zipper or Velcro. Or sew a medium-size button both above and below the pocket opening. Loop a piece of shoestring or other strong string around the buttons when carrying valuables.

Don't leave cash, cameras, and other valuables in the hotel room or locked up in a suitcase. Take them with you or leave them in the hotel safe. We advocate leaving expensive jewelry at home, but if you must take it with you, leave it in the hotel safe when you're not wearing it.

Don't dangle your camera from around your neck or wrist; keep it in an inexpensive-looking camera bag.

Don't designate one individual to carry everyone's passports or other valuables, and don't carry all of your own valuables in one place. Split up documents and money in various locations.

Stay alert. Pickpocketing most commonly occurs in crowded public areas. Be leery of being bumped or someone causing a distracting incident.

For all that, don't be alarmed—just be aware and take proper precautions. Actually, pickpocketing is fairly mild compared to what could happen to you on Main Street in your own home town in broad daylight.

For further peace of mind we suggest reviewing the Web pages at http://travel.state.gov/asafetripabroad.html for insightful tips and suggestions for "A Safe Trip Abroad." This site contains ideas on what to bring and leave behind, what to learn and arrange before you go, and also contains helpful tips for public transport safety.

Remember, visitors are always subject to the law of the land; therefore it may be helpful to pay attention to media reports and research some of the local laws and customs prior to departing for a foreign country. Also consider visiting the U.S. State Department's internet site, http://state.gov, which contains up-to-date information on foreign affairs. You may also contact the U.S. Department of State Consular's Office for information on travel warnings and public announcements by calling (202) 647–5225, faxing (202) 647–3000, or visiting http://travel.state.gov.

Several pamphlets are available as well from the Superintendent of Documents, U.S. Government Printing Office, Washington, DC 20420; *Tel:* (202) 512–1800. They average about $1.00 each in cost and include *Your Safe Trip Abroad, A Safe Trip Abroad, Tips for Americans Residing Abroad,* and *Travel Tips for Older Americans.*

Ariving in Britain

That big moment is about happen. Years of dreaming, months of planning, and weeks of anticip are about to become a reality. The NO SMOKING and FASTEN SEAT 's signs have been illuminated, and the cabin attendants advise that arcraft will be landing at your destination in just a few minutes. If this ur initial visit to Britain, you'll probably be straining to get your first g_e of the land from your window; if you have been to Britain many tim efore, you'll probably be straining to get a glimpse of the land right alo with the others. For most of us, there is always an inexplainable thrill ab arriving in a foreign country. Enjoy the emotion; it's part of the reaso or your journey—to experience the adventure of travel, to probe bey the normal confines of your environment, to meet other people, and njoy a bit more of the world than you had before the FASTEN SEAT BELTS n came on.

The Airports

Within Britain, there are five iernational airports servicing traffic from the United States: Gatwick d Heathrow in the London area, Birmingham and Manchester in entral England, and Glasgow in Scotland.

Gatwick–London: There are two terminals: the North Terminal and the South Terminal. Telephone: (0129 353–5353. The Gatwick Express dedicated rail service departs every thiry minutes (from 0020 to 2350 and hourly through the night) from the South Terminal for London's Victoria Station. Approximate journey time is thirty minutes.

Heathrow–London: There are four terminals—Terminals 1, 2, 3, and

4—with courtesy coaches operating betwe terminals on a regular basis. Telephone: (0181) 759–4321. The astTrain service departs every fifteen minutes from Heathro tion, reaching London Paddington Station in only thirty minutes A1 departs from outside each terminal for Victoria Station (sixty nty minutes journey time) and Airbus A2 goes to Euston Station he Cumberland Hotel in London (sixty to eighty-five minutes jou me).

For more detailed information on ck and Heathrow airports, please consult the chapter on London.

Pick up the free guide, *Central Lond ube,* which is available at the travel information centers and tube s s at Heathrow Airport. The guide is full of information on the Und und network, shopping in the West End, and train connections to oth wns and cities within Britain.

Birmingham: Birmingham Intern al Station is right next to the airport and offers some direct service ondon (Euston Station, about one hour, fifty minutes), Brighton, E rgh, Glasgow, Leeds, Liverpool, Manchester, Oxford, and York. *Tel.:* (0 767–5511.

Manchester: There are three term : Terminal 1 Domestic, Terminal 1 International, and Terminal 2. *Tel.:* ( ) 489–3000. The airport rail station is linked to Terminal 1 by a cove escalator and to Terminal 2 by a twenty-four-hour shuttle bus servic Jp to six trains per hour depart from the airport station for Manche Piccadilly railway station (twenty to twenty-five minutes).

Glasgow: One terminal, no rail nection at the airport, direct coach service connects with Paisley Gilmo reet (2 miles from the airport). *Tel:* (0141) 887–1111. Scottish City Link 0 operates from Glasgow airport to the Buchanan Bus Station in the ci enter about every fifteen to twenty-five minutes.

Clearing Customs

The customs-information card given to you by the flight attendants before landing will expedite you clearance through arrival formalities. Actually, you will go through two rocesses—customs and immigration—although they appear to be integ ted. Immigration officials will want to examine your passport, usually at a barrier gate en route to the baggage-claim area in the airport. After c lecting the checked baggage, you should proceed to the customs-inspection area, where you will find two color-coded lanes: green for NOTHING TO DECLARE and red for TO DECLARE. Everyone has some apprehension about passing through customs. For the most part, the apprehension is based on the question, "Am I doing it properly?" Doing it properly in Britain consists of going straight through the NOTHING TO DECLARE channel (unless you are asked to stop by an officer) and moving through into the airport's general-assembly area.

If the customs officials want to examine your luggage, they will indicate so as you approach them. Don't go through the TO DECLARE lane unless you have brought amounts of tobacco or liquor with you that exceed the allowable limits or have purchased a gift that you will be leaving with someone in Britain with a value exceeding £136.

The type and amount of duty-free goods that you may bring into Britain vary with your point of departure—a European Common Market country or otherwise. For transatlantic passengers, the limit is 200 cigarettes and a liter bottle of liquor or two bottles of sparkling wine and two bottles of still wine. You will have plenty of advance advice on duty-free imports posted in your departing airport and you can check with the cabin attendants on the airplane as well. Know before you go, and the clearing procedures in Britain will present no problem.

The phrase "Know Before You Go" also applies to your return to North America. The U.S. Treasury Department publishes an informative booklet containing customs hints for returning residents. Write to the Department of the Treasury, Washington, DC 20229 for the *Know Before You Go* booklet. For U.S. Customs information while in London, telephone at the American Embassy at (0171) 499–1212.

When clearing through foreign customs, keep in mind that the average customs inspector is more interested in the luggage of a returning national than in yours. Always carry your customs declaration along with your passport and in full view as you unlock your luggage in case it has to be inspected.

British Currency

British currency is based on the pound sterling. The pound (£) is divided into one hundred pence (p), just as the U.S. dollar is divided into one hundred cents. Paper notes are issued in values of £50, £20, £10, and £5. Coins are issued in values of £1, 50p, 20p, 10p, 5p, 2p, and 1p. Scottish pound notes are in circulation in Scotland, but the British pound sterling is used in England, Scotland, and Wales. You might find a few kindhearted English and Welsh merchants who will accept a Scottish note, but not without a bit of ribbing first.

British paper notes, like the majority of world currencies, vary in size according to their value, and a variety of them can wreak havoc on the orderliness of a North American's wallet. Certain notes, the £10 and £20 in particular, will require folding before they will fit into a wallet designed to hold dollars. Use discretion when engaged in this folding process, especially in public.

We proudly pointed out to one of our British friends how neatly organized our American wallets are because the U.S. dollar is the same size whether it's a $100 note or a $1 note. "Yes, that's quite neat," she stated, "but what do your blind people do?"

Although the European Union maintains that Europe is now one market, sort of the "United States of Europe," the British are not fond of relinquishing their pounds sterling to the new "one-Europe" currency, the Euro Dollar. At press time, the debate over Europe's single currency is still a "hot potato."

The move to make Europe one market also calls for the abolition of duty-free shopping by June 30, 1999. Currently, the European tourism and transportation businesses, as well as the manufacturers of duty-free goods, are riding the crest of protest against abolition of this $6.5 billion revenue-generating business. Britain represents about 25 percent of Europe's duty-free sales and is spearheading the protest.

British Telephones

The modern public coin-box telephones in operation throughout Britain are simple—with a bit of explanation, that is. Basic differences still exist between British telephones and ours, particularly in the signals they make. A ringing signal is two short rings, followed by a pause. The busy signal sounds the same—only busier. An all-circuits-busy signal is a rapid series of high-low tones, but when you have reached a telephone number not in use, a high-pitched continuous tone reminiscent of a World War II air-raid siren is heard.

Coin-operated telephones are identified by a red stripe across the phone booth door. They operate much like ours, except that a series of rapid pips will signal more coins must be deposited or your call will be terminated. Keep an eye on the window at the top of the phone box that displays the amount you deposited. That amount will be deducted as time passes during your call. Have more coins ready to insert so you won't lose your connection in mid-conversation.

Phonecard payphones are identified by a green stripe across the door. They require the use of a prepaid Phonecard, which you can purchase in £2 (20 units), £4 (100 units), and £20 (200 units) denominations. The cards are sold at post offices and wherever the distinctive green British Telecom (BT) Phonecard sign is displayed. Instructions for the use of Phonecards are posted inside each booth, or you can ask an information office for the pamphlet, *How to Call Home from the UK*. Credit cards may also be used at this type of telephone.

British Traditions

Some visitors entering Britain for the first time may find some of the British traditions, customs, and way of life a little difficult to understand. Perhaps what follows may assist in the transition.

If a Scot from Edinburgh, a Welshman from Cardiff, and an Englishman from London were traveling together in North America, they would describe themselves as being "British." But among themselves, they would be Scot, Welsh, and English. These three nationalities, joined by the Ulstermen of Northern Ireland, make up what we refer to as the United Kingdom. Since the BritRail Pass is not accepted for rail travel in Northern Ireland, references in this book are to Britain rather than the United Kingdom, and the term British refers to the peoples of England, Scotland, and Wales.

Those who plan to add Northern Ireland and the Republic of Ireland to their rail itinerary should consider the BritRail Pass + Ireland (see Appendix for pass prices).

The British character will wear well on you after a few days. They are generally a well-disciplined and very polite people. If anything is at fault, more than likely it is the visitor, not the host. You might spill your tea the first time a waitress calls you "Dearie," but you'll soon learn that such figures of speech are actually a kind of politeness. You'll also learn very quickly that the British queue is the quintessence of "first-come, first-served." The British can face crises and keep their cool, and they maintain a fierce loyalty to Her Majesty, Queen Elizabeth II.

On the surface, Britons may seem reserved, even humorless. In fact, many Britons enjoy some very bold and bawdy humor, as their tabloids will attest. Once their facade is penetrated, however, you will find them capable of the highest mark of humor—they can laugh at themselves. This becomes most evident in their observations regarding their weather. "The way to ensure summer in England," snapped Horace Walpole, "is to have it framed and glazed in a comfortable room." Byron's observation was perhaps terser: "The English winter—ending in July to recommence in August." Britain does have a tendency to be damp at times. You won't regret taking a small folding umbrella or a rain hat.

The Language Barrier

By now, you'll notice that there is one! George Bernard Shaw once said that America and Britain are "two nations divided by a common language." Terminology, more so than pronunciation, appears to be the problem whenever an American and a Briton cannot communicate effectively. *British/American Language Dictionary* by Norman Moss (1991, Passport Books, Chicago, Illinois) can be most helpful during an initial visit to Britain.

Reading the daily newspapers and listening to the British Broadcasting Corporation (BBC) or watching the telly (television) are quick remedial methods for learning the language (try the new BBC America). These media communicate through a more or less middle-of-the-road lexicon.

Regional and local dialects can be extremely difficult to comprehend on occasion; even the Brits themselves admit they sometimes have difficulty understanding each other. It has been said that if an Oxford graduate and a Cambridge graduate were locked together in the same room, neither would be able to converse with the other—even after being properly introduced.

One of the first things a visitor from "the Colonies" (we Americans) will notice is the manner in which directions are given. Americans geographically locate a point within a city by referring to the number of blocks distant from the point of inquiry, for example, "two blocks down the street." Britain's early road builders, however, never thought too much about a grid system and permitted their streets to wander along the easiest gradient. Consequently, directions given by a constable or someone on the street will usually be linear, that is, "Straight away for one-hundred meters," "A kilometer or two," and so on. Visual objects are employed as well: "Straight away to the pub," "Keep walking till you come to the third traffic light," and the like. Cabbies (taxi drivers) are particularly good sources for directional information and advice. Every cabby carries a street map in his taxi and will be glad to assist you.

Nuances in the American/British vocabulary can sometimes lead to trouble. In a public place, such as a train station, those in search of toilet facilities will do well to employ the term *lavatory* in their quest. The WC (water closet) seems to be losing its effectiveness in Britain, although it still brings direct results when used in continental Europe. However, if you want to be up on British expressions, you might ask for the *loo*—that's where those in the know go to "spend a penny." (Most public loos charge a few pence for admission.) Requesting directions to the *bathroom*, particularly in a train station, might lead you to the public showers. So take our advice and stick with *lavatory.*

When a Brit asks you for a *rubber*, don't be offended; just hand him an eraser. If you want a cookie, ask for a *biscuit*; potato chips are called *crisps*, and French fries are *chips.*

Terminology in a train station should not present much of a problem. The baggage room is LEFT LUGGAGE, and LOST PROPERTY translates easily into lost and found. Elevators are labeled *lifts*, but *subway* means a pedestrian underground street crossing. The *Underground*, or *Tube*, is the British version of our subway.

A *carriage* is a (rail) coach, and a *coach* is a long-distance bus. Should you hear the term *goods wagon* or *goods train*, that translates to a freight car or a freight train in American. Aboard a train, the conductor usually is referred to as the *guard;* the engineer becomes the train *driver.*

The British measure their body weight in *stones*—a stone being a unit of fourteen pounds. A person weighing fourteen stone six pounds would gross out at 202 pounds avoirdupois. A popular measurement of elapsed time is a *fortnight*, meaning fourteen days or two weeks. Britain's conversion to a decimal currency system has not changed the slang for the pound sterling—it's still a *quid.*

British Pubs

The pub is uniquely British and can be found only on the British Isles, because the ingredient that makes a true "public house" is not its construction, architecture, furniture, or the spirits it dispenses—it is the clientele. The term *public house* means just that. Everyone is welcome, even Americans and Australians.

The local, as most British pubs are lovingly referred to, is an organic part of the community. It ranks in importance along with the local postal office and the town hall—perhaps even higher. The locals who support it generally prefer to stand when they imbibe, for pub etiquette must be observed at all times. Pub etiquette also dictates that you pay for the "round" when served and if you accept a drink, you are expected to buy a round in return.

To accommodate the differences in drinking etiquette of their visitors, most pubs have a second bar area, which is identified as a lounge or a saloon. There are more seats and usually the drinks cost a bit more.

When are the pubs open? Licensing hours now generally permit English pubs to remain open from 1100 to 2300 Monday through Saturday and Sundays from 1200 to 1500 and 1900 to 2230 in England and Wales; 1230 to 1430 and 1830 to 2300 in Scotland. You must be over eighteen to buy or consume alcoholic beverages in a pub. Children fourteen years and older may be admitted legally to a pub and may consume nonalcoholic drinks. Children of all ages are usually admitted to licensed restaurants; they are also admitted to "beer gardens" and family rooms, which many pubs have.

Closing time in a pub is quite an event and frequently can create confusion among the uninformed and the uninitiated. At the appointed hour, the owner or head barkeep announces, "Time, gentlemen!" in a loud, authoritative voice. At that instant, a bar towel is draped over the beer pumps, and everyone quickly attends to drinking up and hastily departing the premises. Without prior knowledge of this procedure, visitors have frequently mistaken closing time for a fire drill and have begun evacuating the building via the closest window!

A pub is usually rated by the congeniality of its owner, and unless "on holiday," he or she is usually found on the premises during operating hours. An entrepreneurial lot, many owners offer "pub grub" in their establishments. Visitors find it a good alternative to Wendy's or McDonald's for a snack or a lunch because a Frosty can never really compete with a good pint of ale or porter.

The personality of a pub greets you at the door. You can tell in an instant whether or not it's your kind of place. If its ambience reaches out to you, enter. No doubt a local or two will note your entrance with a friendly nod as the bartender beams at you and asks, "What'll you have, governor?" When advised, the bartender will then indicate with a slight directional nod of her head that it will be served in the lounge area. Pay when served. Tip the bartender, but never tip the owner if he or she brings the drinks to the table to bid you welcome. The owner is the host; you are the guest. Later, you might join the locals at the bar; but remember, remain standing and pay for a round when it's your turn to buy. Who knows, the locals might suggest that you drop around again.

British Passenger Trains

Over the last decade, the services on the British rail passenger network have come a long way—with yet a long way to go. There is still a discernible difference between the operating speeds and the passenger comforts of the railroads of continental Europe and those of Britain, yet the gap is narrowing. Plus, a great refurbishment is taking place in the more than 2,500 rail stations in Britain, with completion scheduled by the millennium.

The front-runner of the British rail stable is its High Speed Train (HST), the InterCity 125. Nicknamed the "Journey Shrinker," the world's fastest diesel train is shrinking journeys on many of the main routes out of London. From King's Cross Station, for example, the *Flying Scotsman,* an InterCity 125, covers the 393 miles between London and Edinburgh in four hours flat—an average of 98 miles per hour, and that includes a station stop at York and Newcastle in England before crossing the Scottish border.

Hourly service by 125s links the three capitals: London, Edinburgh, and Cardiff. InterCity 125 service also extends from London to Plymouth and Penzance. Leading the 125 fleet to England's west is the *Golden Hind,* appropriately named after Sir Francis Drake's famous sailing vessel.

InterCity 125 trains offer comfort as well as speed. They have a whole range of luxury features, including air-conditioning, soundproofing, automatic interior doors, and a wide choice of meals, snacks, and drinks. The trains are powered by two 2,250-horsepower diesel-electric engines, one at each end of the train. The 125 coaches are identified by letter (A, B, C, etc.), and the stations they serve have their platform positions marked accordingly.

The light at the end of the tunnel grows brighter and brighter. By InterCity 125 service from London, you can now reach Cardiff, Wales, in one hour, fifty-seven minutes. Running times are being slashed on all major British rail lines. A train trip from London to Glasgow used to take six hours; now you're there in only five hours and fourteen minutes!

Aside from the InterCity 125s and the equally fast and comfortable all-electric passenger trains on major routes, there is a paucity of modern commuter-type trains on many of Britain's intermediate lines. For example, although train service south of London is completely electrified, for the most part it is served by four-car units, some of which have already passed their thirty-eighth "birthdays." These older trains have seen yeoman duty through the years and show more than a fair amount of wear and tear.

Along with Beatlemania, graffiti arrived in Britain accompanied by modern packaging, which produces litter in abundance. The older trains, however, were designed in the days when cleaning labor was plentiful and cheap. Washing as many as eighty windows on a single coach wasn't a problem then, but it is now. Moreover, air-conditioning is nonexistent in the older trains, which is not terrible since summers in the British Isles are generally milder than those in North America. But heating can be a problem. Not many years ago, train passengers set out on their journeys wrapped in heavy overcoats and shod with thick-soled shoes. Full heat in the coach brought complaints of stuffiness.

Today's grumbles from thinly clad travelers are very much the opposite. The "old units" are gradually being replaced by new suburban-type trains, and some of the vintage units are being refurbished with more comfortable seats, better lighting, heating, and soundproofing. Nevertheless, it will be a while before the "generation gap" in British rolling stock is overcome.

Possibly on a day excursion off the main lines, you may ride in a loco-motive-hauled coach with an exit door for each compartment. We've counted as many as nine doors to a side on some coaches. These cars are relics from the days when station porters opened and closed the doors for passengers. Consequently, you won't find any door handles inside the compartment. To get out, lower the window and open the door from the outside.

There are many types of railcars, including sleeping, restaurant, buffet, and Pullman cars, along with the standard passenger carriages (coaches). British Pullman cars differ from the Pullmans of North America in that they do not convert at night to provide sleeping accommodations. Instead, British Pullmans are the elite of the line, the best in daytime comfort, and exclusively first-class.

Even travelers holding first-class BritRail Passes are required to pay a supplemental fare for occupancy, and seat reservations are obligatory. This luxury service operates on the London-to-Manchester/Liverpool route. Basically, it is designed to offer the businessperson morning and afternoon services between England's capital and its leading commercial center. Well worth the experience, but we suggest that you dress appropriately for the occasion if you want to engage in tycoon-to-tycoon conversations or afternoon tea with other passengers. In London, the Pullman trains depart from Euston Station. When accommodations are available, last-minute reservations and supplementary payment can be arranged with the conductor.

First-class sleeping cars have single-berth compartments; economy-class sleepers have two-berth compartments. Sleeping-car charges in Britain are economical: $57 per person for first class and $48 per person for a standard-class double; there is no discounted rate for children. The sleeping cars are equipped with fresh bedding, washing basins with soap and towels, a shaver outlet, and bottled drinking water. Sleeping-car passengers are served with morning tea or coffee and biscuits free of charge, and they generally can remain in the sleeping cars at their destination for an hour after arrival. The charge is standard for all destinations regardless of the distance.

With such attractive prices, an overnight trip aboard a sleeper may outweigh the alternative of seeking a night's lodging in a city and an early morning departure in order to make your destination on time. Consider the sleeping cars for excursions from London to Plymouth, Penzance, and Inverness; available daily, except Saturday. Sleeper services also operate between London and Edinburgh, Glasgow, Aberdeen, and Fort William.

Most InterCity trains haul restaurant cars. If not, there usually is a buffet car from which you can obtain snacks and beverages. Aboard the InterCity fleet, restaurant cars offer a wide range of freshly prepared traditional dishes. Silver Standard restaurant service is available on many 125s and on selected "business" trains—the Manchester/Liverpool Pullman, for example. Passengers holding first-class tickets who wish to take meals can reserve seats in the restaurant car or in adjacent coaches. Breakfast aboard British trains has always been a great attraction. It's hearty, generally very good, and, of course, comes with hot tea or coffee.

Some buffet cars offer "grill" meals, which you may enjoy either there or back at your seat. Seating in the buffet cars is not assignable, thereby providing a reasonable opportunity to be seated while you select from the bill of fare. One innovation found aboard many food-service rail cars is beer and lager on draft. This, according to many railroad buffs, is an outstanding stride forward in the annals of railroad engineering!

Admittedly, dining aboard a speeding train is an unusual gastronomic experience, but it can be on the expensive side. Although food catering aboard a British train is far more economical than similar services on the trains of the continent, those seeking less expensive food may want to utilize the food facilities found at most rail stations in Britain. They range in service from complete restaurants serving a variety of hot and cold dishes to a snack bar–type operation. Some have off-license provisions allowing you to purchase alcoholic beverages for consumption elsewhere, but all bars operating in the stations, unlike those on the trains, must observe the local licensing hours for drinks.

The most economical food you may enjoy on a train in Britain is, of course, that which you bring aboard yourself. Many of the station restaurants will prepare box lunches for you to take on your trip. Ask for the "buffet-pack" service. Your hotel or bed-and-breakfast probably can provide similar service. We suggest that you make your initial inquiry a day ahead of your first planned day excursion.

First Class, Standard Class?

On most British trains you have a choice of first- or standard-class travel. More and more routes are offering strictly standard class or very few first-class carriages. BritRail Passes and Flexipasses are sold for both classes. First-class seats are wider and more spacious. If that is the sort of accommodations you want, then it is worth paying the extra price. Standard class is, however, an excellent standard. All the facilities aboard the trains, such as restaurant and buffet services, are available for both first- and standard-class travelers.

The average British citizen usually travels by standard-class carriage (coach). In fact, it is so much the custom that if you want to purchase a first-class ticket, you must specifically state "first-class"; otherwise, you will automatically receive a standard-class ticket. This does not mean that you will find the standard-class carriages crowded, while the first-class sections remain vacant.

First class offers extra comfort and is less crowded. First-class accommodations for weekend and holiday travel are particularly desirable. Seats may be reserved in both classes, which is a wise move if your journey is a "must" and the distance is great. "Riding the cases" (sitting on your suitcase for lack of a seat) is not comfortable!

Seat reservations may be made in any major train terminal throughout Britain. Some of the twenty-five operating train companies in Britain offer free seat reservations, some charge a £1 to £2 fee, and some do not accept seat reservations at all due to frequency of service. In addition, Birmingham, Cardiff, Gatwick, Glasgow, Heathrow, Manchester, and Stansted Airports have rail ticket booths where you may make reservations immediately after your arrival. You may obtain advance reservations before arriving in Britain, but it is far more economical to make them once on British soil.

Travelers holding first-class BritRail passes may travel in either first- or standard-class carriages, which is a nice option when the good-looking person you've been yearning to chat with boards the standard-class section. It's a disaster, however, if he or she moves to the first-class section while you're holding a standard-class ticket!

You will find some single-class trains operating on branch lines. This means that the first-class accommodations are not available aboard that particular train. It is a nice, polite British way of avoiding the somewhat unrefined term, "second class only."

Similar to those on the continent, first-class British rail cars are marked distinctively by a yellow band running the length of each car above its doors and windows. On other-than-mainline service, where both first- and standard-class accommodations may be provided in the same car, a yellow band will be shown for only the first-class portion of the car. Restaurant cars, buffets, and cars containing other forms of food-catering facilities are identified by a red band above their doors and windows.

Except for those of the InterCity 125s and 225s, it is difficult to determine exactly where the first-class coaches will halt during an en route station stop. The non-English-speaking nations of Europe generally provide a diagram of each train's composition and where it will stop in the station.

Not so in Britain. According to the equipment in use, the first-class section of a British train can be at the head, the rear, or the middle of the train. Through experience, we have devised a system that is relatively effective in determining where the yellow-striped cars will stop.

Position yourself midway on the platform and scan for the yellow band as the train enters the station. Should it pass you, take off to the head of the train; if it doesn't, head in the other direction. Should the yellow-striped car stop directly in front of you, fate has been kind to you this day, but you can bet it won't happen again soon.

There is an increase in the nonsmoking accommodations aboard British trains. The overall percentage of nonsmoking seats currently is about 75 percent, reflecting the noticeable change in the public attitude toward smoking. There is a stiff fine for violating the rule. So if you are a smoker, keep your eyes alert for the red nonsmoking signs and smoke only in the areas so designated.

Train Schedules

British timetables are generally divided into sections according to the pattern of services provided. A typical two-part division is "Mondays to Saturdays" and "Sundays." You may run across a mix, however, including "Mondays to Fridays," "Mondays to Saturdays," or "Saturdays and Sundays." All days stated are inclusive. In other words, "Mondays to Saturdays" includes all six days. (The schedules appearing in *Britain by BritRail* are stated as "Mondays through Saturdays.")

Always be certain that you look at the correct part of the schedule for the particular day of the week on which you wish to travel, and always double-check departure times and platform number of the next train you wish to take when you arrive into a station. Sometimes alterations are necessary. Another caution: services may be modified on days preceding and immediately following Bank Holidays. The best bet for a "must" trip, a late night return, or an early morning departure is to check your plans with the train personnel in the station Travel Centers. Extensive engineering work is often conducted on the British rail system on weekends, which frequently affects passengers' schedules. Telephones may also be employed for inquiries. Useful telephone numbers are listed in *Britain by BritRail* for this purpose.

You should experience little difficulty in verifying the departure time of your selected train or locating the platform from which it departs once you've made it to the station—providing that in London you've gone to the proper station. Airport-style digital displays are the usual source for such information in most British stations. You will find them in the main station halls and also on the train platforms in many stations. Even the old-fashioned train bulletin boards, however, can still provide the needed information. Augmenting displayed train-departure information are the usual vocal announcements in the station halls and on the platforms. For the most part, they differ from those made by Amtrak because you can understand them. Perhaps it's the accent that makes it possible.

Ask the Guard

Every British passenger train travels with a conductor aboard. As previously explained, his official title is *guard*. This person carries with him (or her)—in either his handbook or his head, a potpourri of valuable information. For example, if you are required to change trains in order to arrive at your final destination, talk to the guard. The London day excursion to Lincoln is one in which you should change trains at Newark Northgate, approximately one and one-half hours after departing London. Will the train departing there for Lincoln Central be standing across the platform from the train you arrive on from London, or will a platform change be necessary? The guard has this information, and it's yours for the asking.

Perhaps en route you learn that the train you are traveling on will be passing a famous British landmark, say a castle. On which side of the train will it pass? If you are a castle buff, maybe you would like to come back on another day to visit the castle. Is there a local train station near the castle? Is there a local bus to take you there if the castle is beyond walking distance? Is there a pub or inn in the vicinity? Surprisingly, you'll probably get responses to all of the above plus a condensed history lesson on the castle and its surroundings—all from the guard.

The guard becomes invaluable when you decide to change your itinerary or vary the time to return to your hotel. With a quick reference to his handbook, he will be able to tell you the time of the next train or the last one you may take that evening. He is also an excellent source of the correct time, for his watch is always set to the second and checked with the station's master clock. In many ways, the guard becomes your unofficial tour guide—or guardian angel, as the case may be.

The Channel Tunnel and Crossing the English Channel

The newest method of crossing the English Channel is to go under it via the tunnel (affectionately known as "The Chunnel") connecting England with France and the rest of Europe. Direct rail service from London to Paris or Brussels takes you from city center to city center in only three hours to Paris and three hours, fifteen minutes to Brussels.

Other convenient ways of crossing the English Channel between England and France is by P&O Stena Line Sea France or Hovercraft and SeaCat Catamaran by Hoverspeed between Dover and Calais. Hoverspeed SeaCat operates between Folkestone and Boulogne. For information, visit the Ferry Terminal pages at the Web site http://www.seaview.do.uk.

Choosing a Channel Crossing

Since there are various ways of crossing the English Channel and the North Sea en route to Europe, which one should you select? The fastest route from London to Paris or Brussels is through the tunnel under the Channel, utilizing the Eurostar passenger services departing London's Waterloo International Eurostar Terminal.

For those who prefer to skim over the channel rather than under it, the fastest means of crossing the English Channel for direct rail connections between London Charing Cross and Paris is by Hoverspeed's SeaCat or catamaran service through Folkestone and Boulogne.

As previously described, London to Paris by P&O Stena Line ferry takes you from London's Victoria Station or Charing Cross Station to Folkstone Harbor by special boat train right to the dock. After the crossing, a French National Railroads train waiting in Calais continues your journey on to Paris. You will arrive in the Gare du Nord (North Station) of Paris approximately four hours after you reach the French port.

The "Chunnel" and Eurostar Trains

In 1888, Louis Figuier proclaimed that "linking France and England will meet one of the present day needs of civilization." On May 6, 1994, England's Queen Elizabeth II and France's President François Mitterrand brought Figuier's words to life and inaugurated a new era in European train travel: the linking of England and France via a 31-mile tunnel that runs underground and under the English Channel. More than 17 million tons of earth were moved to build the two rail tunnels (one for northbound and one for southbound traffic) and one service tunnel.

Plagued by delays and billions of dollars in cost overruns, the Chunnel has proven to be one of the world's largest undertakings. The project cost more than $13 billion and took seven years to complete. Napoleon's engineer, Albert Mathieu, planned the first tunnel in 1802, incorporating an underground passage with ventilation chimneys above the waves. For obvious reasons the British were nervous. Later, in 1880, the first real attempt at a tunnel was undertaken by Colonel Beaumont, who bored 2,000 meters into the earth before abandoning the project. When work on another tunnel began in 1974, the Beaumont tunnel was found to be in good condition. Construction of the current tunnels, which are 38 kilometers in length undersea and have an average depth of 40 meters under the seabed, began in 1987.

Operated by the British, French (SNCF), and Belgian (SNCB) railways, the Eurotunnel provides three different types of service between England and the continent. Eurostar provides passenger service, and Le Shuttle provides automobile, coach, and lorry service between Folkestone and Calais. International rail freight rounds out the list.

Eurostar service is offered from London's Waterloo International Eurostar Terminal to Calais, Lille, Brussels, Paris, the French Alps, and Disneyland Paris. Travel times from London to Paris are reduced from more than five hours to three hours; Brussels is only two hours and forty-five minutes away, thus making a European Capitals tour nothing more than a day excursion. BritRail Pass holders receive a discount on Eurostar tickets; call Rail Pass Express at (800) 722-7151 or for more information visit http://www.railpass.com.

Eurostar services include departures from Glasgow, Edinburgh, York, Manchester, Birmingham, and cities in between that link them to Paris in either direction. These direct daytime Eurostar Regional Services reduce travel times from Edinburgh to Paris, for example, from more than twelve hours to about nine hours.

Plans are to add European Night Services for those wishing to arrive in Paris or Brussels in time for breakfast. Night services will include departures from London to Amsterdam, as well as to Dortmund and Frankfurt in Germany. Both seated and sleeper accommodations will be offered for overnight departures, featuring on-board catering and luggage storage compartments.

The sleek Eurostar trains (Trans Manche Super Trains) each carry 779 passengers (206 in first class and 548 in second class, plus 25 premium first-class seats) and reach speeds of 186 miles per hour in Europe, with speeds through the Chunnel of 80 miles per hour. The train is based primarily on the TGV (Train à Grand Vitesse) but was redesigned to accommodate the three different voltage types encountered en route. The trains are accessible to handicapped passengers and provide sufficient storage for luggage.

Those taking advantage of a trip from Paris or Brussels to London on a Eurostar train are in for a treat. The trains offer the comfort and amenities comparable to few trains in the world. From the moment of departure you're in for a smooth, quiet ride, and even when you enter the tunnel the only noticeable change is the sudden darkness. Those concerned with changes in air pressure needn't worry. Air flow through the tunnel is regulated to minimize changes in pressure, and few, if any, passengers are uncomfortable.

Eurostar staff members are multilingual and are available to provide assistance the minute you enter the terminal to the minute you exit the platform. You'll notice them right away, with their navy blue uniforms accented by yellow scarves or ties. If you have any questions, don't be shy—they're there to serve you, and serve you they do.

Passengers traveling first class are treated to an onboard meal ranging from breakfast to dinner depending on the time of day. Second-class passengers won't starve either, as a buffet car and roving refreshment cart services are available at nominal costs. Whichever service you choose, you're in for a moving experience!

Given the frequency of rail service and the speed of travel, it's easy to see how a "quick trip" to Paris, Brussels, or any continental destination can be accomplished. Following is the schedule for Eurostar trains running between London and Paris. To purchase Eurostar tickets or for scheduling information on trains to other cities, *Tel.:* (800) 722–7151, *Fax:* (614) 764–0711, or visit http://www.railpass.com/eurostar.

Note: Be certain to check in at your departure station *at least* twenty minutes prior to departure.

LONDON–PARIS

Monday–Friday Train #	Depart	Arrive	Saturday Train #	Depart	Arrive	Sunday Train #	Depart	Arrive
9078	0515	0923	9078**	0515	0923	9010	0810	1223
9002	0619	1023	9002	0619	1023	9012	0853	1253
9006	0723	1123	9006	0723	1123	9014	0953	1353
9008***	0753	1147	9008***	0753	1147	9018	1010	1417
9010	0823	1223	9010	0823	1223	9024	1157	1556
9012	0853	1253	9012	0853	1253	9028	1253	1653
9014+	0923	1323	9014+	0923	1253	9030	1314	1720
9016	0953	1353	9016	0953	1353	9032	1357	1756
9018	1023	1417	9018	1023	1417	9038	1510	1923
9020	1053	1453	9020	1053	1453	9040	1553	1947
9024	1157	1556	9024	1157	1556	9042	1623	2023
9028	1253	1653	9028	1253	1653	9046	1723	2117
9032	1357	1756	9032	1357	1756	9048	1753	2153
9038	1523	1923	9038	1523	1923	9050	1823	2223
9040+	1553	1947	9042	1553	1947	9052	1853	2247
						9054	1923	2323

PARIS–LONDON

Monday–Friday			Saturday			Sunday		
Train #	**Depart**	**Arrive**	**Train #**	**Depart**	**Arrive**	**Train #**	**Depart**	**Arrive**
9005	0637	0845	9005***	0637	0839	9011	0807	1030
9007	0716	0909	9007+++	0710	0909	9015	0910	1130
9011	0813	1013	9011	0813	1013	9019	1019	1230
9015	0910	1113	9015	0910	1113	9025	1143	1347
9017***	0943	1143	9017	0943	1143	9027	1219	1430
9019	1019	1213	9019	1019	1213	9031	1304	1526
9025	1143	1343	9025	1143	1343	9035	1416	1609
9027	1219	1413	9027	1219	1413	9037	1443	1643
9031	1304	1509	9031	1304	1509	9039	1519	1713
9035*	1416	1609	9037	1443	1643	9043	1607	1813
9037	1443	1643	9039	1519	1713	9047	1710	1913
9039	1519	1713	9043	1607	1813	9049	1743	1943
9041++	1543	1743	9047	1710	1913	9051	1819	2013
9043	1607	1813	9051	1819	2013	9053	1843	2043
9047	1710	1913	9053	1843	2043	9055	1919	2113
						9059	2007	2213

*Fridays only
** Mondays and Fridays only
*** May 25–Sept. 5
+ July 3–Sept.6
++ Friday only, July 3–Sept. 6
+++ Sept. 12–26

LONDON–BRUSSELS

Monday–Friday			Saturday			Sunday		
Train #	Depart	Arrive	Train #	Depart	Arrive	Train #	Depart	Arrive
9108	0614	1002	9108	0614	1001	9116	0814	1210
9110	0653	1037	9110	0653	1037	9124	1014	1405
9116	0827	1210	9116	0827	1210	9132	1214	1610
9124	1027	1405	9124	1027	1405	9140	1410	1802
9132	1227	1610	9132	1227	1610	9148	1627	2010
9140	1423	1802	9140	1423	1802	9152	1727	2106
9148	1627	2010	9148	1627	2010	9156	1827	2210
9152	1719	2106	9152	1723	2106	9160	1927	2310
9156	1827	2210	9160	1927	2310			
9160	1927	2310						

BRUSSELS–LONDON

Monday–Friday			Saturday			Sunday		
Train #	Depart	Arrive	Train #	Depart	Arrive	Train #	Depart	Arrive
9109	0702	0850	9109	0702	0843	9117	0856	1043
9113	0803	0939	9113	0803	0939	9125	1102	1247
9117	0856	1039	9117	0856	1039	9133	1302	1447
9125	1102	1243	9125	1102	1243	9141	1456	1639
9133	1302	1443	9133	1302	1443	9149	1702	1843
9141	1456	1639	9141	1456	1639	9153	1756	1939
9149	1702	1843	9149	1702	1843	9157	1856	2039
9153	1756	1939	9157	1856	2039	9165	2102	2239
1957	1856	2039	9165	2102	2243			
9165	2102	2243						

EUROSTAR FARES

Eurostar fares are provided in U.S. dollars one-way, in either direction. Please contact Rail Pass Express, Inc. at (800) 722–7151 or www.railpass.com. Call (614) 793–7650 for Eurostar fares to other cities serviced.

London to Paris

	FIRST CLASS	SECOND CLASS	
Adult Fare	$199	$139	
Senior Fare	$149	$115	Senior: Age 60 and Over
Youth Fare	NA	$75	Youth: Age 12–25 Railpass discount not available for youth.
Child Fare	$99	$55	Child: Age 4–11 Railpass discount not available for children.
Adult Fare w/rail pass	$139	$79	Discounted ticket available with the purchase of a Eurail Pass, Europass, BritRail Pass, FrancePass, or Benelux Tourrail Pass

London to Brussels

	FIRST CLASS	SECOND CLASS	
Adult Fare	$199	$139	
Senior Fare	$149	$115	Senior: Age 60 and Over
Youth Fare	NA	$75	Youth: Age 12–25 Railpass discount not available for youth.
Child Fare	$99	$55	Child: Age 4–11 Railpass discount not available for children.
Adult Fare w/rail pass	$139	$79	Discounted ticket available with the purchase of a EurailPass, Europass, BritRail Pass, FrancePass, or Benelux Tourrail Pass

Seat reservations are mandatory on all Eurostar trains and refunds are subject to a 15% cancellation fee.

P&O Stena Line

P&O Stena Line services (http://www.stenaline.com) on the English Channel are one class only; both first- and second-class accommodations, however, are available on the boat trains between London and Dover. The BritRail Pass is accepted for the rail portion of the journey from London to the port. Separate tickets, however, must be purchased for the sea portion.

These tickets are available at the ticket offices of London rail stations or at the P&O Stena Line Travel Centre at the head of Platform 2 in the Victoria Station. Seat reservations are advisable throughout the year for the boat trains departing from this station. The term "boat train" applies to those trains departing from London's Charing Cross to Dover Priory for direct sailing connections at Dover's Eastern Docks with P&O Stena ferries crossing to the French port of Calais. The trains traveling from London to Dover Priory are met by a courtesy bus service to the docks.

Boat trains go from London's Charing Cross and Waterloo East directly to the pier at Folkestone Harbor. Boat trains going to the port of Folkestone for Hoverspeed SeaCat services (http://www.hoverspeed.co.uk) do not stop at Folkestone's Central Station. Regular train service is available to Dover, terminating at Dover Priory (Dover's main station), and to Folkestone, where trains call at Folkestone Central but not at Folkestone Harbor. Due to the myriad sailings to the continent, we suggest that you check with the Stena Line Travel Centre at the head of Platform 2 in the Victoria Station for additional information, reservations, and current schedules.

Hoverspeed's SeaCat

A SeaCat vessel is 242 feet in length with a beam of 85 feet. It can carry 450 passengers and 80 vehicles on a separate car deck. It is powered by four diesel engines housed in the vessel's side hulls that generate jets of water for steering and for propulsion at speeds of up to 42 knots, making it the world's fastest passenger ferry. Known as a wave-piercing catamaran, it has a narrow hull that is designed to pass through waves rather than ride over them. In 1990, the Hoverspeed Great Britain earned its place in history by making the quickest crossing of the Atlantic by a passenger ship since 1952. This record-breaking voyage took just three days, seven hours, and fifty-two minutes at an average speed of 36.6 knots. It also holds the record for the fastest crossing of the English Channel by a passenger ship.

Aboard a SeaCat, you get the sensation of traveling in a wide-body jet airplane. You can settle into an aircraft-style seat, or you can stroll around the cabin, which is four times wider than the largest jumbo jet, or you can watch the captain and the crew through windows just behind the bridge as they guide the ship across the busy English Channel at a cruising speed of 35 knots. Passengers are advised of the SeaCat's safety and emergency procedures by a video demonstration quite similar to the way that such briefings are now conducted on transatlantic aircraft.

Because the cabin of the SeaCat is on flexible mounts and the engines are positioned down in the side hulls away from the passenger area, the levels of noise and vibration are greatly reduced. The stylish interior is more like an airliner than a ferry boat. You can stretch your legs by taking a stroll on deck and watch the waves whiz by, pick up a sandwich in the snack bar, or enjoy a drink in the panoramic stern bar. A duty-free shop is also available to help you stock up on bargains.

What we found most amazing about the SeaCat was its maneuverability, which is made possible by having steering and reversing controls on waterjets fitted on both outboard hulls of the craft. On the evening prior to our crossing to Boulogne, we observed our SeaCat arriving in the harbor in Folkestone, where it turned about on its own length and then docked sideways! This same maneuver was repeated as we landed in Boulogne the following day. The SeaCat's maneuverability, together with fast check-in, boarding, and disembarkment procedures adds up to an enjoyable high-speed crossing of the English Channel.

Even with the opening of the English Channel Tunnel, Britain's ferry operators are optimistic about what the future holds in store for them. We are of the opinion that with watercraft like the SeaCat and the P&O Stena Lynx—and even bigger ones are on the drawing board—crossing the Channel by ship will always remain a delightful alternative.

Other Crossings

Dover–Ostend (Oostende). A courtesy bus connection is available between Dover Priory and the Hoverspeed terminal at Dover Hoverport. The Hoverspeed SeaCat catamaran (http://www.hoverspeed.co.uk) crosses between Dover and the Belgian port of Ostend with train service connecting with Brussels and Cologne (Köln). The crossing takes two hours, and there are up to seven crossings per day during peak season.

Train departures for the Hoverspeed leave from London's Charing Cross to Dover Priory Station. Passengers must report to track 14 for a boarding card at least twenty minutes before train departure. This route is the most direct sea connection with Brussels. By rail and Hoverspeed, the average time between London's Charing Cross and the Midi (South) Station in Brussels is seven hours.

Newhaven–Dieppe. If you are looking for an alternate route between Britain and France, P&O Stena Line ship and Lynx catamaran services are available from the English port of Newhaven, east of Brighton, to the maritime terminal of Dieppe in France. The sea route is 71 miles and the crossing takes four hours by ship and two hours, fifteen minutes by catamaran. Night crossings are made throughout the year.

If the English Channel is not in a huffy mood, this can be a very pleasant crossing. Victoria Station is the point of departure from London. The boat train calls at Gatwick Airport en route to the Newhaven harbor. The French National Railroads' express-train service between Dieppe and Paris takes slightly more than two hours. St. Lazare is the rail terminal in Paris. The entire trip takes approximately nine hours.

Harwich–Hook of Holland. This is an excellent routing for travelers ranging between Britain and the Netherlands by sea. Ships are provided by Stena Line HSS Fast Ferry. It is the most direct sea link between London and Amsterdam. Convenient connections may also be made from the Hook of Holland (Hoek Van Holland) to Brussels, Belgium.

Day crossings only are now available on this route. Departure out of London is from the Liverpool Street Station.

Many famous express trains utilize this North Sea crossing as well as regular through-train service to Belgium, Germany, Russia, and Switzerland. If you are looking for international intrigue, you'll be most likely to find it on the Harwich-Hook of Holland crossing. Running between the Liverpool Street Station and the Harwich harbor takes one hour and twenty minutes.

Portsmouth–Cherbourg/Le Havre. Trains depart London's Waterloo Station and arrive in Portsmouth Harbor rail station in about one hour, thirty minutes. P&O European Ferries provide ship services. Arriving in Portsmouth, passengers are advised to use the bus service between the Portsmouth Harbor rail station and the Portsmouth Continental Ferry Port. The crossing from Portsmouth to Cherbourg takes four hours and forty-five minutes (eight hours, thirty minutes to nine hours, forty-five minutes at night); the sailing to Le Havre requires five hours and forty-five minutes (seven to nine hours at night). Both routes to the French capital pass through Normandy, where the Allies stormed ashore on 6 June 1943 in the invasion of Hitler's "Fortress Europe."

Please note:

• Holders of BritRail, Eurail, Europass, France Pass, and Benelux Tourrail passes receive discounted fares on Eurostar services.

• BritRail Passes are NOT accepted by P&O Stena Line, Hoverspeed, or any of the privately owned shipping companies operating on either the English Channel or the North Sea.

• Point-to-point tickets must be purchased for all sea voyages and continuing rail travel once you have departed Britain.

• BritRail Passes cannot be utilized for rail travel in continental Europe.

• If you also hold a Eurailpass, you may have it validated at the rail station of the European port upon arrival and then continue your rail trip without the inconvenience of having to purchase point-to-point tickets.

Crossing the Irish Sea

Some of the ferry crossings on the continent of Europe involve actually loading the passenger-rail cars aboard the ferry. When this occurs, the passengers need not even disembark. But at all ferry ports in Britain, passengers are required to leave the train and board the ferry. Then they board another train after landing. You will find that this change of transportation mode is no great hardship. In fact, it can be a very enjoyable experience by including drinks and dinner aboard the ferry, followed by a chat with fellow passengers. The salon of a ferry is a good place for meeting people. Everyone has a common interest in travel, and everyone is going to the same destination.

Crossing the Irish Sea is very much like crossing the English Channel by ferry, except you cannot forward your luggage on to the Republic of Ireland. What you take is what you carry. So, adhere to our admonition to "go lightly" when it comes to luggage. Porter service is almost nonexistent at the marine terminals, except by prearrangement. It is best not to expect porter service. Furthermore, the trolleys (baggage carts) found in the majority of British rail stations are missing at the piers because their use is impractical on the sloping ramps and gangways used for access to the vessels.

When you visit Ireland, keep in mind that the Republic of Ireland and Northern Ireland are two separate political states. Northern Ireland is a part of the United Kingdom, while the republic is independent. There are no customs to contend with when arriving in Northern Ireland from England, Scotland, or Wales. On the other hand, customs formalities entering the Republic of Ireland should present no problem for the bona fide traveler. The efficient "declare" or "nothing-to-declare" system is used by Irish customs.

Duty-free shops are operated on all of the shipping lines crossing the Irish Sea between Britain and the Republic of Ireland. Crossing times are adequate enough to permit shopping at leisure. Except for tobacco and alcoholic beverages, however, there are few bargains. Check with the salespersons to be certain that you are not exceeding the import limits. Duty payments on excesses can be stiff. Tax-free shops are not available on routes to Northern Ireland.

BritRail Pass + Ireland covers the complete network of trains in England, Scotland, Wales, Northern Ireland, and the Republic of Ireland. Choose five or ten days of travel to be completed within one month in first or standard class with this pass.

The pass also includes a round trip on the Stena Line between Holyhead and Dun Laoghaire by HSS (High Speed Sea Service), between Fishguard and Rosslare by ship or LYNX catamaran, and between Stranraer and Belfast via ship. The new HSS ships cruise between Dun Laoghaire and Belfast at twice the speed of conventional ships. If you prefer a more leisurely cruise, by all means choose Stena's ships.

Sea Links to Ireland

Stranraer–Belfast. The new HSS ships cruise between Stranraer and Belfast in only one hour, thirty minutes. The Hoverspeed's SeaCat departs from Stranraer West Pier and arrives at Belfast Donegal Quay. Conventional ship service takes three and a half hours. Food and beverage services are available aboard. There are no customs formalities for entering Northern Ireland from Scotland and no tax-free shops aboard.

Train connections from London through Euston Station with overnight sleeper service are available between London and Stranraer. A change of trains is required at Glasgow Central Station. Access to England, Scotland, and Wales by rail is through Glasgow. Direct train service from the Glasgow Central Station to Stranraer Harbor takes two hours, six minutes. Note that BritRail Passes are not accepted on trains in Ireland unless you have purchased the BritRail Pass + Ireland option.

Sailing to Ireland

	Services per Day	Approx. Journey Time (house)	Approx. One-way Fares, $U.S.	
			First	Standard
FROM LONDON BY TRAIN AND HSS (HIGH-SPEED SEA SERVICE)				
Dun Laoghaire (via Holyhead)	1	6½	$126	$96
Rosslare (via Fishguard)	1	7	$124	$85
Belfast (via Stranraer)	1	9½	$184	$126
FROM LONDON BY TRAIN AND SHIP				
Dun Laoghaire (via Holyhead)	2	10	$162	$132
Rosslare (via Fishguard)	2	9	$160	$121
Belfast (via Stranraer)	1	11	$216	$166
SEA CROSSING ONLY BY SUPERFERRY				
Holyhead–Dublin	1	3½	$28	$28
Fishguard–Rosslare	2	3½	$28	$28
SEA CROSSING ONLY BY HSS/CATAMARAN				
Holyhead–Dun Laoghaire (HSS)	5	1½	$36	$36
Fishguard–Rosslare (Stena Lynx)	5	1½	$28	$28
Stranraer–Belfast (SeaCat)	4	1½	$41	$41
Stranraer–Belfast (HSS)	5	1½	$36	$36

Note: For round-trip: double one-way price. Special fares available on some routes upon request. One class only on ship. Reservations (approx. $5.00 per person per journey) are required. Sleeping berths available on some overnight services for an additional fee.

Holyhead–Dún Laoghaire. This crossing is from Holyhead in Wales to Dun Laoghaire (a suburb of Dublin) in Ireland. The elapsed time from port to port is three hours, thirty minutes. Stena Lynx catamaran service is also available, taking only one hour, thirty minutes. Food and beverage services are available aboard the ferries, and tax-free shops are open during the crossing. Customs formalities are observed upon disembarkation. There are daytime connections from London's Euston Station to Holyhead. The ferries offer one-class accommodations.

Connections from the port at Dun Laoghaire into Dublin can be made by train, city bus, or taxi. All of these transportation modes are available at the pier. Eurailpass and BritRail Pass + Ireland options are accepted on the trains of the Republic of Ireland; the BritRail Classic and Flexipass, however, are not.

Fishguard–Rosslare. This Stena Line ferry crossing is recommended for train travelers bound for Cork, Killarney, and the Shannon Airport. Conventional ship service takes about three hours, thirty minutes; Stena Lynx catamaran service takes only one hour, forty minutes. Food, beverages, and tax-free shops are available during the voyage. Customs formalities are observed at disembarkation.

Train connections from London's Paddington Station to Fishguard take about four hours (daytime service only); train time from Rosslare Harbor into Dublin is three hours; to Limerick for connections to Shannon Airport, three hours, twenty-five minutes; and transportation time from Limerick to Shannon Airport is about forty-five minutes.

Special Itineraries/ Tours

In addition to the day excursions offered by this edition of *Britain by BritRail*, there are some special itineraries and tours that are made possible through the unique features of British rail services and its associated transportation facilities. The BritRail by Night excursion is our own concoction. Remember to carry your passport on these adventures! (Note: All tour descriptions are for 1998; 1999 offerings were unavailable at press time.)

BritainShrinkers

BritainShrinkers were first developed in 1995 as wonderful, value-packed ways to make day trips with finesse to the romantic cities of Paris or Brussels, or to elegantly visit the marvelous countrysides of England and Scotland. These successful tours are offered in several options and are all fully escorted from London and back.

Each is very easy to take, after confirmation to the phone number on the voucher at least twenty-four hours in advance—just arrive at the London rail station indicated on your voucher. A guide in a red uniform will take your voucher at the BritainShrinkers check-in point, which is easily identified by its sign. And you are on your way....

The tours are usually fully booked in advance, so you should make your tour reservations as early as possible prior to your departure. For detailed information or to make reservations, call toll-free (888) TOUR–404

(888–868–7404) or visit http://www.europeanvacation.com on the Internet. For other BritRail products, contact Rail Pass Express, Inc., an authorized U.S. sales outlet, at (800) 722–7151 or visit http://www.britrailpass.com on the Internet.

Continental Quickies

The Eurostar Day Tours take you from England to France or Belgium and back on the Eurostar, state-of-the-art super train, and go through the 31-mile long Channel Tunnel. (See "Channel Tunnel and Crossing the English Channel.") Trains depart London's Waterloo International Terminal for Paris at 0630 (return at 2113) or for Brussels at 0615 (return at 1939). We wish you well on making a choice among these high-speed treks; perhaps you can squeeze them all in.

Day Trip to Paris. Want to take in the Louvre and see Leonardo da Vinci's *Mona Lisa* or do a little shopping à la Paris? Ride from London to Paris in only three hours on this fully escorted adventure.

All the tours described below include a guided panoramic tour of Paris, including the Champs Élysées, Arc de Triomphe, and the Eiffel Tower. From May through October, the tours run daily except Sunday. March through April departure is on Monday, Wednesday, and Saturday. During January, February, November, and December, tours depart on Wednesday and Saturday.

Tour P—Standard class on the Eurostar, no meals

Tour PL—(as per Tour P) includes guided visit to the Louvre★★

Tour PB—(as per Tour P) plus guided Seine Cruise★

Tour PF—First class on the Eurostar, breakfast and dinner included

Tour PFL—(as per Tour PF) includes guided visit to the Louvre★★

Tour PFB (as per Tour PF) plus guided Seine Cruise★

(★Available April through October only; ★★ not available on Tuesday).

Day Trip to Brussels. Want to shop for famous Belgian chocolate and lace or tour the Grand Place, Common Market Building, and Art Nouveau Houses, visit the thirteenth-century Cathedral of Saint Michael and Saint Gudula, or see the largest collection of vintage cars in the world at Autoworld? Or would you prefer to wander off independently to discover Brussels' other treasures? Ride the Eurostar from London to arrive just two hours and forty-five minutes later in Brussels. This fully-escorted tour departs every Thursday from May through October.

Tour R—Standard class on the Eurostar, no meals

Tour RF—First class plus meals on Eurostar

Eurostar Overnighter to Paris. Imagine actually going to the most romantic city in the world for an evening! The lights, the views, the sounds, the mood. Ooh la la! You cannot say you have really lived until you're experiencing the aroma of Paris in the morning—a delicious combination of fresh croissants and coffee.

After your fully guided tour of the Arc de Triomphe, cruise down the River Seine before having the entire evening to do whatever lovers do. (Well, after enjoying the nightlife of the city.) In the morning, your tour will take you back to the intricate lace work of the Eiffel Tower so you can view Paris from its heights. Then you will visit the largest museum in the world, the Louvre, including the glass pyramid addition, before venturing back to London.

Tours run May through October and depart Tuesday/return Wednesday or depart Friday/return Saturday. Accommodations at a four-star hotel and buffet breakfast are included.

Tour PN—Standard class on the Eurostar, no meals

Tour PFN—First class plus meals on Eurostar

British Day Trippers

It won't take you long to find out that each of these tours is packed with pure enjoyment for history buffs, castle fiends and shopping connoisseurs alike.

BritainShrinker Day Tours are fully escorted day excursions taking travelers to some of the most historic sites of England and Scotland. All trains depart from London in the morning and return in the late afternoon to early evening hours. Choose the elegance of Bath and mystery of Stonehenge; the magnificent castles of Leeds and Sissinghurst; the birthplaces of Shakespeare and Churchill; or the Royal Mile from Edinburgh Castle to the Palace of Holyroodhouse.

Tour A: Country Tour (May through mid-October on Wednesday and Friday) Bath, Longleat House, Stonehenge

Tour B: Castle Explorer (May through mid-October on Thursday) Leeds Castle, Sissinghurst Castle Garden

Tour C: The Shakespeare Explorer (May through mid-October on Monday and Thursday) Warwick Castle, Stratford-upon-Avon, The Cotswolds, Blenheim Palace, Oxford

Tour E: Scotland Express (May through mid-October on Tuesday) Edinburgh

British Pullman Day Tours

The **Venice Simplon Orient–Express British Pullman Day Tours** offer travelers a refined day or weekend excursion. Dress code calls for smart daywear (no jeans, please); formal attire, of course, is the appropriate choice for attending the Royal Ascot races; golfing apparel for the British Open; or sensible yachting outfits for sailing week at Cowes.

Originated by George Mortimer Pullman over a century ago, these trains were designed as "palaces on wheels," with upholstery plush enough for royal standards. Add the intricate mosaic flooring, shiny brass features, and soft glow of beautifully shaded lamps atop starched white tablecloths covered in glistening crystal, and the setting becomes the perfect backdrop for your experience of the luxury of a bygone era.

Lunch and dinner trips offer about three hours and thirty minutes of "marvelous indulgence as the train travels through Britain's undulating landscape, passing fields, meadows, and towns rich with history." Top service and delectable meals make travelers comfortable en route to fine hotels for weekend excursions in many of Britain's historical towns.

BritRail by Night

Here's something that you can do with your eyes closed. British sleeper services are excellent and inexpensive—a great way to save both time and money. British rail sleeper services operate between London and the main centers in Scotland, the north of England, Plymouth, and Penzance.

First-class sleepers accommodate one person; connecting bedrooms are available. Standard-class sleepers offer double accommodations—the two berths are stacked one over the other like bunk beds. Both services provide wall-to-wall carpeting, hot and cold running water, soap and towel, a comfortable mattress, and that all-important call button that will bring you a nightcap or your wake-up coffee.

The cost of sleeper accommodations based on single occupancy is $57 for first class; $48 for standard class. Usually, you can take occupancy thirty minutes before departure time and stay aboard until 0730 or 0800, even if the train arrives at your destination several hours earlier. No sleeper service is offered on Saturday evenings.

The *Caledonian* sleepers depart London's Euston Station for Edinburgh, Glasgow, Aberdeen, Inverness, and Fort William. The *Night Riviera* sleeper departs London's Waterloo Station for Plymouth and Penzance.

Overnight sleeper service opens a new door to the adventurous rail traveler. The sleeper charge compares favorably to economical hotel rates, so you can make the sleeper your "hotel on the move." By reserving sleeper accommodations for successive nights, an itinerary could be planned for a night on the train; a day at the destination; a night on the train returning to London; sightseeing, shopping, or a short day excursion out of London; and a night to another destination. Call the Point-To-Point and Reservation Line at (614) 793–7650 to arrange for your night rides.

Expanding on the above, an adventurous traveler could depart London's Waterloo Station about midnight, arriving early morning in Penzance to begin an all-day sightseeing trek extending to Land's End. Back in Penzance, the adventurer could board the sleeper that evening for London, spending an entire day there before boarding another sleeper in Euston Station for Aberdeen, Britain's "oil city." After spending the day in Aberdeen, our traveler could journey to either Edinburgh or Glasgow, and then finally board a sleeper bound for London, or take the Aberdeen sleeper direct to London.

Another option is via Inverness. After arriving in Edinburgh overnight from London, there's ample time in the day to entrain to Inverness, search for "Nessie" on Loch Ness, then return to Edinburgh on a late train out of Inverness in time to board the Edinburgh-to-London sleeper for the last of four nights' sleeper travel.

England

They came, they saw, and they conquered—Celts, Romans, Anglo-Saxons, Danes, and Normans constitute the major ancestry of the modern-day Briton. From the mysterious megaliths at Stonehenge to the formidable fortress at Hastings, the ancient English proved to be a capable people. Despite the size of their island and its limited resources, the English became a nation of traders fostering not only an exchange of commodities but also of cultures, giving rise to one of the most powerful empires in history.

England represents about 57 percent of the total land area of the island, or 130,439 square kilometers (50,363 square miles). We normally think of England as gently rolling green countrysides, but its terrain is diversified—from mountains in the northern and western portions to a deeply indented coastline providing excellent natural harbors.

When we think of England, we automatically think of royalty. Never make the mistake of thinking that Her Royal Majesty Queen Elizabeth II is merely Queen of England; she reigns over many other countries and territories as well. In recent years, the older members of the House of Windsor have been puzzled, then distressed, by the world's fascination with the goings-on of its younger generation. The titillating misadventures of Fergie and Prince Andrew as well as the very public feuding of the Prince and Princess of Wales set the stage for the almost unthinkble divorce of Prince Charles from Princess Diana.

And then one fateful evening in Paris, near the end of August 1997, the world lost its Diana, "the People's Princess." Her death impacted not only her family and all the Brtish: People everywhere grieved for this young, vibrant woman. In some peculiar way, the British monarchy actually seemed to belong to all of us. With the approaching millennium, one wonders if Princess Diana's death portends the demise of the House of Windsor.

Base City . . .

London

The City of London is a wonderful combination of ancient elegance and modern technology, of old traditions and vestiges of its past mingling with contemporary conveniences. While plumed guards mount jet black horses in Whitehall, bankers examine computer printouts on Lombard Street. This mixture provides a provocative, fascinating atmosphere in one of the largest and most sophisticated cities in the world.

Although London is Europe's largest city, most of its historical sights are clustered in a compact area. Central London sits astride the Thames River, about 40 miles inland from its estuary on the North Sea. By strolling through the oldest section of Central London, you'll see its first-century Roman walls, the Tower Bridge and infamous Tower of London, Saint Paul's Cathedral (where Prince Charles and Princes Diana were wed under the second largest cathedral dome in the world), and the city's financial center.

In the so-called newer (it's only about 1,000 years old) section of Central London, you can visit such famous sites as Buckingham Palace, the Houses of Parliament, Palace of Westminster, and Westminster Abbey. It also includes Trafalgar Square, Soho, and Piccadilly Circus.

In addition to Central London, the city is composed of thirty-two other boroughs. Since the streets seem to follow no particular pattern, use postal designations appearing with the addresses on maps to identify a particular region.

Arriving by Air

London's Heathrow and Gatwick Airports are America's primary gateways, with Stansted International Airport as well as London City and Luton Airports primarily providing service within continental Europe and Great Britain.

Heathrow Airport. Information Desk: 0181–759–4321. Heathrow

Airport is connected by FastTrain with Paddington Station in Central London. Journey time: thirty minutes; cost: £5 each way. Trains depart every fifteen minutes daily from 0510 to 2340. Hop on a FastTrain connecting bus outside your terminal (1, 2, 3, or 4) to Heathrow Junction Station. Tickets are available onboard FastTrain and at Rail, Speedlink, and selected sales points throughout Heathrow Airport. For more information, *Tel:* (0845) 600–1515; Internet: http://www.heathrowexpress.co.uk.

Using the Underground (the "Tube"), the Piccadilly Line has access to all four terminals. (Terminal 4 has a separate station.) Tube service to Piccadilly Circus and Central London runs about every ten minutes from approximately 0545 to 0020 Monday through Saturday; Sundays 0700 to about 2325. Journey time: forty-five minutes; cost: £3.90. The airport information number is 0181-759-4321; London Transport information, 0171–222–1234.

"Airbus" transportation to Heathrow is available aboard the A1 to and from Victoria Station and the A2 to and from Russell Square. Adult fare is £6 single, £10 return. Depending on the departure terminal, the Heathrow–Victoria Station journey time may be forty-five to ninety minutes. The A1 Victoria Station airbus departs every thirty minutes from about 0830 to 2045, with occasional late afternoon lapses. The A1 airbus also makes stops at Hyde Park Corner Stop L, at Harrods, and three stops on the Cromwell Road: the Forum Hotel, the Swallow International, and near the junction of Earl's Court Road. Purchase tickets from the driver, the Airbus lounges at Terminals 3 and 4, Travel Information Centres in London, or at the airport. For more information, call (0181) 400–6655.

Depending on the departure terminal, the Heathrow–Russell Square run may take between an hour and an hour and a half. The A2 Russell Square airbus departs approximately every thirty minutes from 0540 to 2030. Stops are also made near the Underground stations of Euston, Great Portland Street, Baker Street, Marble Arch, Lancaster Gate, Paddington, Queensway, Notting Hill Gate, and Holland Park. Some buses also call at King's Cross Station.

Golden Tours provides airport shuttle service from hotels direct to any Heathrow terminal every forty-five minutes at a cost of £10 per person. Book by calling (0171) 233–7030.

Gatwick Airport: Information Desk: (0129) 353–5353

Gatwick Airport, about 27 miles south of London, provides easy-to-access, efficient, and swift train service into London's Victoria Station aboard the Gatwick Express. The express train departs Gatwick's South Terminal rail station every fifteen minutes from 0530 to 2000 and then every thirty minutes until 2300.

Victoria Station–Gatwick Express departures from London to the airport follow the same schedule with additional early departure times of 0430 and 0500. A single fare is £8.90.

For train transportation to and from Gatwick during the remaining night hours, contact Connex South Central trains, which run an hourly night service. Information on this or the Gatwick Express is available in London at (017) 128–5100. Gatwick Express tickets may be purchased in advance in the U.S. by calling (800) 722–7151.

Flightline 777 coaches also provide transportation to and from London's Victoria Station and Gatwick Airport. Coaches run about every hour from 0520 to 2200. In addition, there are 0630, 2125, and 2325 departures from Victoria Station. The fare is £7.50 for a single, £11 return. For information in the United Kingdom, *Tel:* (099) 074–7777; for Flightline information in the United States, *Tel:* (310) 568–0009 or *Fax:* (310) 338–0708; Internet: http://www.speedlink.co.uk; e-mail: info@speedlink.co.uk.

Golden Tours provides minibus service to and from your hotel to the Gatwick Express at Victoria Station, with porterage at both London and airport stations and reserved seating aboard the train for £16 per person per trip. You can contact Golden Tours at (0171) 233–7030.

Stansted Airport: Information Desk: (01279) 680–5100

Stansted Airport, located about thirty-one miles northeast of London, has fast and frequent links to London via its Stansted Skytrain (formerly the Stansted Express) train service. The Skytrain from the airport to London's Liverpool Street Station takes about forty-five minutes, with departures running every thirty minutes Monday through Saturday from 0600 to 2300. Sunday and holiday departures are from 0800 to 2330. Liverpool Street Station departures to Stansted airport are every thirty minutes Monday through Saturday from 0500–2300, with Sunday and holiday departures from 0700 to 2300. One-way fare is £10.

Arriving by Train

London is a hub of rail travel for the Western world and a great introduction to the wonders of European train travel. With speed, little expense, and relative comfort, you have the opportunity to access some of the most stimulating sights of one of the world's most beautiful cities.

London's seventeen primary rail stations provide an abundance of travel opportunities within the city, to other cities, and to the countryside and seasides. For the readers of *Britain by BritRail,* eight of these stations are well worth knowing:

Victoria Station is an international rail terminal linking Gatwick and various other airports with London. It also provides easy access to the south and southeast of England. The International Rail Centre is located to the left of platforms 3 and 4 when making sea-rail connections with Belgium and France. Station facilities include shops, eateries, money exchange, and tourist information, which is located in the station forecourt. To reach it, follow the corridor running from platform 15.

Euston Station is closely grouped with St. Pancras and King's Cross Stations for rail services to England's Midlands, northern England, and Scotland. Trains to *Britain by BritRail's* base cities Edinburgh and Glasgow depart from this station. It serves as the terminal for Stena Line ship and ferry services to Belfast via Stranraer and to Dublin via Holyhead. The Travel Centre is open year-round Monday through Saturday 0700–2330 and Sunday 0800–2330. Waiting rooms, restaurants, and other conveniences are located on the far side of the station hall from the Travel Centre.

St. Pancras Station is the departure point for *Britain by BritRail's* day excursions to St. Albans, Nottingham, and Sheffield. The station is undergoing renovation to provide regional Eurostar passenger service from Glasgow, Edinburgh, Manchester, and Birmingham to Paris and Brussels via the Channel Tunnel. Directional signs for the Euston and King's Cross stations, as well as the London Underground, are prominent throughout the station.

Charing Cross Station is London's rail terminal for direct train service to Folkestone, Hastings, Dover, and other ports for P&O Stena Sealink and Hoverspeed services to Boulogne and Calais on the continent.

King's Cross Station is the London terminal for InterCity 125 train service to Aberdeen and Edinburgh. The Travel Centre is open 0700–2300 daily. Full information, reservations, and advance ticketing services are available. Outside the station, to the left, a money exchange service is open daily, 0800–2000.

Paddington Station serves the west InterCity 125 service through Plymouth and Penzance and into *Britain by BritRail's* base city of Cardiff in Wales. It also is the London terminal for Stena Sealink services to Ireland via Fishguard to Rosslare. The Travel Centre is located in front of platforms 1 and 2. Hours: 0800–2130 Monday–Saturday and 0900–2000 Sunday.

Liverpool Street Station, one of the oldest rail terminals in London, has undergone extensive renovation. The Underground (London Transport) Travel & Tourist Centre is in front of tracks 4 and 5, directly behind the stairs.

This station is the gateway for rail and ship traffic between London and the Netherlands, northern Germany, and Scandinavia. Trains departing Liverpool Street Station proceed to Harwich, where passengers then embark from the Parkeston Quay by ship to Hook of Holland, a small peninsula jutting out into the North Sea. There, trains wait to take them to such destinations as Amsterdam, Hamburg, Berlin, or the Scandinavian capital cities of Copenhagen, Oslo, and Stockholm. The ship crossing is now made by Stena Line HSS fast craft in only three hours and forty minutes. Visit http://www.stenaline.com for more information.

Waterloo Station is primarily for trains to the south of England, including the Isle of Wight. The Travel Centre is at the end of platforms 15 and 16 just opposite the Underground Entrance. It is open from 0800 to 2200 daily. Waterloo International Eurostar Terminal for direct service to Paris, Brussels, or Amsterdam via the Channel Tunnel occupies tracks 20 through 24. Eurostar is the passenger service provided by the railways of Britain, Belgium, and France.

More than fifteen passenger trains make the daily runs through the "Chunnel," providing tourists and business travelers with quick, efficient travel to London, Paris, Brussels, and Amsterdam. Maximum speed through the tunnel is 100 mph and 186 mph on the Continent. For more detailed Eurostar information, please see "The Channel Tunnel and Crossing the English Channel."

Getting Around in London

London is meant for walking. Charming nooks, side streets, stores, and vistas all await your discovery. Of course, time constraints may force you to consider other options. To orient yourself, first-time visitors especially will find an introductory guided bus tour helpful. London Coaches makes it convenient for you to become familiar with the various sections of the city by operating "The Original London Sightseeing Tour." The tours run every fifteen minutes in summer and every thirty minutes in winter around a 20-mile circular route in about one and a half hours. They pass most of London's major historic and contemporary landmarks, with commentary in several languages. Board the tour at Piccadilly Circus, Victoria, or Baker Street Underground station locations. The cost is about $15 (U.S.) for adults, $8 for children.

For a more personalized, albeit more expensive, introduction to London, hail a taxi. London's taxicab drivers, known as "cabbies," are a special breed. They are not issued a taxi operator's license just because they can drive a car. An extensive knowledge of the city and its history is an important part of their taxi-licensing examination. Cabbies usually have fixed rates for such sightseeing excursions.

Tour London with "The Happy Cabbie"—an exclusive offer for *Britain by BritRail* readers. Jack Bernstein, London's original "Happy Cabbie" offers *Britain by BritRail* readers customized tours of London at special discounted rates. He'll start by picking you up at the airport if you wish. We learned more about life and sights in London in a two-hour tour with "The Happy Cabbie" than is possible with the typical prepackaged sightseeing tours. Just "ring him up" on (097) 628–2234 for a truly interesting experience.

Another picturesque way to get acquainted with London is via a river tour. These tours provide a view of London and its surroundings from an entirely different perspective. In central London, there are piers at the Tower of London, Westminster, and Charing Cross. Ask for a leaflet containing prices and sailing times at any of the tourist offices. Buy your tickets at the pier. There are also lunch and dinner cruises. For *Bateaux London*, call (0171) 925–2215; *Catamaran Cruises* (0171) 839–3572; or *Tidal Cruises* (0171) 839–2164.

After an introductory tour, you will be better able to get around on London's Underground, the Tube. Don't let the enormous size of the Tube overwhelm you—it's really very user-friendly. Composed of ten basic lines, the Tube's train system provides an easy and fast way to get around London from 0530 until midnight Monday–Saturday and 0730–2330 on

Sundays.

If you plan to travel on the Tube for more than one day, consider the London Visitor Travel Card (available from Rail Pass Express, Inc. toll free at (800) 722–7151 or via Internet at http://www.railpass.com) or one of the other passes that provide access to the Tube trains and buses. Maps of the London Underground are included with the Travel Card and are posted in all the Underground stations; or obtain them from the BTA or any London tourist office.

When in London, you can obtain the most up-to-date information on many subjects about the city by dialing the London Tourist Board's "VisitorCall." Dial (0839) 123 plus the last three numbers shown below:

400 – What's on this week

401 – What's on during the next three months

403 – Current exhibitions

404 – What's on (for children)

406 – Summer in the parks

407 – Sunday in London

411 – Changing of the Guard

413 – Lord Mayor's Show, State Opening of Parliament, and Trooping the Color

416 – Popular West End shows

418 – Christmas and Easter events

420 – Bespoke Guided Tours

422 – Rock and pop concerts

424 – Places to visit (with children)

428 – Street markets

429 – Museums

430 – Getting around London

431 – Guided tours and walks

432 – River trips/boat hire

433 – Getting to the airports

434 – Beyond the West End

435 – General advice (accommodations)

438 – New productions—how to book

480 – Popular attractions

481 – Palaces (such as Buckingham Palace)

482 – Greenwich/Military Museum

483 – Famous houses and gardens

484 – Day trips from London

485 – London dining

486 – Shopping news

The bookings hotline is (0171) 932–2020.

The Metropolitan Office forecast for Greater London weather is (083) 950–0951.

The Gay and Lesbian London Line is (089) 114–1120.

London—At Your Service

Professional tourist officials from the London Tourist Board provide visitors with detailed information about hotel accommodations, points of interest around the city, and their new twenty-four-hour information line on using London's extensive transportation network of the Underground, bus, and rail services.

London Tourist Board locations at your service:

Victoria Station: Located in the forecourt on the street side outside platform 15. Operates 0800–1900 daily, April–October; November–

March, 0800–1800 Monday–Saturday and Sunday 0900–1600. *Tel:* (083) 912–3456.

Liverpool Street Station: Located at the Underground Station Concourse. Open Monday–Friday 0800–1800; Saturday and Sunday 0845–1730. *Tel:* (083) 912–3456

London Visitor Centre: Located at Waterloo International Station's arrivals hall. *Tel:* (0171) 620–1550.

Heathrow Airport: Located at the bottom of the passenger ramp in the concourse leading to the Underground station in Terminal 2. April–September, open Monday–Saturday 0800–1830 and Sunday 0800–1800; September–March 0800–1800 daily. *Tel:* (0181) 759–4321.

The London Tourist Board also operates a telephone accommodations reservations service for credit-card holders only Monday–Friday 0930–1730. *Tel:* (0171) 932–2020.

London Limelights

There are, of course, some "must sees" in London, particularly if you're a first-time visitor. Even if you've been to London several times, here's an update on some "basics."

BBC Experience, Broadcasting House, London W1A 1AA; Bookings *Tel* (0870) 603–0304. This new exhibition provides a look at the past, present, and future of the British Broadcasting Corporation. Visitors can star in and produce a radio play or even try their talent at being sports commentators.

Buckingham Palace, The Visitor Office, Buckingham Palace, London SW1A 1AA; *Tel:* (0171) 839–1377; *Fax:* (0171) 930–9625. Take the Tube to Victoria, Green Park, or St. James's Park station.

Changing of the Guard: 1130 daily, April 1–August 7; every other day, August 8–March 31.

Tours of the Palace State Rooms: £9 adult; £5 children five to sixteen; £9 students. Open every day August 6–October 4, 0930–1630. Tickets, which guarantee entry to the State Rooms at a specific time, may be purchased for any day in person from the Buckingham Palace Ticket Office in Green Park (August and September only) or by telephoning (0171) 321–2233 or by writing to the Visitor Office at the above address.

Ironically, Queen Victoria's favorite palace was originally built in 1702 on the site of a notorious brothel as the home of the Duke of

Buckingham. In the early nineteenth century, the flamboyant architect John Nash rebuilt it as a palace for George IV. But Nash became hash when he excessively exceeded the redesign budget and Edward Blore finished the building.

You can visit eighteen of the palace's 661 rooms from early August to the end of September, when the royal family is at Balmoral in Scotland. Same-day tickets for the tour are sold on a first-come first-served basis from a booth at the end of Green Park, which faces the plaza outside the palace. The ticket booth opens at 0900. Be prepared to stand in line for as long as two hours. The tour includes the prominent vaulted Picture Gallery, which houses part of the royal collection of 10,000 paintings.

Cabinet War Rooms, Clive Steps, King Charles Street, SW1; *Tel:* (0171) 930–6961. The entrance is across from St. James's Park. Take the Tube to St. James's Park or Westminster station. Hours: 0930–1800 daily. Admission: £4.40 adult; £2.20 child; £3.30 senior or student. Free headset with commentary.

Few Americans are aware that a memorial to their World War II president, Franklin Roosevelt, exists in London's Grosvenor Square; perhaps even fewer are aware that the place where Prime Minister Winston Churchill of Britain held secret telephone conversations with him is open to the public.

In 1936, when the storms of the war were gathering, the British began constructing a communications center, or war room, beneath the government offices in Whitehall. Building a 10–foot layer of concrete above a labyrinth of wine cellars and connecting tunnels, workers toiled at night so as not to arouse suspicions of what was being constructed. Virtually bombproof, the Allies' direction of the war was conducted from this communications center. It is interesting to see the place where the most dramatic decisions in the history of humanity were made. The Map Room and Churchill's combined bedroom, office, and broadcasting room remains just as they were during the war.

Imperial War Museum, Lambeth Road, SE1. *Tel:* (0171) 416–5000. Hours: 1000–1800 daily. Admission: £4.50 adult; £2.25 child; £3.50 senior or student. Free admission after 1630. Take the Tube to Lambeth North, Waterloo, or Elephant and Castle station.

Appropriately so, the early nineteenth century's most famous lunatic asylum, Bedlam, houses the country's memorial to the two World Wars. A rotating clock hand in the basement represents the cost of war in terms of human lives, and the body count exceeds 100 million. Operation Jericho supposedly simulates a World War II bombing mission, but seems more like an unamusing amusement park ride. However, two thought-provoking "experiences" include the Trenches and the Blitz, which portray the horror of war.

Jewish Museum, 129–131 Albert Street, Camden Town, NW1 7NB. *Tel:* (0171) 284 1997. Hours: Sunday–Thursday, 1000–1600; closed Friday and Saturday. Admission: £3 adult; £1.50 child or student; £2 senior. Take the Tube to Camden Town Station, then a three-minute walk. There's also a branch at 80 East End Road, N3 2SY (Finchley). *Tel:* 0181 349 1143.

The refurbished Raymond Burton House, the site of the Jewish Museum, explores the history and religious life of the Jewish community in Britain and beyond. It has one of the finest collections of antique ceremonial art.

Kensington Palace, High Street, Kensington, W84 PX. *Tel:* (0171) 937–9561. Take the Tube to Bayswater, High Street Kensington, Lancaster Gate, or Queensway station. Admission: £7 adults; £3.50 children.

Serving as the last home of Diana, Princess of Wales, the palace has been converted into a memorial to the Princess and a home for a portion of the Royal Art Collection.

London Docklands, London Docklands Visitor Centre, 3 Limeharbour, London E14 9TQ. *Tel:* (0171) 512–1111 or *Fax:* (0171) 537–2549. Docklands Light Rail, http://www.d/r.co.uk. See Day Excursion to Greenwich.

London Transport Museum, Covent Garden Piazza, WC2; *Tel:* (0171) 379–6344; Hours: Saturday–Thursday 1000–1800; Friday 1100–1800 (last admission 1715). Admission: £4.95 adult; £2.95 child.

See and hear the exciting story of London's famous transportation system—from the red double-decker buses to the masterpiece Underground system, the Tube. Try the Tube train simulator or practice driving a bus.

Madame Tussaud's, Marylebone Road, NW1. *Tel:* (0171) 935–6861. Hours: 0930–1730 daily; May–September 0900–1730 daily; October–April 1000–1730 Monday–Friday and 0930–1730 Saturday and Sunday. Admission: £ 9.95 adult; £6.95 child. Purchase tickets in advance if possible. To get there, take the Tube to Baker Street Station.

Here's a place where you can mingle with top celebs and top criminals at the same time. More than 400 lifelike wax figures of the famous and the infamous beckon to you. The figure of the late Princess Diana is a star attraction. Take in the dazzling "Spirit of London" time travel ride and the chilling "Chamber of Horrors." Be certain to only look—don't touch. Too many female gropings did in the Pierce Brosnan–James Bond figure in 1997 and he had to be sent out for a little retouching work, so to speak.

Museum of London, 150 London Wall, EC2. *Tel:* (0171) 600–3699; Internet: http://www.museum-london.org.uk. Hours: Tuesday–Saturday, 1000–1750; Sunday 1200–1750. Admission: £4 adult; £2 child; free after 1630. Take the Tube to Barbican or St. Paul's, or take the Tube/rail to Moorgate.

Visit the London Now gallery, trace London's history from prehistoric times up to the present day, and relive the Great Fire that destroyed London in 1666. The most comprehensive city museum in the world and one of the most imaginatively designed, the Museum of London should be on your "must-see" list.

Pepsi Trocadero, Piccadilly Circus, W1. Take the Underground to Piccadilly Circus. The Trocadero is a two-acre enclosed entertainment, shopping, and restaurant complex. The Pepsi IMAX Theatre is a real visual and sensory treat. An IMAX projection system uses the largest film frame in history—a 70mm, 15 perforation format, ten times larger than ordinary 35mm film. This is the United Kingdom's largest screen—seven stories high. Put on the Personal Sound Environment 3D headset and you truly are transformed into the heart of the action. The IMAX ticket hotline is (071) 494–4153.

Other attractions include Segaworld, Funland, and Lazerbowl, and Showscan's Emaginator which offers a variety of simulated rides, including a space-age roller coaster and desert buggy race. Rock Circus is the rock 'n' pop version of Madame Tussaud's wax museum.

Planet Hollywood, also at the Trocadero, provides Hollywood memorabilia and an occasional appearance by celebrities along with a variety of the newest cuisine. Other eateries at the Trocadero include Ed's Easy Diner and Rainforest Café.

The Royal Opera House, currently being refurbished, is scheduled to reopen at the end of 1999.

Shakespeare's Globe Theatre and Exhibition, New Globe Walk, Bankside, London SE1 9ED. *Tel:* (0171) 902–1500; *Fax:* (0171) 902–1515. Education Centre (for lectures, workshops, etc.): *Tel:* (0171) 620–0202. Hours: May–September 0900–1215 and 1400–1600; October–April

1000–1700.

To get there, take the Underground to Mansion House or take bus 11, 15, 17, 23, 26, or 76 to Mansion House, cross over the Thames River via Southwark Bridge. The Theatre is along Bankside about 500 yards to the right of the bridge.

Shakespeare's Globe Exhibition was voted "Best of Europe" by the European Federation of Associations of Tourism Journalists. The Globe Theatre was rebuilt as the focal point of the International Shakespeare Globe Centre, an educational, entertainment, and cultural complex. The original Globe burned down in 1613 and the Puritans closed the second one in 1642. Third time's a charm?

The Education Centre and workshops will be completed in 1999, the 400th anniversary of its first recorded performance. If you want to know what an Elizabethan audience would have experienced, find out what a "bodger" is, or learn about "penny stinkards," this is the place. A guided tour will bring England's most important theatrical heritage to life. According to Mark Rylance, Artistic Director of Shakespeare's Globe, "The theatre you will see is, to the best of our abilities, the space in which Shakespeare wanted us to meet his plays. It is unique in the world."

Tower of London, Tower Hill, EC3. *Tel:* (0171) 709–0765. Hours: March–October 0900–1700 Monday–Saturday; 1000–1700 Sunday. November–February, 1000–1600 Sunday and Monday; 0900–1600 Tuesday–Saturday. Admission: £9 adult; £5.90 child. To get there, take the Tower Hill Tube.

Throughout London's history, the Tower has been a fortress, a palace, and a prison. Free one-hour guided tours depart every half hour. The oldest part of the Tower complex, the White Tower, was begun in 1076 and contains the Chapel of St. John, the oldest church in London. Other main attractions include the Bloody Tower (where twelve-year old Edward V and his ten-year-old brother were incarcerated by their uncle, the future Richard III) and the Jewel House, which houses the Crown Jewels.

Victoria and Albert Museum, Cromwell Road, SW7. *Tel:* (0171) 938–8441. Take the Tube to South Kensington Station. Hours: Monday 1200–1750; Tuesday–Sunday 1000–1750. Admission: £5; children under 18, free.

The famous Victoria and Albert Museum, informally called the "V&A," is considered the finest decorative-arts museum in the world and includes exquisite collections of jewelry, furniture, and oriental carpets. Principal attractions include the Photography Gallery, Art & Design galleries, and a collection of more than 400 years of European fashion.

Royal Parks. Manicured gardens and pastoral grounds within London's vast Royal Parks, once the hunting and recreational property of the Royal Family, now provide the people of London and their visitors with something few megalopolises have: peace and quiet. The lake of St. James is so serene that it is a breeding ground for birds. Boats cruise the Serpentine River in huge Hyde Park, where there is room for riding trails and open-air concerts.

Westminster Abbey, Broad Sanctuary. *Tel:* (0171) 222–5152. Take the Tube to Westminster or St. James's Park Station. Admission to Royal Chapels and Poets' Corner: £4 adult; £1 child; £2 senior or student.

Every king and queen of England since 1066 has been crowned here, and more than 3,000 of the nation's most highly valued figures are buried here. You'll see the Tomb of the Unknown Soldier, Elizabeth I's tomb, the Coronation Chair in use since 1300, Poets' Corner commemorating Britain's greatest writers, the Chapter House containing examples of medieval English sculpture, the eleventh-century Pyx Chamber, and the Abbey Museum.

Shopping

Shopping can be quite traditional—even stuffy—at Harrod's in Knightsbridge, where the Royals shop. You will find exclusive leather goods at Asprey's and can seek out rare antiques at Sotheby's, on Bond Street. Oxford Street and Regent Street shopping is the most diverse and the most crowded, featuring famous London department stores such as Marks & Spencer and traditional British fare at Aquascutum, Austin Reed, and Burberry's. For those who desire a princely wardrobe, visit Gieves & Hawkes at No. 1 Savile Row, London.

The Piazza near the Covent Garden Underground Station replaced the Covent Garden flower and vegetable market, which was in age-old times the convent gardens of the Abbey at St. Peter at Westminster. The new Covent Garden is a boisterous compound of antiques, clothing, and craft stores, amid a plethora of indoor and outdoor cafes, pubs, eateries, and clubs.

Restaurants and Pubs

Ten years ago, many visitors to London might have regarded English food as overcooked and boring, according to Lawrence Isaacson, Director of London's Tourist Board and one of the city's top restaurateurs. "Now we have more than 5,500 restaurants," which, he explained, includes pubs that serve food, "with *sixty* different cuisines."

"You could eat a different meal every day for thirty years," Isaacson said, adding, "We're much more exciting than Paris." Isaacson attributes the dramatic change to the rise of economic standards. "We have more households with two wage earners and more people traveling abroad and experimenting with different foods. And there is an appreciable rise in fine young British chefs with great expectations who are not departing for the Continent," Isaacson explained. The result has been adventurous foods in glamorous settings.

Isaacson's Soho Soho ground-floor cafe and upstairs formal dining room on Frith Street in Soho exemplifies the new food mood. The food here is freshly prepared, light fare—salads and omelettes with cheeses—in a simple decor of clay tile floors and vivid art work. Such gourmet cafes and bistros set the trend for the new Soho and West Soho, with Carnaby Street at its center. Both areas are bedecked with fashionable boutiques, bookstores, craft shops, and expensive private clubs.

Fans of the successful American TV show *Cheers* will feel right at home at the Cheers London Bar & Restaurant at 72 Regent Street. It's located on the ground floor of the Café Royal. For reservations, Tel: (0171) 494–3322; Fax: (0171) 494–2211.

Rail nostalgia buffs will enjoy Chez Gerard on 64 Bishopsgate. The restaurant is imaginatively decorated with lamps and luggage racks that are reminiscent of the golden days of the railways. For reservations, Tel: (0171) 588–1200.

Day Excursions from London

After you've seen London, explore more of this wonderful country where, among its many advantages, everyone speaks English. Well, sort of. You cannot get to know Britain without experiencing the charms of its other cities as well and seeing first-hand the lovely rural areas that separate them. Of course, there's no better way to do that than aboard a train, viewing the passing scene and conversing with the British themselves.

Like the road builders of Rome, Britain's rail builders laid their tracks leading to London—or, more properly, out of London. London serves as the center of a somewhat lopsided spider web with its radials running east and south to the sea on the short side of the web and the longer extensions running west to Wales and north into Scotland. Thirty-two day excursions from London await your pleasure.

As with any knight of old, you may want to sally forth on a short sortie or two before departing on a crusade. In that case, you will find the Greenwich, Windsor, and St. Albans day excursions to your liking. Ranging southeast out of London, Kent beckons with its towns of Canterbury, Dover, Folkestone, and Ramsgate. Southward, rail trails lead along the English Channel to the port/resort towns of Hastings, Brighton, Portsmouth, and Southampton and to the Isle of Wight.

Having whetted your appetite with those excursions, you should now be ready to venture farther afield. Everything you plan to see has been there for quite some time—usually at least a century or two—so relax and enjoy your longer travels throughout Britain.

West from London, excursions to Salisbury, Stonehenge, and Gloucester await the train traveler. Excursions to Bath, Plymouth, and Penzance may be made from either Cardiff or London. See the chapter on Cardiff for these three-day excursions; schedules from both Cardiff and London are included there.

In the heart of England excursions to Birmingham, Stratford-upon-Avon, Coventry, Nottingham, Sheffield, Lincoln, and York await you. Farther west beckons Chester.

Northeast of London is East Anglia, where historic King's Lynn, Bury St. Edmunds, and Ipswich abound in museums and memories of World War II. For academic flavor, visit Cambridge or Oxford, and school-tie types will appreciate Eton—a stone's throw away from Windsor.

London–Edinburgh

Services shown operate from London King's Cross via the so-called eastern route to Scotland. Other service is available from London Euston station using the so-called western route, most trains stopping at Glasgow before continuing to Edinburgh. The eastern route provides significantly faster service to Edinburgh.

DEPART KING'S CROSS STATION	ARRIVE EDINBURGH WAVERLEY STATION	NOTES
0700	1122 (1135 Sa)	M–Sa
0730	1159	M–F
0800	1216 (1240 Sa)	M–Sa
0830	1307 (1305 Sa, 1339 Su)	Daily except Sa
0900	1331 (1324 Sa, 1409 Su)	Daily
0930	1413 (1417 Su)	Sa, Su
1000	1411 (1429 Sa, 1453 Su)	Daily

and other services after 1000 at 30 or 60 min intervals until 1800 or 1900.

DEPART EDINBURGH WAVERLEY STATION	ARRIVE KING'S CROSS STATION	NOTES
1400	1836 (1841 Sa, 1844 Su)	Daily
1430	1908 (1851 Sa, 1913 Su)	Daily
1500	1912 (1932 Sa, 1938 Su)	Daily

and other services at 30 to 60 min intervals until 1730 (Sa), 1800 (Su), or 1900 (M–F).

Distance: 393 miles/632 km

High-speed; food service available; reservations recommended for all above-listed trains.

London–Glasgow

Services shown operate from both London Euston and King's Cross stations: Services from Euston Station are labeled ES and those from King's Cross are labeled KC. All trains run to Glasgow Central Station.

DEPART LONDON ES or KC	ARRIVE GLASGOW CENTRAL STATION	NOTES
ES 0630 (0620 Sa)	1212	M–Sa
KC 0700	1240	Sa
KC 0800	1317	M–F
KC 0830	1412 (1449 Su)	Sa, Su
ES 0835 (0825 Sa)	1357	M–Sa
ES 0925	1521	Sa
KC 0900	1515	Su
KC 0940	1514	S
KC 1000	1517	M–F
KC 1030	1635	Su
ES 1035 (1025 Sa)	1531	M–Sa
KC 1100	1626 (1631 Sa)	M–Sa
KC 1130	1711	M–Sa
KC 1200	1750	Su
ES1235 (1225 Sa)	1749	M–Sa
KC 1300	1848	Sa
KC 1330	1916	M–F
KC 1400	1950	Su
ES 1435 (1425 Sa)	1950	M–Sa
KC 1500	2005 (2039 Sa)	M–Sa
ES 1635 (1625 Sa)	2204 (2216 Sa)	M–Sa
KC 1700	2242 (2244 Su)	Sa, Su
ES 1735 (1725 Sa)	2253	M–Sa
KC 1800	2328	M–F
ES 1835	2354	M–F

Distance: 450 miles/725 km

High-speed trains; food service available; reservations recommended for all above-listed trains.

Day Excursion to

Birmingham   HEART OF ENGLAND

Depart from Euston Station

Distance by train: 113 miles (182 km)
Average train time: 1 hour, 30 minutes
Train information and InterCity services: (034) 548–4950
Birmingham Tourist Information Centre: 2 City Arcade B2 4TX; *Tel:* (0121) 643–2514;
  Fax: (0121) 616–1038.
  130 Colmore Row, Victoria Square, B3 3AP; *Tel:* (0121) 693–6300; *Fax:* (0121)
  693–9600.
Internet: http://www.birmingham.org.uk
Hours: Monday through Saturday 0930–1730; closed on Sunday.
  To reach the Birmingham tourist information center on City Arcade, make your
way to Corporation Street in front of the station. The tourist information center and
ticket shop is behind the Superstore C&A.

  Birmingham has more canals than Venice. This is rather unusual because
Birmingham claims to be Britain's "city at the center." Although it is in the
approximate geographic center of the British Isles, it was once the center
of England's waterways, which carried most of the nation's industrial traffic. With the development of other forms of transportation, particularly
rail, canal transportation dissipated. Most of the canals were developed into
recreation areas with walks, pubs, and restored buildings along their rights-
of-way.

  For decades, Birmingham was recognized internationally as one of the
world's great industrial cities. Along with that recognition came the image
of a smoke-filled, grimy Victorian sprawl of a city. Since World War II,
Birmingham has made spectacular progress in developing a beautiful residential city. The center of the city was completely rebuilt.

  One of the best ways to see Birmingham is on foot. Begin a self-guided
tour at **Brindley Place,** the main canalside development situated at the
rear of the International Convention Centre. You'll see the old, original
canal locks, as well as the newer **Water's Edge.** Your walk will also lead
you to the **National Sealife Centre,** restaurants of all nationalities, and
the newly opened **Ikon Gallery.** If you prefer to experience the canals on
water, barge trips are available at the rear of the Convention Centre.

  Birmingham is said to have several haunted pubs, and you can sample a
pint when you join the **Ghost Trail** tour. You'll just die to get on this next
tour—the **Graveyard Trail,** guided by Birmingham's most popular

corpse, John Baskerville. You can sign up for any of the tours at the tourist information center. *Tel:* (0121) 643–2514.

If walking doesn't appeal to you, you can see the main attractions in the city's center from an open-topped bus. Pay only once and hop off and on whenever you please. Fare: £7 adults; £2.5 children; family with two adults and up to three children, £14. It operates from May to September.

One of the most striking landmarks marking the city center is the Rotunda, a 250-foot tower. Beneath the tower is the world's first under-one-roof shopping complex. It includes The Bull Ring, The Palisades, The Pavilions, and the City Plaza. The complex is also filled with restaurants and hosts a market on Tuesdays, Fridays, and Saturdays. The multilevel, temperature-controlled shopping center is linked by subways with the major shopping streets of the city. It connects directly with the New Street railway station, where you will arrive from London on your day excursion.

London–Birmingham

Direct service from Euston Station only; other service is available from Paddington Station via Reading and Oxford.

DEPART EUSTON STATION	ARRIVE NEW STREET STATION	NOTES
0700	0851	Sa
0715	0850	M–F
0735	0920	Sa
0735	1038	Su, see note below
0745	0920	M–F
0805	0950	Sa

M–F service continues at half-hour intervals until 1945, then departs at 2045, 2145, 2245, and 2345; Sa service continues at half-hour intervals until 1935, then 2030, 2130, and 2255; Su service is at hourly intervals until 1335, then, hourly from 1440 to 2240. Sunday trains will be routed from London Euston Station to Wolverhampton Station and then to Birmingham New Street Station from May 24 to June 7, on June 21, and from July 5 to 19. On June 14 and 28 and from July 26, Sunday trains will be routed directly to Birmingham, journey time being approximately 2 hr 10 min. These changes are a result of major signaling and other engineering improvements on the main line from Rugby to the Birmingham vicinity.

Birmingham–London

DEPART NEW STREET STATION	ARRIVE EUSTON STATION	NOTES
1415	1551 (1600 Sa)	M–Sa
1430	1705	Su
1445	1620 (1632 Sa)	M–Sa
(See notes below for later service on M–Sa.)		
1530	1820	Su, see below
1555	1831	Su, see below
1630	1902	Su, see below
1655	1929	Su, see below
1805	2104	Su, see below
1905	2152	Su, see below
2005	2256	Su, see below
2135	0015	Su, see below

M–F Service continues at half-hour intervals to 1845, then departing at 1945, 2045, 2155, and 2309; journey times as shown above. Saturday service continues at intervals until 1845, then departs at 1945, 2049, 2158, and 2309; journey times as shown above. Sunday service is the reverse of the note above, except on June 14 and 28, trains will be routed from Birmingham New Street to Wolverhampton and then to London Euston Station, with journey times as shown above; normal Sunday direct service will resume on July 26. At press time, this information was accurate. Minor seasonal changes may occur to these schedules.

If you experience difficulty in gaining your bearings in the vast New Street Station, consult the travel center (train information) in the station's main hall on the extreme far right as you exit from the train platforms.

Birmingham's National Exhibition Center is a modern exhibition-and-conference center on a 310-acre site readily accessible by rail. Rail connections to the exhibition center may be made through the New Street Station on any trains departing in the direction of London. The stop, Birmingham International, is a short, seventeen- to twenty-minute ride. Obtain full details from the tourist information center. With 1.2 million square feet of air-conditioned exhibition space in twelve halls, it is by far the largest complex in Britain, and it's still growing.

Located in the Victoria Square vicinity and worthy of a visit for its classic elegance and Victorian style is the Town Hall. Opened in 1834, it was designed by Joseph Hansom, the inventor of the Hansom cab. It is the concert hall in which Mendelssohn conducted the first performance of *Elijah* in 1846. Many distinguished musicians have appeared there since, including Sir Edward Elgar. The Town hall is presently closed for renovation and hopes to reopen in 2001.)

Sarehole Mill on Cole Bank Road (served by Hall Green Station) is an eighteenth-century water mill restored to working order, and would become an exciting adventure for J.R.R. Tolkien fans. So inspired by this mill was Tolkien that he chose it as the setting for his *Middle-Earth*. The mill is open 1330 to 1730 Wednesday through Saturday, between April and September. This particular area of Birmingham was where Tolkien, author of *The Hobbit*, spent his childhood. His family's home, Gracewell, is now privately owned, but you can visit Edgbaston, a house he often used for holiday lodging. For a beautiful view of the hills and trees where Tolkien may have seen his first hobbit, you must stop at Lickey Hills in Rednal, just outside Birmingham.

Blakesley Hall, Blakesley Road, Yardley (Stechford Station), is a delightful sixteenth-century timber-framed yeoman's house, furnished in period style, with an interesting garden, barn, and historical vehicles. It's open daily 1400-1700 from April to October. Two and a half miles north of the city center on Trinity Road is a seventeenth-century gem, Aston Hall (Wilton Station). The magnificent Jacobean mansion was begun in 1618 and took seventeen years to complete.

For rail buffs, a visit to the Birmingham Railway Museum is a must. It houses the world's oldest steam engine, which was built in 1784, along with displays of early machinery, engines, and motorcars. You can even learn to drive a main line express yourself.

Birmingham's Civic Centre is a modern contribution to the city's skyline. It includes a repertory theater and one of the largest and best-stocked libraries in Europe, featuring a comprehensive Shakespeare collection. The city's Central Museum and Art Gallery houses paintings and sculpture by Van Gogh, Botticelli, and Gainsborough, and its pre-Raphaelite painting collection is the best.

After all the sightseeing, you may develop a thirst. You came to the right city. Birmingham has long been one of Britain's major brewing centers, and its beer is recommended highly by both locals and visitors. There are plenty of pubs in which you can conduct your own taste tests.

Birmingham is justly proud of its restaurants, which cater to every palate and purse. The city has stylish theater-restaurants with entertainment by international cabaret stars, as well as a wide selection of eateries providing French, Italian, Spanish, Greek, "Balti" (from northern India), Chinese, and traditional English cuisine. There's no reason to leave Birmingham with an empty stomach or an unquenched thirst.

Birmingham has undergone many structural changes in recent years and, undoubtedly, it is becoming one of Europe's outstanding cities.

Day Excursion to

Brighton   COLORFUL SEASIDE RESORT

Depart from Victoria Station

Distance by train: 51 miles (82 km)
Average train time: 55 minutes
Train information and InterCity services: (034) 548–4950
Brighton and Hove Tourist Information: Bartholomew Square, Brighton BN1 1JS;
   Tel: (0127) 329–2599; *Fax:* (0127) 329–2594
   Internet: http://www.brighton.co.uk/tourist
   E-mail: brighton-tourism@pavilion.co.uk
   Hours: Daily (except Christmas) 0900–1700, with extended evening hours in summer.

   Brighton's tourist information center is located in Bartholomew Square next to the Town Hall, about a ten-minute walk from the station. Walk directly out of the rail station down Queens Road to the sea. Turn left at that point onto Kings Road. Where Kings Road becomes Grand Junction, turn left again and proceed to the Town Hall to the tourist information center.

Brighton is, and always has been, much more than a traditional seaside resort. Since the earliest days of travel, visitors have been attracted by the resort's unique sense of style and architectural splendor. Having merged with its neighbor, Hove, in 1997, these special qualities are as strong as ever. But they are only part of a continuing success story that secures Brighton's position as Britain's liveliest seaside city.

Perhaps Brighton would have remained a tiny, humble fishing village originally known as Brighthelmstone were it not for the efforts of Dr. Richard Russell and the Prince Regent who later became King George IV. In 1750 Dr. Russell, a Brighton resident, published a book extolling the magical effects of sea air and saltwater. This started a fashionable trend that

London–Brighton

Services shown are from London Victoria Station; other service on Thameslink Trains is available from London Blackfriars and London Bridge Stations.

DEPART VICTORIA STATION	ARRIVE BRIGHTON STATION	NOTES
0732	0847 (0849 Su)	Sa Su
0752	0852	M–F
0808	0857	Sa
0832	0933 (0947 Sa, 0949 Su)	Daily
0908	0957	M–Sa
0938	1034	M–Sa

M–Sa service continues at half-hour intervals to 1508; Su service continues at hourly intervals until 2132.

DEPART BRIGHTON STATION	ARRIVE VICTORIA STATION	NOTES
1450	1539	M–Sa
1500	1618	Su
1518	1611	M–Sa
1550	1641	M–Sa
1600	1718	Su
1618	1711	M–Sa
1650	1743 (1738 Sa)	M–Sa
1700	1818	Su
1718	1811	Sa
1722	1822	M–F
1750	1839	M–Sa
1800	1918	Su
1818	1911	Sa

M–Sa service is then hourly at 1850, 1950, 2050, 2150 (Sa only), then 2200, and 2302. Su service is hourly to 2200, then 2302.

---

brought royalty and commoner alike to Brighton. The good doctor prescribed bathing in the sea and drinking a pint and a half of seawater daily as a cure for glandular diseases. Such a prescription, incredible as it seems, must have initiated a whole new series of maladies. Chronicles of that period, however, have failed to note them.

The gifted and wayward Prince Regent first visited Brighton in 1783. Enamored by it all (and well heeled with royal funds), he ordered his Royal Pavilion constructed there. Completed in 1822 from an architectural style taken somewhere east of the Suez, it has been termed one of the most bizarre and exotic palaces in all Europe. The Royal Pavilion's ostentatious onion-domed exterior, looking very much like a series of hot-air balloons about to ascend, is only surpassed by its even more amazing interior. It is fully furnished in its original style and open to the public daily from 1000 to 1800 June–September and 1000 to 1700 October–May.

Queen Victoria, not at all amused by the pavilion's architecture, was permitting it to fall into ruin when Brighton's citizenry saved it from demolition in 1850. The Royal Pavilion underwent a £10 million refurbishment to restore the seaside palace to its original condition.

Visit The Lanes, where you take a step backward into the old fishing-village days. The buildings in these narrow, twisting passages were fishermen's cottages in the seventeenth century. Today they house quaint and fascinating antiques, jewelry, and high-fashion shops, as well as pubs and cafes.

Part of the changing scene in Brighton has been the introduction during the last twenty years of English-language schools, which attract international students from a score of foreign lands. This youthful input has made it one of the most vibrant resorts in Britain.

Brighton's train terminal is being renovated, with completion expected by spring 2000. The station's rail information center is currently located at the entrance.

In English-style directions, had you denied yourself the turning at Grand Junction, you would have come quickly upon the gates of the Palace Pier, which extends out into the English Channel like a silent sentinel. Constructed in 1899, the pier has been restored and features free entrance, free deck chairs, and free entertainment. It opens daily at 0900. Have a look. It's quite enjoyable.

If you would like to participate in a guided walking tour of Brighton's "Old Town," obtain details from the information center. From June through mid-September, the tours start at the tourist information center. Or you can pick up the *Brighton and Hove's Visitor Guide* at the information center. The town plan in it shows where to go and what to see.

The shopping center, Churchill Square Pedestrian Precinct, is unique to southern England.

Swank designer shops can be found in Brighton's east side and the adjoining Regent Arcade. For the more bizarre, shop the Upper Gardner Street Junk Market on Saturday mornings and the station car park's "carboot" (junk and antiques) sale on Sunday mornings. Or visit the North Lane's quirky shops for unusual gift items.

Young and old alike should take a ride along the sea front on the Volks Railway, Britain's first public electric railway. Open daily between Easter and Labor Day, the railway travels along the beach on Madeira Drive to Black Rock. Lacking the speed of the InterCity 125s, the Volks Railway makes up for it with its nostalgia. The kids will love the Sea Life Centre and Peter Pan's Playground. Because of the city's number and variety of shopping areas, Brighton is often referred to as "London by the Sea." New bars, cafés, and restaurants in the Victorian sea front arches offer an uniterrupted view of the sea along the beach front and boardwalk. While exploring try not to miss the Artists' Quarter or the Fishing Museum.

Brighton's Marina is one of the largest in Europe. Whether you are a boating enthusiast or not, a visit there is well in order. A complete village is now the centerpiece of the marina, with an eight-screen cinema, elegant shops, quayside restaurants, bowling complex, and, of course, traditional British pubs on the waterfront. The marina also stages many colorful events, such as boat shows and sailing regattas throughout July and August. Time permitting, we suggest a stroll along the Hove with its elegant Regency squares and crescents. Visit the Museum and Art Gallery, home to the "Hove to Hollywood Gallery"; or stop by the Brunswick Town House for fascinating insight into Regency lifestyle. For steam enthusiasts, do *not* miss the British Engineerium.

If you're caught up in Brighton's buoyancy, check with the tourist information center for hotel accommodations and catch a morning train back to London. Hove also has its own train station with regular services to London.

Day Excursion to

Bury St. Edmunds   Magna Carta

Depart from Liverpool Street Station

Distance by train: 74 miles (119 km)

Average train time: 2 hours

Train information and InterCity services: (034) 548–4950

Bury St. Edmunds Tourist Information Centre: 6 Angel Hill, IP33 1UZ; *Tel:* (0128) 476–4667; *Fax:* (0128) 475–7084

Minicom: (0128) 475–7023

Internet: http://www.stedmundsbury.gov.uk

E-mail: eloise.appleby@burybo.stedsbc.gov.uk

Hours: Open from Easter through October from 0930–1730, Monday through Saturday, and 1000–1500 Sunday (June–October only). Winter hours and bank holidays are 1000–1600 Monday–Friday and 1000–1300 Saturday.

    The Tourist Information Centre is located immediately opposite the Abbey Gate entrance to the ruins of the Abbey of St. Edmund, a short distance from the train station. The information map is displayed in the station (map dispensers available also); or station personnel will gladly provide directions. Taxi rank is located outside.

    For centuries, the East Anglian town of Bury St. Edmunds has been the scene of a fight for freedom of conscience, speech, worship, and the rights of the individual.

    In his *Pickwick Papers*, Charles Dickens described Bury St. Edmunds as " . . . a handsome little town of thriving and cleanly appearance." So it remains today.

    A monastery was built on the present site of Bury St. Edmunds in A.D. 633. In 903, thirty-four years after King Edmund of East Anglia was killed by the Danes at Hoxne, his body was brought to the town by Bishop Theodred. Thus, the town became known as Bury St. Edmunds (town of St. Edmund). The abbey church was built soon afterward to honor the memory of the king. For many, Bury St. Edmunds is regarded as one of the most famous towns in all England. It is said that in 1214, barons gathered at the high altar of the abbey to take a solemn oath to force King John to grant a charter of liberties, one of the events leading to the granting of the Magna Carta in 1215.

    The town center is most notable for its pleasant Georgian atmosphere, recalling the days when the town was a leading social center within East Anglia. The great Abbey of St. Edmund was one of the largest in Europe

London–Bury St. Edmunds

Service shown is from London Liverpool Street Station via Ipswich and requires a change of trains in Ipswich; other service is available via Cambridge, with a change of trains necessary in Cambridge, with service from both London Kings Cross and Liverpool Street Stations.

DEPART LIVERPOOL STREET STATION	ARRIVE BURY ST. EDMUNDS STATION	NOTES
0800	1027	Su (1)
0830	1016	M–Sa (1)
0920	1108	Su (1) (2)
0920	1146	Su (1) (3)
0930	1141	M–Sa (1)
0950	1141	M–F (1)
1030	1249	M–Sa (1)
1050	1249	M–F (1)
1120	1351	Su (1)
1130	1311	M–Sa (1)
1220	1425	Su (1)
1230	1426	M–Sa

DEPART BURY ST. EDMUNDS STATION	ARRIVE LIVERPOOL STREET STATION	NOTES
1351	1548	Su (1)
1444	1648 (1640 Sa)	M–Sa (1)
1522	1730 (1740 Sa)	M–Sa (1)
1557	1756	Su (1)
1647	1855 (1852 Sa)	M–Sa (1) (4)
1702	1855 (1852 Sa)	M–Sa (1) (5)
1704	1856	Su (1)
1748	1948	Su (1)
1846	2052 (2040 Sa)	M–Sa (1) (6)
1904	2057	Su (1)
1920	2214 (2226 Sa)	M–Sa (1)
2204	0021	Su (1)

(1) Change trains in Ipswich
(2) Requires a 3-minute connection time in Ipswich
(3) Requires a 35-minute connection time in Ipswich
(4) Arrival in Liverpool Street station at 1840 may be possible, with a 9-minute connection time in Ipswich
(5) Requires a 5-minute connection time in Ipswich
(6) Requires a 6-minute connection time in Ipswich

during medieval times. Sacked in 1327 by townspeople protesting against monastic control, and again in 1381 during the Peasants' Revolt, the Abbey Gate was severely damaged and many monks were killed. In 1465, a severe fire damaged the church, and it had to be extensively repaired. The abbey was subsequently robbed of much of its stone for use in other buildings. A placard on the Abbey Gate indicates that the gate was destroyed and the abbey badly damaged by the townspeople in 1327 but was rebuilt on a spot adjacent to the old one in 1347.

Across from the Abbey Gate is the Angel Hotel, more than 500 years old, known for its association with Charles Dickens. His room, No. 15, is preserved exactly as it was more than a century ago. The site has seen three East Anglian inns over the years. Unique attractions of the Angel Hotel include its tavern room, dating back to 1433—fifty-nine years before Columbus discovered America—and the restaurant located in the medieval vaults of the structure.

During World War II, Bury St. Edmunds was ringed with American air bases. Today, the U.S. Air Force European Command operates a base at Mildenhall, west of Bury St. Edmunds. Visitors are welcome there if they have contacted the base information office or its community relations advisor before going. The Tourist Information Centre can provide tour bookings and further details.

Sightseeing in Bury St. Edmunds focuses on the Abbey ruins and gardens. St. Mary's Church, the southern boundary of the abbey precinct, is also popular. The Borough Council's Museum of Local History is housed in Moyse's Hall. Constructed in the latter part of the twelfth century, it is a fine example of Norman domestic architecture and houses eclectic collections from archaeology to crime and punishment exhibitions. The Manor House Museum faces the great churchyard. This restored Georgian mansion houses clocks, paintings, costumes, and objets d'art from the seventeenth to the twentieth century.

There are two distinct parts to the town. As was customary in most medieval towns with a monastic foundation, there was a division between the monastery and the townspeople—possibly the first example of separation of church and state. This division resulted in the business section and public buildings standing on a hill only 100 meters away to the west of the Abbey Ruins today.

The Theatre Royal, one of three surviving Georgian playhouses in Britain, was built in Bury St. Edmunds during 1819 by English architect

William Wilkins. He also designed Downing College at Cambridge University. Almost a miniature version of West End London Theatre (seating only 352 people), the Theatre Royal's architecture displays in elegant fashion the style and form for which the Georgian architects were famous. This historical theater's repertoire features a broad range of entertainment, plays, dance, opera, and every form of music from classical to jazz and rock. In 1892, the Theatre Royal made international headlines by presenting the world premiere of *Charlie's Aunt*, a comedy that is still performed in every major language throughout the world.

Bypassed by time, Bury St. Edmunds is essentially a country town that was spared the industrial expansion of the Victorian Age. But the town stands tall in history. The principles of the Magna Carta, which had their foundation in Bury St. Edmunds and were developed over the centuries into English Common Law, have become the heritage not only of the British Isles but of countless millions throughout the world. As history records, the grant of the Magna Carta by King John is the basic source of the constitutional liberties of English-speaking peoples.

One of Bury St. Edmunds's local products is ale. Although the city boasts numerous pubs, we suggest that you sample a pint in the Nutshell, the smallest pub in England. Its single barroom measures 12 feet by 7 feet.

Ask at the Tourist Information Centre about tours of Bury St. Edmunds. Modestly priced, all are guaranteed to be enjoyable and educational. Audio tapes may be picked up at the center, allowing you to be led through the sites by the historical voices of Brother Jocelin, Abbot Samson, and other town notables. Another tour to consider is the *Summer Excursion tour* (during the school summer holiday), which offers a carefree day touring the beautiful countryside, with visits to villages and attractions in Heritage Suffolk.

Day Excursion to

Cambridge

UNIVERSITY CITY

Depart from King's Cross Station

Distance by train: 56 miles (90 km)

Average train time: 1 hour

Train information and InterCity services: (034) 548–4950

Cambridge Tourist Information Centre: Wheeler Street, CB2 3QB; (0122) 332–2640; Guided group tours, (0122) 345–7754; *Fax:* (0122)345–7588

  Internet: http://www.cambridge.gov.uk/leisure/tourism.htm

  E-mail: tourism@cambridge.gov.uk

  Hours: April–October, Monday–Friday 1000–1800; Saturdays 1000–1700; Sundays (Easter–September) 11–1600; November–March, Monday–Friday, 1000–1730; Saturdays 1000–1700.

  To reach the center, take the bus (No. 1) located immediately in front of the railway station to St. Andrew's Street. After getting off the bus at St. Andrew's Street, ask for directions to the tourist information center on Wheeler Street (behind the Guildhall) a few short blocks away.

Oxford graduates often refer to Cambridge as "the other place." Both universities hold one thing in common: Organized along the classic federal structure, they house a number of largely autonomous colleges. Comparisons stop here. Cambridge is Britain's "University City." It is said that if you visit only one other English city besides London, it should be Cambridge.

Cambridge is a complex blend of market town, regional center, tourist attraction, and university. It is situated on the River Cam around the original bridge over which all trade and communications passed between central England, East Anglia, and Continental Europe 1,000 years ago. It was a natural spot for travelers to pause to exchange news and opinions, thereby preparing the ground for a center of learning.

Several religious orders, including the Franciscans and Dominicans, established monasteries and affiliated schools in Cambridge early in the twelfth century. Students from the University of Oxford and the University of Paris left to study in Cambridge during the thirteenth century. The present-day colleges originated at that time, when students began residing in hostels and halls.

Daily walking tours with qualified guides can tell you about the university and its colleges. Schedules may be obtained from the Tourist

London–Cambridge

Frequent service is available between London and Cambridge. Trains depart from both King's Cross and Liverpool Street stations. Trains that take 61 minutes or less, depart from London King's Cross Station; trains from Liverpool Street station take 75 to 90 minutes.

LONDON TO CAMBRIDGE

M–F   Depart London King's Cross Station at 0645, 0715, and every half-hour until 2015.

Sa   Depart London King's Cross at 0745, 0815 and every half-hour until 1945.

Su   Depart London King's Cross at 0915 and hourly until 1415, then more frequently.

CAMBRIDGE TO LONDON

M–F   Depart Cambridge at 0545, 0615, and every half-hour until 1945, then at 2027; later trains are slower, the last train departing at 2318.

Sa   Depart Cambridge at 0745, 0815, and every half-hour until 1945, then at 1927, 2027, and 2127.

Su   Fast trains depart at 1145 and 1615; other service is hourly at 27 minutes after the hour until 2227; still other trains depart at 1654 and then hourly until 2054.

Information Centre. The main colleges are closed to visitors from mid-April until the end of June. A note of academic etiquette: College members are happy to welcome you to the grounds and their historic buildings, but they ask you to respect their need for quiet and privacy.

Ask at the tourist office for the *Cambridge Mini-Guide* (nominal fee). It provides basic information about the colleges and museums and includes a street plan of the city. Other books and gifts are available for those wanting to know more about the history of Cambridge and places of interest outside the city.

If you plan to see Cambridge on your own, planning an itinerary may be difficult because there is so much to see. King's College Chapel is regarded universally as one of Cambridge's finest architectural structures. It was constructed in stages over a period of nearly seventy years and was completed in 1536. The chapel (£3.00) displays the carved coats of arms of Henry VIII. His initials, along with those of Anne Boleyn, can be seen on the screen. The chapel's stained-glass windows depict stories from the Old Testament and the New Testament. Rubens's *Adoration of the Magi* is the altarpiece.

Trinity College's great court is one of the largest collegiate quadrangles in England. It's so large that much of its detail goes unnoticed. It is said that taking advantage of this situation, Byron bathed nude in the fountain and shared his room with a pet bear, which he claimed he kept for the purpose of taking examinations. Sir Isaac Newton first measured the speed of sound in the great court by stamping his foot in the cloister along the north side.

The admission qualifications to the University of Cambridge are exceptionally demanding. Each year, approximately 8,000 students apply for admission. In the end, however, only about 20 percent are admitted.

The Cam River, the source of Cambridge's being and delightful in any season, deserves a portion of your visit. A tour of the city by boat along the "backs," as the placid stretch of the river is called, is an experience not to be missed. You can hire a punt, rowboat, or canoe to boat along the backs. If your selection is the punt—which is propelled with long wooden poles—be aware that these poles frequently stick in the mud and have been known to vault a punter into the river. A "chauffeur punt" service is also available.

Visitors have a wide choice of museums covering a wide range of interests. Allow yourself time to wander in at least one of them. The Fitzwilliam Museum on Trumpington Street features Greek and Roman artifacts and a famous collection of paintings. The Folk Museum on Castle Street contains a vast array of domestic articles. Another point of interest is Kettles Yard Art Gallery at Castle Street on Northampton with its fine collection of modern paintings and sculpture.

Steeped in history, Cambridge has a reminder of a more recent historical event—Duxford Airfield, which is located 8 miles south of the city. Duxford is now the site of the Imperial War Museum and the American Air Museum. During World War II Allied aircraft flew raids from Duxford to continental Europe. The American Military Cemetery, 4 miles from Cambridge, contains the graves of 3,811 American airmen who operated from bases in Britain. The cemetery and the museum may be reached by bus. For some preliminary knowledge, visit the Imperial War Museum's Web site at http://gazetteer.interdart.co.uk/east/visit/duxfrd.htm.

Day Excursion to

Canterbury

AND THE CATHEDRAL

Depart from Victoria Station

Distance by train: 62 miles (99 km)

Average train time: 1 hour, 25 minutes

Train information and InterCity services: (034) 548–4950

Canterbury Tourist Information Centre: No. 34 St. Margaret's Street, Kent CT1 2TG; *Tel:* (0122) 776–6567; *Fax:* (0122) 745–9840.

    E-mail: 101523.510@compuserve.com

    Accommodations: (0122) 745–1026

    Theatre–Concert Bookings: (0122) 745–5600

    Internet: http://www.canterbury.co.uk

    Hours: Open Monday through Saturday 0930–1730 in summer; Sundays 1000–1600; July through August Monday through Saturday 0930–1800; Sunday 1000–1700. Winter hours are 0930–1700, Monday–Saturday and 1000–1600 Sunday.

    Canterbury has two railway stations: West Station and East Station. There's a taxi queue just outside the station entrances, or you can walk to the city centre and the cathedral in about fifteen minutes.

Canterbury, the Metropolitan City of the Anglican Communion, has a history going back to prehistoric times. It was a Roman settlement and the Saxon stronghold of the men of Kent. Here in 597 St. Augustine began the conversion of the English to Christianity, where Ethelbert, King of Kent, was baptized.

Only ruins remain of the Benedictine St. Augustine's Abbey, burial place of the Jutish Kings of Kent, but St. Martin's Church, on the eastern outskirts of the city, is still in use. This church is said to have been the place of worship of Queen Bertha, the Christian wife of King Ethelbert, before the arrival of St. Augustine.

In 1170 the rivalry of church and state culminated in the murder in Canterbury Cathedral, by Henry II's knights, of Archbishop Thomas à Becket. His shrine became a great centre of pilgrimage, as described by Chaucer in his *Canterbury Tales.* After the Reformation the pilgrimage ceased, but the prosperity of the city was strengthened by an influx of Huguenot refugees from the Continent, who introduced weaving.

Trains departing London's Charing Cross and Waterloo Stations arrive at Canterbury West. Those departing London's Victoria Station arrive at

London–Canterbury

Service shown is from London Victoria Station to Canterbury East Station; other services available are from London Charing Cross Station and Waterloo East Station to Canterbury West Station. Passengers should be aware that trains may be split at Faversham, some coaches going to Canterbury East and others going elsewhere; passengers should be sure they are in a coach going to Canterbury before the train reaches Faversham. Consult the conductor if you are unsure.

DEPART VICTORIA STATION	ARRIVE CANTERBURY EAST STATION	NOTES
0735	0859 (0858 Sa)	M–F (1)
0805	0929	Daily (1)
0833 (0835 Sa)	0958	M–Sa
0905	1029	M–Sa (1)
0935	1058	M–Sa

and then at half-hour intervals until 1335; Sunday service continues at hourly intervals until 1905.

DEPART CANTERBURY EAST STATION	ARRIVE VICTORIA STATION	NOTES
1453	1617	Daily (1)
1523	1647	M–Sa
1553	1717	Daily (1)
1623	1747	Sa
1626	1757	M–F
1650 (1635 Su)	1817	Daily (1)
1722 (1723 Sa)	1848 (1847 Sa)	M–Sa
1750 (1751 Su)	1917	Daily (1)

Sunday service continues at hourly intervals until 2205; and then at half-hour intervals until 1335, less frequently thereafter.
(1) Train splits or merges at Faversham. Check with the conductor before reaching Faversham if you are not sure you are in a proper coach.

Canterbury East. For simplicity, day-excursion schedules are given for Victoria and Canterbury East Stations only.

Arriving in Canterbury East Station, use the pedestrian bridge to reach the city walls. The Cathedral, with architecture ranging from the eleventh to the fifteenth century, is world famous. Modern pilgrims are attracted particularly to the Martyrdom, the Black Prince's Tomb, the Warriors' Chapel, and the many examples of medieval stained glass. The Medieval city walls are built on Roman foundations and the fourteenth-century West Gate is one of the finest buildings of its kind in the country.

From the station entrance, you'll see a sign across the street that says, CITY CENTRE–MARLOWE THEATRE–CATHEDRAL. A blue sign showing a person walking indicates where to cross the highway. Proceed along the city's old Roman walls, which enclose Dane John Park. Climb the mound in the park for a view of the town and the cathedral. Farther along, you'll come to the city bus station. Descend from the wall at this point onto St. George's Street. Turn left and walk until the cathedral is in view on your right through the Christ Church Gate. Passing through the gate will bring you onto the cathedral grounds.

The poet and playwright Christopher Marlowe was born and reared in Canterbury, and there are also literary associations with Defoe, Dickens, Joseph Conrad, and Somerset Maugham. The Mayflower was provisioned in Canterbury, before she set sail for Plymouth and her historic journey to America.

During World War II Canterbury suffered a severe bombing raid, but parts of the city centre have been rebuilt. Modern-day Canterbury has a wide range of quality shops and comfortable hotels, many of these small, family-run businesses. The 1,000-seat Marlowe Theatre offers a program of first-class plays, operas, musicals, and one-night shows. Each autumn, Canterbury celebrates the International Arts Festival.

Not far from the Christ Church Gate is the Longmarket, a paved pedestrian area beginning at the intersection of Rose Lane and St. George's Street. Walking directly away from the Christ Church Gate on St. Margaret's Street will bring you to the Canterbury Visitor Information Centre. City tours depart from this point.

From High Street, where it intersects St. Margaret's Street, walk down until you pass over a narrow bridge on the River Stour. On the far right of the bridge you will see the Old Weaver's House, built in 1500. Canterbury was the background for Dickens's *David Copperfield,* so let your imagination take over for a few fleeting moments and transport you back into English history and literature. The structure houses a beautiful collection of English Church brass rubbings from the medieval and Tudor periods.

Unfortunately, as of press time it is closed temporarily to the public due to a change of ownership.

Following World War II, Canterbury became a great educational center. In 1962 Christ Church College was opened adjacent to St. Augustine's College. More recently, the University of Kent was established on a hill overlooking the cathedral and city from the west. Its buildings are modern in design, emphasizing artistic and cultural development.

Recently the Victoria Hotel in London Road has been expanded; a Friday market now takes place in addition to the traditional Wednesday Market in the city center; and easier access has been made to Herne Bay. (Beach bums will want to take this seafront trek, especially around the first two weeks of August when the annual Herne Bay Festival is held—family events, fireworks, live music, and more!) The annual Canterbury Festival is held every October for two weeks also.

We suggest taking in the award-winning Canterbury Tales Visitor Attraction as well; or make a night of it and take the Ghost Tour of Canterbury. This street-theatre spook shows Canterbury in a whole new light and runs every Friday, Saturday, and Sunday from April through August (year-round to prebooked groups).

Canterbury, proud of its historical past, is nonetheless eager to respond to the demands of present "pilgrims"—visitors who come to see the cathedral, the other historical landmarks, and new sites. The city of Canterbury has done an excellent job by exhibiting its history as a living part of a modern community.

Day Excursion to

Chester

A MODERN "MEDIEVAL" CITY

Depart from London's Euston Station

Distance by train: 178 miles (287 km)
Average train time: 2 hours, 30 minutes
Train information and InterCity services: (034) 548–4950
Chester Tourist Information Centre: The Forum CH1 2HS; *Tel:* (0124) 440–2111; (0124) 431–3126 (24 hours/day); *Fax:* (0124) 440–0420
Internet: http://www.chester.gov.uk
Hours: Open 0900–1730 Monday through Saturday and 1000–1600 Sunday all year.
    The railway station in Chester is about a fifteen-minute walk from the city's center. City Road, at the front of the station, will get you started in the right direction. Change at the pedestrian underpass onto Foregate Street, which turns into Eastgate Street and brings you to the center of the city's historic area. Or you can board a bus outside the station. The bus arrives at the town hall in approximately ten minutes for a charge of thirty-five pence. Taxi meters click off around £2.00.

    "All's well" in Chester, but don't take our word for it. Check personally with Chester's Town Crier. He appears at noon (Tuesday through Saturday, April through August) in the center of the city to announce that fact. Chester is one of the few cities in England with its encircling walls completely intact—a splendid example of a fortified medieval town.

    The center of Chester, known as The Cross, takes its name from the stone "High Cross" standing in front of St. Peter's Church. From this point you may view Chester's distinctive landmark, the Rows—two tiers of shops (one at ground level, the other immediately above), each with its own walkway.

    Developed in the thirteenth century, the Rows are unique and justly world famous. The upper levels are great for people-watchers who like to linger undisturbed while observing the stream of passersby in the streets below. The true origin of the Rows has never been satisfactorily explained, but they far exceed any modern-day shopping center in utility and beauty. One opinion is that they served as a means of defense against the incursions of the Welsh raiders, who came to plunder their richer English neighbors.

    The Romans gave Chester its street plan. Walk today along the four main streets within the city's walls, and you will follow the lines laid down

London–Chester

DEPART EUSTON STATION	ARRIVE CHESTER STATION	NOTES
0735 (0725 Sa)	1014	M–Sa (1)
0800 (0750 Sa)	1041 (1123 Su)	Daily (1)
0840 (0830 Sa)	1110	M–Sa
0905 (0855 Sa)	1140	M–Sa (1)
1000	1305	Su
1005 (0955 Sa)	1243	M–Sa (1)
1105 (1055 Sa)	1340 (1418 Su)	Daily (1)
1205 (1155 Sa)	1440	M–Sa (1)

DEPART CHESTER STATION	ARRIVE EUSTON STATION	NOTES
1416	1725	Su (1)
1432	1715 (1720 Sa)	M–Sa (1)
1522	1756 (1805 Sa)	M–Sa
1533	1813 (1826 Sa)	M–Sa (1)
1538	1826	Su (1)
1613	1901	Su (1)
1633	1935	M–Sa (1) (2)
1709	2009	Su (1)
1733	2020 (2027 Sa)	M–Sa (1)
1748	2103	Su (1)
1833	2110 (2145 Sa)	M–Sa (1)
1837	2124	Su (1)
1938	2215 (2240 Sa)	M–Sa (1)
1958	2256	Su (1)

(1) Change trains in Crewe.
(2) On Sa, passengers can connect with either of three trains at Crewe, arriving in Euston Station at 1913, 1945, or 1950.

by Roman engineers almost 2,000 years ago. Part of the Roman wall survives and is incorporated in the massive tenth-century fortifications enclosing the city. You can find out more about the city's Roman heritage at the Dewa Roman Experience, just off Bridge Street (0124–434–3407).

A walk on the walls provides an opportunity to enjoy the vista of the surrounding countryside.

Restoration has thrived on a large scale in Chester. Entire blocks were renovated in massive programs. The city's famous "black and white" Tudor buildings survived the ravages of time but did not escape alterations to their facades by Victorian architects. In all, however, Chester has managed to preserve its pleasant medieval appearance.

Your first call should be at the tourist information center at the town hall on Northgate Street across from the entrance to Abbey Square. The center offers a wide range of facilities including a national room-finder service and ticket agency.

Special guided walks are also available: Pastfinder Tours depart daily year-round at 1045; the Ghosthunter Trail departs from Chester Visitor Centre at 1930 on Thursday, Friday, and Saturday from May through October; and the Roman Soldier Wall Patrol sets forth at 1400 on Wednesday, Friday, and Saturday from June through September. Other tours may be made by special arrangement.

Opposite the town hall is Abbey Square, an island of quiet in the center of the city. By entering the square through its massive fourteenth-century gateway, you will find various buildings constructed anywhere from the sixteenth to the nineteenth century.

Chester Cathedral is within sight of the town hall. An abbey was founded on this site in the tenth century. It remained as a monastery until its dissolution in 1540, when the building was made a cathedral. The bell tower of the cathedral is a concrete structure that was finished in 1974, the first freestanding bell tower for a cathedral built since the fifteenth century.

Chester's prestigious event—the Chester Mystery Plays—occurs in July once every five years. This medieval tradition draws from stories of the Bible. Chester's Mystery Plays texts are the most complete, with the earliest surviving records dated 1546. For more information contact the Chester Tourist Information Centre at (0124) 440–2111 or http://www.chester.gov.uk.

An interesting observation point that provides a splendid view of the city, the River Dee, and the locks of the Chester canal is located at the north end of the city walls. A spur wall connects there with the water tower, which was built to protect the port of Chester. Another vantage point is from Bonewaldesthorne's Tower, about 100 feet from the water tower. If you participate in the Roman Soldier Wall Patrol tour, you will be able to enjoy this view.

Also in view at a bend in the River Dee is the Roodee, home of the Chester racecourse, the oldest in Britain. The main racing season is held in May and its richest prize, the Chester Cup, was first awarded 1824. As a matter of interest to sportive North Americans, the Roodee was, before horse racing, a football field. But due to the violent nature of the football matches, the city assembly members voted to terminate the sport in 1540.

Day Excursion to

Coventry

LADY GODIVA–SHOW & TELL

Depart from Euston Station

Distance by train: 100 miles (161 km)
Average train time: 1 hour, 10 minutes
Train information and InterCity services: (034) 548–4950
Coventry Tourist Information Centre: Bayley Lane CV1 5RN
　Tel: (0120) 383–2303 or –2304; *Fax:* (0120) 383–2370
　Hours: The center operates Monday through Friday, 0930–1700; Saturday and Sunday, 1000–1630. It remains open on Bank Holidays (except Christmas), 1000–1600.

　Coventry's rail station lies outside its "ringway," a circular superhighway surrounding the city. At the bus stop, you'll find a city map and information regarding Coventry's information center. Buses marked "Pool Meadow" (No. 17 or 27) will take you to the center of town in five minutes along a route that requires about twenty minutes to walk. Dismount at the Broadgate stop near the shopping square by the Leofric Hotel. The Tourist Information Centre is located at Bayley Lane and may be found via well-placed direction signs.

This is a city of myth and magic, from St. George the Dragon Slayer to the legend of Lady Godiva! Did she actually put everything on a horse—or has this tale, retold through the ages, changed with the telling? Was there really a "Peeping Tom"? Was he late for the show? Coventry holds the answers.

Coventry is best described as a modern city with ancient roots. Among its tall office buildings, new streets, and attractive shops, there is a scattering of old homes and churches, Coventry's remnants of its far-reaching past

Coventry's new cathedral, consecrated in 1962, stands as visible proof that today's craftsmen can, in fact, create memorable works of supreme beauty, as did their medieval counterparts. In the new cathedral you will

London–Coventry

(Because of engineering modifications near Coventry, passengers are advised to get current information at Euston Station before planning a summer trip to Coventry, particularly on a Sunday in June or July.)

Note: Signaling and other engineering modernization on the main line from London Euston Station to Birmingham New Street precludes train service to and from Coventry *on Sundays only* between May 24 and July 19, except on June 14 and 28. A bus service will convey train passengers from Rugby to Coventry train station or vice-versa when there is no train service to or from Coventry.

DEPART EUSTON STATION	ARRIVE COVENTRY STATION	NOTES
0735	0845 (0918 Su)	Sa, Su–see note above
0745	0856	M–F
0805	0926	Sa
0815	0926	M–F
0835	0954 (1015 Su)	Sa, Su–see Note above

M–F service continues after 0815 at half-hour intervals until 2345; Sa services continues after 0835 at half-hour intervals until 1935, then at 2030, 2130, and 2255. Beginning July 26, Sunday service will continue after 0835 at hourly intervals until 1645, then every half hour until 1945, then hourly until the last train at 2345.

DEPART COVENTRY STATION	ARRIVE EUSTON STATION	NOTES
1407	1520 (1532 Sa, 1539 Su)	Daily–see Note above
1437	1551 (1600 Sa)	M–Sa
1507	1620 (1632 Sa, 1636 Su)	Daily–see Note above

M–F service continues after 1437 every 30 minutes until 1907, then at 2007, 2106, 2218, and 2332; Sa service continues every 30 minutes until 1907, then at 2007, 2110, 2219, and 2331. Beginning July 26, Sunday service will depart at 7 minutes after the hour and continue at hourly intervals until 1707, then at half-hour intervals until 1907, then at 2007, 2107, and 2337.

see outstanding examples of the finest modern works of art, including the Baptistery Window, the largest piece of modern stained glass in the world. The tapestry "Christ in Glory" hangs behind the altar. Weighing nearly a ton, it is the largest tapestry in the world; ten men worked for three years to complete it. The cathedral, open from 0900 to 1930 in summer, closes at 1730 in winter.

Alongside the new stands the old Cathedral of St. Michael, reduced to ruins by one dreadful air raid in November 1940. An altar of broken stones surmounted by a charred cross stands at the eastern end of the ruins, backed by the words, "Father, forgive." In the nineteenth century John Ruskin wrote, "The sand of Coventry binds itself into stone which can be built half-way to the sky." Attesting to this, the tower and spire of the old cathedral survived intact after the bombing. Built in the fifteenth century, it is the third highest spire in England. A visit to both cathedrals should not be missed.

Lady Godiva was the wife of Leofric, the "grim" Lord of Coventry. Evidently, she bugged him about the heavy tax burdens he had levied on the townspeople. Legend says Leofric, weary of her nagging, agreed to decrease the tax rate if Her Ladyship would increase the town's morale by riding naked through its streets. Modern historians seriously doubt that Godiva made her gallop without benefit of even a riding crop. They believe her husband challenged her to ride stripped of her finery and her jewels and to ride humbly as one of his people and in full sight of them.

Stripped of her rank—or just plain stripped—Her Ladyship did make the ride and taxes were lowered, but she commanded the people to remain indoors with windows barred. Legend says that one town resident called "Tom" unbarred his window to peep as she rode by. Before he could satisfy his gaze, he was struck blind, poor man!

In modern-day reenactments, Lady Godiva now rides her horse through Coventry wearing a body stocking—a considerable improvement of the event over when it was conducted in Victorian days and she was dressed in billowing petticoats.

Oddly enough, the Godiva story was told for some 500 years before the "Peeping Tom" version was added. In any case, a stunning bronze statue perpetuates Her Ladyship's memory in Broadgate Park as Tom peeps out at her on the hour from the Broadgate clock. We can't help but wonder what effect Lady Godiva's ride would have on our modern-day Internal Revenue Service.

Lady Godiva's statue stands under the Cathedral Lanes Shopping Centre's canopy and immediately opposite the Leofric Hotel near the Tourist Information Centre. Be certain to read the inscriptions on the east and west sides of the statue's pedestal. They were written by Alfred Lord Tennyson, England's poet laureate.

Among many informative publications, be sure to acquire the *Coventry and Warwickshire Visitor's Guide* from the Tourist Information Centre. It contains a plan of the city's central area, along with a brief description of places of interest. It will lead you from Broadgate to a number of interesting places, including the two cathedrals. The *City Centre Attractions Guide* provides also a map and key to attractions.

For the more ambitious visitor, a two-hour walking tour accompanied by a guide leaves the information center Saturdays at 1400, if pre-booked. The tour passes Fords Hospital, a fine example of sixteenth-century almshouses, several sections of the remaining city wall, and Cook Street Gate, one of the twelve ancient gates erected in the fourteenth century. You will also be able to see some of Coventry's new buildings, including the Retail Market and the Belgrade Theatre. The price of the tour is £2.50 per person. Factory tours, if pre-booked, are also available on weekdays. When returning to the rail station, board the bus at the shelter directly in front of the Holy Trinity Church, opposite the hotel.

Day Excursion to

Dover

ON THE WHITE CLIFFS

Depart from Charing Cross Station

Distance by train: 77 miles (124 km)
Average train time: 1 hour, 30 minutes
Train information and InterCity services: (034) 548–4950
Dover Tourist Information Centre: Townwall Street, CT16 1JR; *Tel:* (0130) 420–5108; *Fax:* (0130) 422–5498.
   Hours: The center is open daily, 0900–1800.

   Taxis are available at the Dover Priory Station to take you to the Tourist Information Centre. If you prefer to walk and do not have cumbersome luggage, it takes about fifteen minutes. As you leave the station, walk to the first roundabout and turn right. Continue to the second roundabout and turn left. The center is 200 meters further, on the left side of the street.

For centuries Dover has been one of Britain's major channel ports. In theory, this is where England ends and the Continent begins, where countless Englishmen have been parted from, or united with, their homeland. Here stand the white cliffs of Dover. Below, on the beaches, the legions of the Roman Empire stormed ashore in 55 B.C., only to be repelled and to land again, successfully, at Deal.

Atop the cliffs broods Dover Castle. Initially constructed in the 1180s by Henry II to repel invaders, it has been reinforced at every threat to England's shores, including Hitler's in 1940. From its ramparts, on a clear day you can look across the 21 miles of the English Channel and see France. Approaching from the sea, a dramatic panorama unfolds as the white cliffs slowly rise from the horizon.

You cannot deny it—Dover is dramatic. Brooding hangs over it on a rainy, windswept day; grandeur surrounds it on a clear one when, for example, Boulogne in distant France becomes discernible. Although the deafening ramjets of the World War II German V-2 "buzz bombs" were replaced by the humming vacuums of the hovercraft, the screams of the gulls and the relentless crashing of the sea continue on, unchanged by time. If you are one to "stand in history," Dover becomes a must visit during your stay in Great Britain. Few other places on earth swell the imagination as do the white cliffs of Dover.

Train service from London to Dover follows two routes. Departures from Victoria Station split destinations at Faversham. Part of the train goes to Dover, the other part to Margate and Ramsgate. As a precaution against "trainsplitting," our rail schedule is based on direct service to Dover from London's Charing Cross Station. Readers can, however, avail themselves of either route. As a suggestion, depart Charing Cross and return via Faversham to Victoria Station. This way, you will be "joined" by the Ramsgate train instead of being "split" by it.

The tourist information center is extensive, since Dover is a major debarkation point for visitors from the Continent. The center can provide information on all of Great Britain, as well as the local area. Pick up the *Days Out* brochure for White Cliffs Country for Visitor Vouchers to get either a free adult or child admission or a free or discounted gift from the many attractions of the area.

Ask for information on Dover Castle and how to reach it. No doubt you will also be interested in visiting the Roman-painted house, Britain's buried Pompeii, discovered by an archaeological unit in 1971. Roman legions took over the structure about A.D. 300 for

London–Dover

Schedules shown are for direct trains that operate from and to London Charing Cross Station. Other services are available from London Victoria Station and may require a change of trains.

Readers who may be planning trips from England to France by train and sea are advised that these schedules are not valid for those services: Trains shown here terminate at Dover Priory Station, which is some distance from the Dover Docks used by ferries.

DEPART CHARING CROSS STATION	ARRIVE DOVER PRIORY STATION	NOTES
0700	0858 (0902 Sa)	M–Sa
0755	0943	Sa
0800	0941	M–F
0855 (0900 Sa)	1040	M–Sa
0900	1043	Su
0930	1130 (1128 Sa)	M–Sa
1000	1140 (1143 Su)	Daily

M–Sa service continues after 1000 at half-hour intervals until 1600 and afterward at other intervals; Su service continues after 1000 at hourly intervals until 2200.

DEPART DOVER PRIORY STATION	ARRIVE CHARING CROSS STATION	NOTES
1422	1606	Su
1451	1635	M–Sa
1512	1709 (1705 Sa)	M–Sa
1522	1706	Su
1551 (1554 Sa)	1738 (1735 Sa)	M–Sa
1603 (1607 Sa)	1806	M–Sa
1622	1806	Su
1653	1835	M–Sa
1705 (1709 Sa)	1906	M–Sa
1722	1906	Su
1750	1937	M–Sa

M–Sa service continues after 1750 at hourly intervals until 2050, then 2203. Su service continues after 1722 and hourly intervals until 2022, then at 2108.

shore-defense purposes. It gains its name from the brilliantly painted plaster of its walls, the oldest and best-preserved painted walls in Britain. Incredible as it seems, the Romans even installed an elaborate under-the-floor heating system in the house. The house is a permanent museum, open every day except Monday from 1000 to 1700 (April through October). Admission is £2.00 for adults and £1.00 for children.

Legend has it that if Romans are left alone long enough, they will build something. Apparently, this was the case in the second century, when the Roman legions constructed two lighthouse beacons on Dover's cliffs for the purpose of guiding their galleys into the sheltered anchorage below. The surviving lighthouse, reaching to a height of more than 40 feet, is the tallest surviving Roman structure in Britain.

Dover can hardly be compared with the Continent's Riviera. Its beaches are small, tiny enclaves in the rugged face of the looming cliffs. And the height of the surf frequently becomes more than the average bather cares to contend with. Dover and its environs, however, lend themselves well to sunbathing, walking, and viewing. It is a point that more people pass through than pause to enjoy, but there is no other point in all of Britain more majestic than Dover. It is the very cornerstone of Britain.

During World War II, Dover was subjected to long-range artillery shelling from the Pas de Calais German gun emplacements. Dover's residents dug cellars deep into the cliffs as bomb shelters. The surviving structures, most of which are now small hotels, still maintain the shelters for use as wine cellars, bars, and boutiques. In addition, Hellfire Corner, a top-secret operations and command center used by the British to mastermind the evacuation from Dunkirk, were declassified and the tunnels opened to the public.

Have you ever been to France? If not, now's your chance! Take the train to Folkestone, a short distance to the west of Dover. From there you can whisk across the English Channel to Calais in about fifty catamaran minutes; to Boulogne, in fifty-five minutes. Day trips from Dover to the Continent are very popular. Stock up on wine and cheese, plus a yard or so of crusty French bread during your visit, and load up with duty-free tobacco and booze on the return journey, provided that duty-free shopping is still available. Plan ahead by asking any train information office for information on ferry, hovercraft, or catamaran services. (also see "The Channel Tunnel and Crossing the English Channel").

Day Excursion to

Folkestone
TRADITIONAL SEASIDE RESORT

Depart from Charing Cross Station

Distance by train: 70 miles (113 km)

Average train time: 1 hour, 20 minutes

Train information and InterCity services: (034) 548–4950. Also departs Waterloo East Station 3 minutes after Charing Cross departure time.

Folkestone Tourist Information Centre: Harbour Street, Kent CT20 1QN. *Tel:* (0130) 325–8594; *Fax:* (01303) 259–754.

E-mail: shepway.dc@shepwaydc.gor.uk

Hours: Daily 0900–1800 from June–September; October–March, Monday–Saturday 0900–1750, Sundays 1000–1600; closed 1300–1400 for lunch.

Walk from the Folkestone Central Station to the town center, along the pedestrian precinct and down to the Old High Street (which is paved with cobblestones and was a favorite haunt of Charles Dickens).

Folkestone is a "multiple treat" seaside resort—enjoy a delightful day of sightseeing, shopping, and seafood; take a memorable journey across Romney Marsh on the world's smallest public train, the Romney, Hythe and Dymchurch Railway; go antiques shopping in quaint English villages; or take a day trip to Boulogne, France, aboard Hoverspeed's SeaCat. Any of these options will take at least one full day. So you may plan on making several trips out of London to Folkestone during your visit. With so many possibilities, we suggest that you make your way to Folkestone's tourist information center immediately upon arrival, especially if you decide to look into accommodation information and stay over for a day or two.

The opening of the Channel Tunnel in 1994, with the terminal situated on the outskirts of Folkestone, has given car travelers to France another option. Cars are driven straight onto shuttle trains and arrive at Cocquelles in France, between Calais and Boulogne, in thirty-five minutes. Special arrangements for rental cars have been made with Hertz and Eurotunnel to exchange left- or right-hand drive vehicles at the Hertz/Eurotunnel terminal in Calais. This information is also useful if you have purchased a BritRail Pass + Car package. For Le Shuttle Information, call *Tel:* (099) 035–3535.

Once down in the harbor area, you can stroll under the arches and imagine what life must have been like in the Napolean era when the smuggling of contraband was prevalent. Or make your way into the dock area and visit Folkestone's latest attraction, a Russian submarine. Commissioned during the Cold War period, it gives visitors an insight into the secret world of the Russian Navy.

From there it is just a stone's throw to the Hoverspeed pier office where tickets for the catamaran are available (or purchase them at the tourist information office). If you are tempted to set foot on French soil, the office will provide you with current fares and schedules if you choose to cross the Channel "topside" rather than go under it. Hoverspeed's SeaCat catamaran service takes just fifty-five minutes.

The scenery along the seawall of Folkestone's outer harbor is enjoyable, to say the least. From there, you will have a commanding view of the harbor. Once across the Channel in Boulogne Harbor, visit the renowned sea life center, Nausicca, where sharks swim all around you in a water-filled glass dome. Or take a short walk into the bustling town center, with pavement cafes, restaurants serving mouth-watering French cuisine, and a street market; then for the hearty, a steep walk up to the Old Town is well worth the effort. Visit the thirteenth century Chateau, the most complete and best-preserved example of medieval fortification and memorabilia so magnificent that it was considered one of the finest museums in France by the nineteenth century.

Back in Folkestone, history and heritage abound. Folkestone has a dual distinction. As a cross-channel port, it is second only to Dover in total passenger traffic. For beauty of location, it probably stands second to none. The Bayle area was said to be the site of a fort built around A.D. 659 and also the site of a castle built around 1068. The pub in the square, the British Lion, claims to be one of the oldest in the country and asserts that it has served ale since the fifteenth century—it was certainly frequented by Charles Dickens, who resided just around the corner on The Leas.

The Leas, Folkestone's famous mile-long, cliff-top promenade, served as an inspiration for some of H. G. Wells's finest works and surveys the town's beach from a vantage point of more than 200 feet above. From there, one can view the landscape from Dover to Dungeness. Stretching behind The Leas are the spacious, well-planned business and residential quarters.

The Leas is the most popular attraction for visitors to Folkestone. With its breathtaking views of the English Channel, colorful flowers, and intriguing pathways zigzagging down to the lower Coast Road, it is a tranquil reminder of Victorian and Edwardian elegance. At the west end of The Leas are steps that lead down close to Spade House, H. G. Wells's home

London–Folkestone

DEPART CHARING CROSS STATION	ARRIVE FOLKESTONE CENTRAL STATION	NOTES
0700	0858 (0902 Sa)	M–Sa
0755 (0800 Sa)	0943 (0941 Sa)	M–Sa
0855 (0900 Sa & Su	1040 (1032 Su)	Daily
0930	1115	M–Sa
1000	1128 (1132 Su)	Daily

Continuing service at hourly intervals until mid to late P.M. Monday–Saturday; hourly on Sunday.

DEPART FOLKESTONE CENTRAL STATION	ARRIVE CHARING CROSS STATION	NOTES
1406	1535	M–Sa
1419 (1434 Su)	1606	Daily
1503	1635	M–Sa
1523	1709 (1705 Sa)	M–Sa
1534	1706	Su
1603 (1606 Sa)	1738 (1735 Sa)	M–Sa
1615	1806	M–Sa
1705	1835	M–Sa

M–Sa service continues after 1705 at approximately 1-hr intervals until 2216; Su service continues after 1534 at hourly intervals until 2034 and then at 2120.

from 1900 to 1910. Midway along, The Leas Cliff Hall is one of Kent's leading entertainment centers, while a little further down is the Bandstand—constructed in 1895 and still in regular use! Before leaving this delightful area you should experience a trip on the Cliff Lift. The second oldest of its kind in the country, this original water-balance lift operates from the top of The Leas down to the lower end.

Sandgate, on the western outskirts of Folkestone and on the Coast Road, has become one of the major antique centers in England. Numerous antique and curio shops beckon from narrow High Street. Also competing for shoppers' attention are several old-world inns and the Sandgate Castle, which has retained its English village atmosphere with friendly residents, as well as affording visitors a brisk sea-air promenade before continuing the journey towards Hythe.

A bus service operates from Folkestone, along the coast road and into Hythe, approximately twelve minutes from Folkestone town center. There the young—and those not so young—may board the fascinating Romney, Hythe and Dymchurch Light Railroad for a delightful journey by steam traction to New Romney, with stops in Dymchurch and St. Mary's Bay. At New Romney there is a wonderful model railway museum. Service is generally every hour, you may pick up a timetable at the tourist information center beforehand.

Before leaving Hythe, visit the crypt of St. Leonard's Church. Warning: This is not for the faint of heart! It houses a fascinating, macabre collection of hundreds of skulls and thousands of other bones dating back to before the Norman Conquest of 1066. St. Leonard's Church, built in A.D. 1080, is beautiful and has several architectural features similar to those found in Canterbury Cathedral, as well as its own very special and unique Saxon, Norman, and medieval historic features. Hythe has many small specialty shops and restaurants and is renowned for its Royal Military Canal and Martello Towers.

Stop en route at Dymchurch, England's "children's paradise," or at St. Mary's Bay, where boating and fishing are two highlights of that holiday center. The RH&D Railroad terminates its service at Dungeness, another 5½ miles down the RH&D "road," where you'll find great contrast between its fishermen's shacks and its atomic plant.

Those with the use of a car should explore the peaceful flatlands of Romney Marsh. Hundreds of years ago this area was part of the English Channel, and ships were moored to the castle walls at Lympne. Now drained by a series of dikes, the marsh is a haven for wildlife. Dotted around the waterways, fields of sheep and crop pastures nestle little villages. Although never densely populated, there is a surprising number of old churches here, with their own mysterious pasts steeped in smuggling tales. The thirteen medieval churches dotting this land each have unique features and are well worth a visit. Notices inform visitors where the church keys can be obtained: Some are kept by local homeowners, some in the nearby pubs, and some require almost an expedition in themselves to locate the ancient artifacts!

Day Excursion to

Gloucester

On the River Severn

Depart from Paddington Station

Distance by train: 114 miles (184 km)

Average train time: 1 hour, 50 minutes

Train information and InterCity services: (034) 548–4950

Gloucester Tourist Information Centre: 28 Southgate Street, GL1 2DF; *Tel:* (0145)
242–1188; *Fax:* (0145) 230–9788

Hours: Open 1000–1700 Monday through Saturday.

Gloucester's Central Station is within walking distance of the city center or you
may hail a taxi or ride a city bus. To reach the tourist center on foot, walk toward the
cathedral from the Central Station until you reach Northgate Street. Then turn left
to where it intersects Eastgate Street at The Cross. (Northgate and Eastgate Streets
take their names from the ancient city routes through the Roman wall.) Carry over
The Cross into Southgate Street.

Gloucester is steeped in history. First to arrive were the Romans, following their invasion of the British Isles. A legion fort was erected at the
site of the present city center, and by A.D. 96–98, the Roman city of
Glevum (now Gloucester) was established and flourishing. Little remains
of the Roman presence in modern Gloucester. None of the Roman wall is
now visible above ground, but its line is still followed by the principal
streets of the city.

Although Gloucester is situated some distance from the open sea, by the
construction of a ship canal in 1805, Queen Elizabeth I granted the city a
charter and declared it a "port." Oceangoing ships of up to 5,000-ton
capacity are able to dock at Sharpness, the terminal dock of the city's port
system. The entire dock complex has been given a new lease on life: An
ambitious redevelopment program is converting the site into a haven of
recreation, education, and commerce.

The National Waterways Museum is the principal tourist attraction in
the dock complex. Two hundred years of history, which shaped the fortunes of Britain, may be viewed there, housed in an imposing three-story
building. The historic docks are also home to three other museums, an
antiques center, shops, restaurants, and pubs. Following this, ride in a horse-
drawn wagon around the dockland area.

Gloucester's showplace is, of course, its cathedral, the oldest building
in the city. It consists of a Norman nucleus (1089–1260) incorporating

additions in every known style of Gothic architecture. Topped by a towering fifteenth-century pinnacle rising 225 feet above ground level, Gloucester's Cathedral is judged to be one of the six most beautiful buildings in Europe. If you have a limited amount of time to spend sightseeing in Gloucester, make the best use of it by concentrating on the cathedral and its surroundings.

The cathedral's origins began in 679, when the Saxons founded the Monastery of St. Peter on the site. In 909, Alfred the Great's daughter gave relics to the priory, making it the Church of St. Oswald. It is a magnificent example of medieval architecture with its great Norman piers still in the cathedral nave. Although craftsmen have continued to work on the structure since the fifteenth century, gracing it with an elegant exterior of later architectural designs, it remains a Norman edifice.

Sightseeing in Gloucester has been made easy by the Via Sacra, a walkway around the city center that follows the lines of the original city wall. It is described in several publications, among them the *Gloucester Mini Guide,* available in the information center. Follow the pattern of dark paving placed in the sidewalk to keep visitors from going too far astray.

At the beginning of the walking tour, you will observe a considerable variety of early English architecture, ranging from fifteenth-century timber-frame structures to the Tudor facades of the present county offices. You will pass Blackfriars, the best-preserved medieval Dominican friary in Britain. Although it is under restoration, a portion is open to the public. Greyfriars is also on the route. Unlike Blackfriars most of it stands in ruins.

Stopping in the city museum and art gallery affords the opportunity to examine many archaeological items, including a part of the original Roman city wall. The museum is open 1000–1700 Monday through Saturday. It is also open 1000–1600 on Sunday from July through September.

Just beyond the city museum, you will see the Eastgate Shopping Centre, which provides traffic-free areas at ground level. The tour ends at the cathedral in St. Lucy's Garden, the approach to the college green.

Gloucester abounds with interesting eating establishments ranging from McDonald's to such ancient eateries as the New Inn on Northgate Street. Don't let the name fool you. The New Inn was built by St. Peter's Abbey to accommodate pilgrims in 1450. The inn courtyard was used for staging plays during the time of Queen Elizabeth I, and in the eighteenth century the inn became renowned for its association with traveling menageries and

London–Gloucester

DEPART PADDINGTON STATION	ARRIVE GLOUCESTER STATION	NOTES
0715	0929	M–F (1)
0815	1017	Sa (1)
0827	1012	M–F
0915	1135	M–Sa (1)
0930	1129	Su (1)
1020	1207	Su
1100	1254 (1253 Sa)	M–Sa
1152	1353	Su (1)
1215	1417	M–Sa

DEPART GLOUCESTER STATION	ARRIVE PADDINGTON STATION	NOTES
1422	1630	M–F (1)
1432	1637	Su (1)
1526	1725 (1735 Sa)	M–Sa (1)
1614	1808	M–F
1621	1815	Su
1632	1830	Sa (1)
1747	2000	M–F (1)
1748	2007	Su (1)
1757	2005	Sa (1)
1900	2100	M–F (1)
1915	2113	Su
1933	2135	Sa (1)
1956	2150	M–F
2026	2230	Su (1)
2105	2305	Sa (1)
2112	2315	M–F (1)

(1) Change trains at Swindon

exhibitions of "curiosities." It is said to be the finest medieval open-gallery inn in England, and the food served there today matches the excellence of its medieval decor.

Day Excursion to

Greenwich   IT'S TIME TO MAKE A DIFFERENCE

Depart from Charing Cross Station

Distance by train: 7 miles (11 km)
Average train time: 15 minutes
Train information and InterCity services: (034) 548–4950
Greenwich Tourist Information Centre: 46 Greenwich Church Street SE10 9BL; *Tel:* (0181)
    858–6376; *Fax:* (0181) 853–4607
Internet: http://www.mx2000.co.uk
Hours: Open 1015–1645 daily throughout the year.
    Upon arrival in the Greenwich railway station, use the pedestrian subway
(underpass) to the main station and the street. Turn left and walk along the road into
the town. Follow the signs guiding you to the National Maritime Museum and the
Cutty Sark. Where they split, continue to follow the *Cutty Sark* signs until the ship's
masts come into view. The local Greenwich Tourist Information Centre is just
before the entrance of the *Cutty Sark* Gardens on Greenwich Church Street. Or, if
you prefer, take the Historic Greenwich Shuttle Bus at the station to visit all the
principal sites. Guided walking tours leave from the tourist office.

In addition to its intrinsic historical significance, Greenwich will be the
site for what is heralded to be one of the most fantastic new millennium
events. "It's Time to Make a Difference" is its theme, and it promises to
leave a lasting legacy for the future. The Millennium Dome, the largest
structure of its type anywhere, is scheduled to open on December 31,
1999. The dome's 10,000-seat arena will feature a spectacular light-and-
sound show using the latest interactive technology to take you on a journey from the past and into the future. Of the various publications available
at the Greenwich Tourist Information Centre, the *Greenwich Visitor's Guide*
has the latest information on the development of this Millennium
Experience.

A visit to Greenwich reveals the city known as the cradle of Britain's
maritime history. Queen Elizabeth II knighted Sir Frances Chichaster for
his solo circumnavigation of the world at a public ceremony at the Royal
Naval College, which now stands on the site of the Royal Palace of
Greenwich, where both Henry VIII and Elizabeth I were born.

The *Cutty Sark,* launched in 1869 as one of the fastest sailing ships, now
lies in dry dock at Greenwich. The clipper served in the China tea trade as
well as the Australian wool trade. Her curious name, which means "short

chemise," originated in "Tam O' Shanter," a poem by Robert Burns in which the witch Nanny appeared in a cutty sark. The ship's figurehead represents Nanny. Admission to the *Cutty Sark* is £3.50 for adults and £2.50 for children.

A short distance away stands the 54-foot ketch *Gypsy Moth,* which Sir Francis Chichester sailed solo around the world. Sir Francis sailed from Plymouth on August 27, 1966. He completed his circumnavigation of the world on May 28, 1967, when he sailed into Plymouth harbor to a tumultuous welcome. During his voyage, he covered a distance of 28,500 miles.

A few yards beyond the *Cutty Sark's* stern is the entrance to the Royal Naval College. Built during the seventeenth-century reign of William and Mary, the present buildings were used as a hospital for disabled and aged naval pensioners. In 1873, it became the Royal Naval College to provide for the higher education of naval officers.

Visitors are admitted to the Royal Naval College's Painted Hall and Chapel daily except Thursday from 1430 to 1645. Admission is free (*Tel:* 0181–858–2154). The Painted Hall is now used as the officers' mess of the college.

After the Battle of Trafalgar, the body of Lord Nelson lay in state in the Upper Hall. The interior decorating, by Sir James Thornhill, took nineteen years to complete. (You'll find out why when you see it.) Benjamin West's painting of the shipwrecked St. Paul in the college chapel is one of the highlights of that beautiful structure.

The world's largest maritime museum, the National Maritime Museum of Greenwich, has in its fascinating collection the paddle tug *Reliant,* often described as "the world's largest ship in a bottle." To reach the museum, turn left on King William Walk, leaving the Naval College. Walk past the Seamen's Hospital to Romney Road. Cross it and turn left. The museum entrance is a few yards beyond. The museum tour leads you through its west wing where you can view the *Reliant* and the state barges once used on the River Thames. The museum houses an amazing display of old ship models and features naval history of the nineteenth and twentieth centuries. Also included are two galleries of Victorian paintings and Arctic exploration exhibits.

Adjacent to the National Maritime Museum stands The Queen's House, a royal villa from the time of Charles I. Reopened by Queen Elizabeth II in May 1990, the palace has been restored to its former glory

London–Greenwich

All services shown here operate from London Charing Cross Station and also stop at London Waterloo East Station approximately 3 minutes from Charing Cross.

DEPART CHARING CROSS STATION	ARRIVE GREENWICH STATION	NOTES
0728	0742	M–F
0742	0756	Sa
0757	0811	Su
0805	0820	M–F
0812	0826	Sa
0824	0840	M–F
0827	0841	Su
0844	0900	M–F
0913	0927	M–F
0942	0956	M–F
1012	1026	M–F
1042	1056	M–F

M–F service continues after 1042 at half-hour intervals until midafternoon, more frequently afterward; Sa service continues after 0812 at half-hour intervals until 1642, then more frequently; Su service continues after 0827 at half-hour intervals until late P.M.

DEPART GREENWICH STATION	ARRIVE CHARING CROSS STATION	NOTES
1401	1418	M–Sa
1428	1446	Su
1431	1448	M–Sa
1458	1516	Su

M–F service continues after 1431 at half-hour intervals until 1601, then 1607; later trains depart at 1627, 1638, 1707, 1727, 1737, 1805, 1831, and 1901 and arrive at London Bridge Station, after which service resumes to Charing Cross with departures at 1927 and then every half hour until 2327. Sa service continues after 1431 at half-hour intervals until 1901, and then at half-hour intervals from 1927 until 2257. Su service continues after 1458 at half-hour intervals until the last train at 2258.

with sumptuous furnishings and rich silk hangings reflective of its heyday when Henrietta Maria, wife of Charles I, was in residence. It is the earliest example of English Palladian architecture.

An admission ticket of £5.50 (children £3.00) will gain you entrance to the museum, The Queen's House, and the Old Royal Observatory.

In Greenwich Park, next to the museum, you may enter the Old Royal Observatory (0181–858–4422), an integral part of the museum. It is open daily 1000–1700. The *Prime Meridian,* marking the line of zero degrees longitude on which GMT (Greenwich Mean Time) is calculated, is located in the courtyard of the observatory's meridian building.

While at Greenwich, you can take the opportunity of viewing it from the Island Gardens on the Isle of Dogs, located on the opposite bank of the River Thames. To get there, take the Greenwich foot tunnel under the river. It takes only about four minutes to get to the opposite bank. From this vantage point, it is possible to photograph the entire Greenwich complex. The domed entrance to the tunnel lies in front of the *Cutty Sark.*

The Greenwich and Docklands International Festival is held annually at the end of May and presents the finest in music, dance, literature, theater, and visual arts from around the world. A full program of events is available from the tourist office in early April.

Greenwich has no shortage of eating establishments—choose from over sixty restaurants offering a wide variety of cuisine ranging from the traditional English cooking to French haute cuisine or exotic oriental. Try the historic riverside Trafalgar Tavern. Located in a beautiful riverside setting beside the Royal Naval College, the Trafalgar has been providing traditional ales and fine foods since 1837. *Tel:* (0181) 293–3337 or 858–2437.

Day Excursion to

Hastings
FAMOUS BATTLE SITE

Depart from Charing Cross Station

Distance by train: 60 miles (87.4 km)

Average train time: 1 hour, 30 minutes

Train information and InterCity services: (034) 548–4950

Hastings Tourist Information Centre: Queens Square, Priory Meadow, East Sussex TN34 1JE; *Tel:* (0142) 478–1111; *Fax:* (0142) 478–1186

> *Hours:* Monday through Sunday 1000–1700 during the winter; extended summer hours.
>
> Leaving Hastings Station walk to the Priory Meadow Shopping Centre where the information center is centrally located.

Undoubtedly, 1066 is one of the most well-known dates in history. When dusk fell near Hastings on October 14, 1066, William the Conqueror, Duke of Normandy, had defeated the Saxon army of slain King Harold and had become the new king of England.

Contrary to popular belief, the actual battle was not fought in Hastings. After landing at Pevensey, the Norman army marched to Hastings and then northward about 5 miles to Senlac Hill where they engaged the Saxons in battle. The castle, formerly a timber form, was converted to stone in 1067, one year after the Battle. Hastings holds the lore of the Battle of Hastings plus the lure of its ancient fishing village and Norman castle.

Harold's troops were not pushovers. Nineteen days prior to the Battle of Hastings, his men had put a Norse army to rout at Stamford Bridge near York. In the initial onslaught at Senlac, the Normans retreated with the Saxons in hot pursuit. In so doing, the Saxons had to break the tight formation of their Saxon wall of shields, and the Norman cavalry quickly took advantage of the hole opening up in the line and inflicted heavy losses upon the Saxons. This tactic was twice repeated and the conflict ended. Today's Super Bowl tactics may have developed in Hastings! To go sightseeing at the battleground, board any "Battle Abbey" bus.

During the Roman occupation, Hastings was one of the famous Cinque (five) Ports where the Caesars moored their galleys. Later in history, however, the harbor was silted up by a series of violent storms, culminating with the great tempest in 1287. As a result, Hastings was reduced to the status of a small fishing community during the following four centuries.

The tourist information center has an excellent brochure titled *Discover Hastings*. With it in hand, you can easily visit the Norman Castle via the West Hill lift. After visiting the castle, venture a few more paces to St. Clement's Caves for the Smugglers' Adventure. Set in a labyrinth of caverns and secret passageways beneath West Hill, the smugglers are brought to life.

Hastings is home to Britain's largest fleet of beach-launched boats, which continue to operate in the traditional manner. In addition to its rich historical heritage and fishing industry, Hastings has been an attractive seaside resort since the mid-eighteenth century, when London physicians began prescribing sea air and saltwater as a panacea for all their patients' ills. Three miles of promenades line its beaches, many of them two-tiered with sun-trapped shelters overlooking the English Channel. Sun is more sought after than surf in Hastings because the water is very cold. Examine any photo of an English seaside resort and you'll see that the majority of the bathers are on the beach, not in the sea!

After drinking in the panoramic sights from atop the hill, you can drift back toward the sea and Hastings's "Old Town." On Hill Street, observe the two cannonballs on either side of St. Clement's Church belfry. The right one was shot into the tower by the French; the one on the left was added by the locals to balance things off.

The French artillery attack in 1337 also leveled the All Saints Church in the Old Town. Undaunted by the French shelling, the locals got busy and re-erected the church in 1436. The interior of the church contains a well-preserved fifteenth-century mural depicting the *Last Judgment*, with the devil casting souls into hell. The mural was intended to portray a lesson in morality for illiterate people of the Middle Ages. Today, television is utilized for the same purpose.

You'll pass many interesting points on your walk. Stop for a closer examination of the Old Town Hall on High Street, which is now a museum. Drop by the Stables Theatre opposite the Old Town Hall. It originally served as the stables for the Old Hastings House, which was spared demolition by being converted into a cultural center.

Your next stop should be Shovells, circa 1450, reputedly the oldest house in town. If you're desperate for a libation, you might try the Stag Inn opposite Shovells, where remains of mummified cats and rats decorate the bar. Nearing the end of the Old Town walk, you will pass an unusual wedge-shaped house called the "piece of cheese," no doubt the funniest

London–Hastings

Direct service from London to Hastings departs from Cannon Street Station early in the mornings of M–F only, and departs from Charing Cross at other times on M–F and on weekends. Some arrivals are also at Cannon Street Station in the afternoons of M–F. Times for those trains that leave from or arrive at Cannon Street Station are preceded by CS in the listings below.

DEPART CHARING CROSS STATION	ARRIVE HASTINGS STATION	NOTES
0740	0918	Sa
CS 0743	0930	M–F (1)
0810	0953	Su
0840	1018	Sa
CS 0843	1026	M–F (1)
0910	1053	Su
0940	1118	M–Sa

M–Sa service continues after 0940 at half-hour intervals from Charing Cross Station until midafternoon; Su service after 0910 is hourly until 2310.

DEPART HASTINGS STATION	ARRIVE CHARING CROSS STATION	NOTES
1352	1521	M–Sa
1411	1557	Su
1452	CS 1619	M–F (1)
1452	1621	Sa
1511	1657	Su
1552	1721	Sa
1552	CS 1730	M–F (1)
1611	1757	Su
1652	1822	M–Sa
1711	1857	Su
1740	1921	M–Sa
1811	1957	Su
1841	2021	M–Sa
1911	2057	Su
1941	2121	M–Sa
2011	2157	Su
2041	2221	M–Sa
2113	2257	Su

(1) Departs from or arrives at Cannon Street Station

house in town. If you have time, head out on Rock-A-Nore Road to Hastings Sea Life Centre and take an incredible 3-D voyage from outer space to the depths of the earth's seas.

Don't miss the 243-foot embroidery in Sussex Hall, White Rock Theatre. It depicts eighty-one of the greatest events of British history since 1066, including the Battle of Hastings, the Boston Tea Party, and the first television broadcast.

The city of Hastings celebrates the famous 1066 battle every year by staging a program of events and attractions over a full week, encompassing the fourteenth day of October.

Day Excursion to

Ipswich

CHARTERED IN A.D. 1200

Depart from Liverpool Street Station

Distance by train: 69 miles (111 km)
Average train time: 1 hour, 10 minutes
Train information and InterCity services: (034) 548–4950
Ipswich Tourist Information Centre: St. Stephen's Church, St. Stephen's Lane IP1 1DP; (0147) 325–8070; Fax: (0147) 325–8072
Internet: http://www.ipswich.gov.uk
Hours: Office hours are 0900–1700 Monday through Saturday, closed Sunday.

The tourist information center is easy to reach. Departing the rail station, proceed straight ahead down Princes Street to Friars Street and turn right. Friars Street curves and turns into Falcon Street. St. Stephen's Church will be on your left. If the weather is inclement, catch the "City Centre" bus or hail a taxi immediately in front of the station.

The architecture of Ipswich reflects its history. Bypassed by the Romans, this town does not display the former grandeur of Rome. A seafaring community long before King John granted the town's first charter in 1200, Ipswich has always been engaged in commerce and has risen or declined along with the fortunes of its citizens' enterprises. The lack of Georgian buildings in Ipswich is evidence of the town's decline during that period, caused by the loss of its famous Suffolk cloth trade. A revitalization of its harbor by the mid-nineteenth century brought new prosperity to Ipswich and accounts for the number of splendid public buildings erected then, as well as the Victorian architecture of its homes.

Ipswich has withstood the onslaughts of the Vikings and other seaborne raiders down through the ages. Starting with World War I, the town's docks became the targets of a new type of raider coming from the sky rather than from the sea. From 1915 to the end of the conflict, there were a number of zeppelin attacks, but damage was light. During the years 1943–45, Ipswich was rimmed by no fewer than sixty-five air bases of the U.S. Eighth Air Force, from which were launched a staggering 3,000-plus bomber assaults against the Third Reich.

Today, with a population of 120,000, Ipswich has a developing port and is an important industrial and commercial center with fine shopping, sports, and entertainment facilities. Ipswich considers its Tudor Christchurch Mansion, set on sixty-five acres of parkland only a five-minute walk from the center of town, to be its finest attraction. The information office will gladly point out the way to you. Obtain a map there before going off to explore the endless streets and enticing alleyways leading off Ipswich's Cornhill.

The town's Leisure Services Department has devised an excellent series of brochures (*Ipswich Historic Churches Trail, Wet Dock Maritime Trail*, and *Ipswich Street Map*) available for a nominal charge. The trails are signposted by black-and-white signs that are numbered to correspond with the descriptions in the brochure. No doubt the trail was laid out for British walkers, for it is much too ambitious a course for the average Yank to complete within the prescribed period of one hour—at least it was for us! The route is circular, so you can join (or leave) at any point.

Places along the trails that may be of interest to you include the junction of Butter Market, St. Stephens Lane, and Dial Lane. As you can probably guess, the Butter Market was once a marketplace for many products, one of which was butter. The Ancient House in the Butter Market will remind you of the Market's age (more than 500 years old), for its windows represent the known world during its time—and Australia is missing because it had not yet been discovered. A seventeenth-century merchant, Robert Sparrow, added the exquisite, ornate plasterwork to the exterior.

Dial Lane is a traffic-free pedestrian area that gets its name from a clock that was once on the St. Lawrence Church. Although most of the church dates back to the fifteenth and early sixteenth centuries, its tower was rebuilt in 1882 to reflect its original design.

London–Ipswich

DEPART LIVERPOOL STREET STATION	ARRIVE IPSWICH STATION	NOTES
0730	0836	M–Sa
0800	0859 (0907 Sa, 0925 Su)	Daily
0820	0938	Su
0830	0933	M–Sa
0855	1004	M–F
0900	1007	M–Sa
0920	1034	Su
0930	1033	M–Sa
0950	1102	M–F
1020	1134	Su

M–Sa service continues after 0950 at half-hour intervals until mid-afternoon. There are two series of Su service after 1020; one continues hourly from 1020 to 1820, the other is every two hours from 1030 to 1830.

DEPART IPSWICH STATION	ARRIVE LIVERPOOL STREET STATION	NOTES
1430	1540 (1548 Su)	Daily
1445	1552 (1601 Su)	Daily
1513	1625	M–F
1530	1648 (1640 Sa)	Daily
1545	1652 (1656 Su)	Daily
1613	1730 (M–F)	M–Sa

and continuing frequent service daily until 2145 and a final train at 2245 daily.

By passing the church and turning left into St. Lawrence Street and then right into Tavern Street, you'll come upon the Great White Horse Hotel. It is the only surviving inn that can be traced in the city records before 1571. Its Georgian brick facade, completed in 1818, covers a basically timber-frame structure from the sixteenth century. A young London news reporter, sent to Ipswich to cover an election, stayed in the Great White Horse and later wrote his recollections in a comic novel that changed the course of his life. The reporter was Charles Dickens; the novel, *The Pickwick Papers*.

Near the end of your walking tour, take time to pause at the junction of Tavern Street and Dial Lane. The view down Dial Lane to the Ancient

House is one of the most photographed areas in Ipswich. The Tudor-style buildings reflect the detail and attention of the city's craftsmen. From this point, a left turn will take you to the Cornhill, the end of your Tourist Town Trail walk.

As you stand at Cornhill, it may be sobering to consider that only 400 years ago, nine people were burned at the stake on this hill for heresy. Before becoming too sober, however, we suggest you visit one of the bars in the Great White Horse Hotel. Distinguished visitors of the past, besides Charles Dickens, included such notables as King George II, Louis XVIII, and Lord Nelson, who quaffed many a draft there. A toast to these gentlemen would seem only proper. So have a go at it, mate, if you can get there before they call "time!"

Day Excursion to

Isle of Wight THE HOLIDAY ISLAND

Depart from Waterloo Station

Distance by train: 88 miles (142 km)
Average train time: 2 hours, 40 minutes
Train information and InterCity services: (034) 548–4950
Shanklin Tourist Information Centre: 67 High Street, Shanklin, Isle of Wight P037 6JJ; *Tel:* (0198) 386–2942; *Fax:* (0198) 386–3047
   Hours: Daily 0900–1800 Easter–October; 0900–1700 November–March.
     To reach the center, as you leave the station, walk straight to Regent Street, then turn right onto the High Street. The center is on the right just up the hill and next to the theater. It's about a ten-minute walk from the Shanklin Station. Taxi service is also available.

"Britain's Miniature" is a term often employed to describe the Isle of Wight. Shaped like a diamond, the island is a veritable jewel, with every feature of the mainland condensed into a mere 147 square miles. It is dotted with historic spots, sandy beaches, thatched villages, rolling countryside—and discotheques, if that's your pleasure. There is fun for everyone on the Isle of Wight, and getting there can be fun.

The majority of trains departing Waterloo Station in London for Portsmouth Harbour are InterCity trains. As they glide through the scenery of southern England bound for the coast, you'll be treated to a delightful kaleidoscope of England's landscape from the wide-vision train windows. Stay aboard when the train halts briefly in the Portsmouth and Southsea Station. Your destination is the Portsmouth Harbour Station, five minutes farther on.

Board the Portsmouth-Ryde catamaran at the end of the harbor station. Your BritRail Pass does not cover the passage. The fare is about £5.40 one way. The crossing takes only about fifteen minutes.

Docking at the Ryde pier head, you have three options of sightseeing on the island by train. The trains, by the way, run right onto the pier and look every bit like those of the Bakerloo Underground Line in London. All the coaches are one class, but try to select one with ventilators at the top of the windows. It can get a bit stuffy aboard the train in summer. The three options? They are Ryde, Sandown, or Shanklin. All three lie along the 9 miles of track extending from the Ryde pier head to the terminal in Shanklin.

Ryde is the Isle of Wight's gateway. Set picturesquely on a hillside, it becomes a wonderful grandstand from which to watch the great ships of the world sailing by. The pier at Ryde is more than 2,300 feet long, so board the train after disembarking from the passenger ferry and ride the train to its first stop, Ryde Esplanade, where you will find the Tourist Information Centre ready to assist you during summer season (*Tel:* 0198–356–2905; accommodations 0198–386–7979). The pier has a pedestrian walk, if you elect to make your way to the shore in a more leisurely manner. Ryde has 6 miles of sandy beach backed by pleasant, wooded gardens. The town is also noted for its Regency and Victorian buildings and for its Royal Victoria Arcade shopping center.

Sandown is the next railway stop after passing the Brading Station. It has all the facilities for a summer holiday, including a new pier complex that offers a modern theater, licensed bars, cafes, and a restaurant. The theater offers a musical revue, which opens in May and runs through the beginning of October. The sheltered Sandown Bay has more than 5 miles of attractive sandy beaches, where you may find such diversions as miniature golf and a canoe lake. Motor-launch trips are popular. Check at the pier or the tourist information center on High Street for details.

Sandown and Shanklin are considered the twin resorts on the Isle of Wight. Because the distance between the two rail stations is exactly 2 miles, you should select one or the other for your day excursion. There is much to see and do in either resort.

London–Isle of Wight

All service to Isle of Wight is by train to Portsmouth Harbour Station, fast ferry to Ryde Head Pier on the Isle of Wight, and train from Ryde Head Pier to Shanklin; the return route is the reverse.

Schedules shown here are for direct trains that depart from London Waterloo Station and travel via Woking, Guildford, and Portsmouth and Southsea Stations; other services are possible from London Victoria Station via Gatwick Airport Station and/or Brighton; these may also require a change of trains at Portsmouth and Southsea Station to reach Portsmouth Harbour Station.

DEPART KING'S CROSS STATION	ARRIVE KING'S LYNN STATION	NOTES
0722 (0720 Sa)	1005	M–Sa
0840 (0815 Su, 0820 Sa)	1105	Daily
0900	1146	M–Sa
0940 (0915 Su)	1205	Daily
1000	1246	M–Sa
1040 (1015 Su)	1305	Daily

and later services at 20, 40, or 60 minute intervals

DEPART KING'S LYNN STATION	ARRIVE KING'S CROSS STATION	NOTES
1413	1654	Su
1415 (1413 Sa)	1649	M–Sa
1513	1754	Su
1515 (1513 Sa)	1745	M–Sa
1535	1827	M–F
1613	1854	Su
1615 (1613 Sa)	1845	M–Sa
1635	1926	M–F

M–F service continues after 1635 at 15 and 35 minutes after the hour until 1935; Sa service continues after 1513 at hourly intervals until 2113; Su service continues after 1613 at hourly intervals until 2013.

Shanklin frequently holds the British annual sunshine record. It is built on a cliff with a sheltered mile-long beach lying below. It is the end of the line for rail travel. It is easy, however, to transfer to the buses operated by the island's bus company, Southern Vectis, for farther points such as Ventnor, Newport, and Cowes. Check with the Southern Vectis Travel Office on Regent Street, two blocks from Shanklin's train station.

Our personal selection of the Isle's options would be Shanklin. It is certainly one of the prettiest towns in Britain. Shanklin's Old Village on Ventnor Road is world-famous for its quiet beauty. From there, you may descend to Shanklin's beach esplanade via a walk through Shanklin's Chine, a cleft in the town's cliff with overhanging trees, plants, ferns, and a cascading stream. Passage through the Chine costs £1.80 for adults; for children, 50 pence. Check first with the town's information center at 67 High Street for all details *Tel:* (0198) 386–2942.

One of the most gifted and appealing of England's nineteenth-century poets, John Keats, found Shanklin's climate congenial to his health and the town's scenic beauty so inspiring that he resided there for a long period of time. Keats Green, a spacious promenade on the cliff top of Shanklin, commemorates his loving association with the town.

Queen Victoria spent her holidays on the Isle of Wight and died there in Osborne House in 1901. This house, built by order of the queen in 1845, is maintained in good order with the queen's furniture still in place. In a shed on the Osborne House property, you can see the gardening tools of the royal children from more than a century ago. Each tool and wheelbarrow is marked with the small owners' initials. The Queen and Prince Albert used Osborne as a country residence, and it is said that the prince had a considerable influence on the design of the residence. The main rooms and many of the private apartments are open to the public between Easter Monday and the end of October. Situated at East Cowes, which is the northern one of the island's twin peaks, you can reach the Osborne House by bus from Ryde Esplanade Station.

Day Excursion to

King's Lynn
RICH IN ARCHITECTURE

Depart from King's Cross Station

Distance by train: 97 miles (156 km)
Average train time: 2 hours, 5 minutes
Train information and InterCity services: (034) 548–4950
King's Lynn Tourist Information Centre: The Old Jail House, Saturday Market Place,
   Norfolk PE30 5DQJ; (0155) 376–3044; *Fax:* (0155) 377–7281
   Hours: 0195–1700 Monday–Saturday; 1000–1700 Sunday.
   To reach the Tourist Information Centre, walk directly away from the front of
the train station (which faces the west) down Waterloo Street. The street undergoes
a name change at every intersection—Market, Paradise, New Conduit, Purfleet—
but if you continue walking toward the west, you will come to King Street. The
Tourist Information Centre is straight ahead in the Custom House.

King's Lynn, once "Bishop's Lynn" and renamed when Henry VIII took
over the bishop's manor, is one of the most historic towns in England. The
old section of town still seems medieval, complete with narrow streets,
guildhalls, and riverside quays, where the gulls reel and scream overhead.
The town's former prosperity has left it with a rich heritage of architecture. Set along the east bank of the wide and muddy Ouse River, King's
Lynn is the northern terminal of the London-Cambridge-Ely rail line.
   King's Lynn came into being during the eleventh century and is situated on the middle of three islands, where four streams ran into the Ouse
River. Water highways became vital to the commerce of the town. With
these waterway connections to the English Midlands, the town of Lynn
became an important trading port, bustling with the romance of foreign
cargoes, sailing ships, and foreign accents. By the thirteenth century, the
town found prosperity in the wool trade between England and the
Continent. This aura of a wealthy medieval town still prevails. Today, the
town is a thriving, modern port, an essential link between Britain and the
rest of the Common Market.
   Streets and alleyways in King's Lynn twist and wind about on a grand
scale, so a town map will be an invaluable aid. Immediately make your way
from the train station to the Tourist Information Centre, about a ten-
minute walk. Nearby, the town boasts England's oldest surviving Hanseatic
Warehouse.

London–King's Lynn

DEPART KING'S CROSS STATION	ARRIVE KING'S LYNN STATION	NOTES
0745	0928 (0919 Sa)	M–Sa
0751	0941	Su
0845	1019	M–Sa
0945	1119	M–Sa
0951	1141	Su
1045	1219	M–Sa
1145	1319	M–Sa
1151	1341	Su

and continuing with the same pattern until mid-afternoon M–Sa and until late p.m. on Su.

DEPART KING'S LYNN STATION	ARRIVE KING'S CROSS STATION	NOTES
1358	1537	M–Sa
1440	1626	Su
1458	1640 (1637 Sa)	M–Sa
1558	1739 (1737 Sa)	M–Sa
1640	1829	Su
1658	1840 (1837 Sa)	M–Sa
1736 (1740 Su)	1929	M–F, Su
1758	1936	Sa
1836 (1840 Su)	2028 (2029 Su)	Daily
1940 (1936 Sa)	2128 (2129 Su)	Daily
2040 (2036 Sa)	2231 (2228 Sa, 2229 Su)	Daily
2140 (2136 Sa)	2330	Daily
2230	0036	M–F

You will be tempted to wander about in Queen Street with its lovely merchants' houses, each with a character all its own. At the information center equip yourself with a copy of the *King's Lynn Town Walk* booklet (20 pence). With it, you'll know where you are. The booklet is a masterpiece of simplicity. It is packed with facts about the town and its buildings. The trail follows a circular route, so you may start and finish wherever it is most convenient for you. We suggest starting at the town hall. Rebuilt in 1421 after a fire, it houses the "Tales of the Old Gaol House" exhibition, as well as King Lynn's regalia, including the magnificent King John Cup and the Red Register, purported to be one of the oldest books in the world.

A focal point in King's Lynn is the Tuesday Market Place, into which King Street leads. True to tradition, a country market is conducted there every Tuesday in the shadow of the Duke's Head Hotel, a most impressive seventeenth-century structure. The market is everything that one would expect it to be—stalls packed with the agricultural and manufacturing products of the area, augmented by absolutely free entertainment as the hucksters bid for attention.

If you miss the Tuesday market, there's another one on Saturday at a location appropriately named the Saturday Market Place. It is just opposite the town hall. A newer shopping center has been established in the center of town, on the site of the old cattle market, which was moved to one of the industrial estates outside of the town.

Visit St. George's Guild Hall at 27 King Street. It's the largest surviving medieval guildhall. When not in use as a theater, it is open Monday through Friday, 1000–1700, and 1000–1230 on Saturday. Built about 1410, it has been used as a theater, a courthouse, and an armory, and it is now a cultural center housing a theater and an art gallery.

King John, who ruled England between 1199 and 1216, granted the town its charter in 1204. The king came to Lynn in October 1215 in pursuit of rebellious barons. One story relates that after he was wined and dined by the burghers of Lynn, the king and his entourage set off in hot pursuit of the baronial rebels. Heading west out of King's Lynn towards Newark, the king and his entourage crossed the Norfolk tidal flats, where the River Ouse empties into The Wash, a shallow bay known for the treachery of its tides.

During the crossing, a high tide from The Wash wiped out the king's baggage train. King John reached the safety of higher shores, but he lost the crown jewels and everything else that went with such a collection in those days. King John was so distraught that he contracted dysentery (a bad "burger," perhaps?) and died a few days later. No one questioned the burghers as to exactly what they fed the king before he left Lynn. We have our suspicions, however, because reportedly all of the burghers felt fine the following morning.

Somewhere near King's Lynn, buried under centuries of silt, lies King John's lost treasure. None of it has been recovered, and no one knows where to look for it. If you have any ideas, perhaps Robert Stack from television's *Unsolved Mysteries* would be interested.

Day Excursion to

Lincoln

HILLTOP CATHEDRAL

Depart from King's Cross Station

Distance by train: 135 miles (217 km)

Average train time: *2 hours, 10 minutes*

Train information and InterCity services: (034) 548–4950

Lincoln Tourist Information Centre: 9 Castle Hill LN1 3AA; *Tel:* (0152) 252–9828; *Fax:* (0152) 256–4506

> *Hours:* Open 0900–1730, except Friday, when it closes a half hour earlier. On Saturday and Sunday, it is open 1000–1700 in the summer and winter.
>
> On arrival in Lincoln's Central Station, go to the city bus station, which is in front and to the right of the main station entrance (use the designated pedestrian walkways, because the vehicular traffic can be heavy at times). From the bus station, take city bus 1, 7, or 8 up the hill to the Cathedral and ask the driver to let you off at the corner of Eastgate and Nettleham Road (next to Forte Posthouse Hotel). Walk along Eastgate until reaching the White Hart Hotel; turn left and the center is at the top of the hill at No. 9 Castle Hill.

Lincoln Cornhill Information Centre: 21 The Cornhill, LN1 3AA; *Tel:* (0152) 2579056

> *Hours:* Open Monday through Saturday from 1000–1600.
>
> Turn left from the rail station and cross over at St. Mary La Wigford Church on High St. The center is in The Cornhill opposite the British Homes store.

Lincoln's greatest landmark is its cathedral. It stands on a ridge, dominating the skyline. The cathedral appears to be half church, half stronghold. Actually, there are two Lincolns—one, the cathedral and castle standing politely on the hilltop; the other, the city below girding the River Witham and buzzing with commerce. We suggest you scale the heights first and later return to the lower level by a dizzy descent down Steep Hill.

On the other hand, if you bound with energy, bear to the left when leaving the station and walk a short distance on St. Mary Street to where it intersects with High Street. Turn right at this point and, keeping the cathedral in sight, start walking in its direction up High Street. Disregard the fact that the street changes names several times. When you reach an area where a ski lift or a cable car would be most welcome, you'll be on Steep Hill—and it's appropriately named. Now gain the high ground (and your breath), and you will find yourself in Castle Square. With a right turn at the Exchequer Gate, you may enter the cathedral grounds.

Walking up the Lincoln hill from the railway station to the cathedral can give you a sense of accomplishment. It can also be hazardous to your health. Use discretion—take the bus or a taxi if there's any doubt in your mind about the climb.

Walking up Steep Hill, you will pass the Norman House, said to be the home of "Aaron the Jew," a moneylender from the twelfth century who reportedly became the richest man in England at that time. Halfway up Steep Hill, and turning off at Danesgate, your visit will be well rewarded by an inspection of the Usher Gallery. You can view an assortment of personal property belonging to England's poet laureate, Lord Alfred Tennyson, born in Somersby, a Lincolnshire village, in 1809. The gallery also houses an extensive collection of paintings by Peter de Wint (1784–1849). Should you arrive at Castle Square in need of lunch or a libation, seek out the Wig & Mitre, a licensed restaurant with a Dickensian atmosphere.

The cathedral is the main point of interest in Lincoln. When you view its exterior and examine the spacious areas under its roof, it becomes rather difficult to comprehend that it was built by medieval craftsmen in only twenty years. The Normans began construction of the cathedral in 1072. In 1141 the roof was destroyed by a fire, and in 1185 the main structure crumbled into ruins as a result of an earthquake. But it survived.

Reconstruction, which began in 1186, returned the cathedral to its original conforms, and, through the ensuing centuries, it was altered frequently. The central tower was completed around 1311. In more modern times, Lincoln's greatest attraction has withstood Cromwell's artillery and Hitler's bombs. If you have but a short period of time to visit in Lincoln, the cathedral must take priority over all else. In the summer, the cathedral is open 0715–2000 weekdays and 0715–1800 Sunday. In the winter, it closes at 1800 weekdays and at 1700 on Sunday. A contribution of £2.50 for adults and £1.00 for children is appreciated.

Lincoln Castle was built by William the Conqueror in 1068. It became the Normans' military stronghold in the area. Its construction is unusual in that it has two mounds: one crowned by the twelfth century Tower of Lucy, the other with Norman structures on which in the nineteenth cen-

London–Lincoln

DEPART KING'S CROSS STATION	ARRIVE LINCOLN CENTRAL STATION	NOTES
0705	0909	M–F (1)
0830	1034 (1103 Sa)	M–Sa (2)
0910	1032	M–F (1)
0930	1202	M–F (3)
1010	1225	Su (2)
1100	1316 (1314 Sa)	M–Sa (3)
1130	1402 (1403 Sa)	M–Sa (3)
1210	1430	Su (2)

DEPART LINCOLN CENTRAL STATION	ARRIVE KING'S CROSS STATION	NOTES
1437	1633	M–F (2)
1453	1729	M–F (3)
1457	1703	Su (2)
1512	1729	M–F (4)
1546	1800	Su (2)
1603 (1604 Sa)	1836 (1829 Sa)	M–Sa (3)
1635	1931	Su (5)
1705	1908	M–F (2)
1715	2010	Sa (5)
1745	2001	M–F (4)
1816 (1815 Sa)	2134 (2109 Sa)	M–Sa (5)
1919	2130	Su (2)
2033 (2030 Sa)	2242 (2237 Sa)	M–Sa (2)
2104	2308	Su (2)

(1) change from train to bus at Newark North Gate
(2) change trains at Newark North Gate
(3) change trains at Peterborough
(4) change from bus to train at Newark North Gate
(5) change trains at Retford

tury an observatory tower was constructed. From either of these vantage points, there are beautiful views of the cathedral and the surrounding countryside.

Today the Lincoln Castle is a huge, walled enclosure of lawns and trees. The crown courts and the old county jail are located in the castle yard. On permanent exhibition is one of only four surviving originals of King John's *Magna Carta*. The castle is open Monday–Saturday 0930–1730, Sunday 1100–1730; winter closing time is 1600. Admission is £2.00 for adults, £1.20 for seniors, students, and children.

If you wish to visit the "other Lincoln," start by descending (or plunging down) Steep Hill with its bow-fronted shops until you again reach High Street. You will find interest in the twelfth-century High Bridge, which crosses the River Witham. It is the oldest one in Britain to still carry a building on its structure, in this case, a sixteenth-century timber-framed house. The route leading from the cathedral down Steep Hill is studded with other interesting structures such as numerous public houses and restaurants. Modern Lincoln blends easily with its historical counterparts.

Day Excursion to

Nottingham TALES OF ROBIN HOOD

Depart from St. Pancras Station

Distance by train: 127 miles (204 km)

Average train time: 2 hours

Train information and InterCity services: (034) 548–4950

Nottingham Tourist Information Centre: 1-4 Smithy Row NG1 2BY; *Tel:* (0115) 915–5330; *Fax:* (0115) 935–5328

> *Hours:* Open Monday through Friday, 0830–1700; Saturday, 0900–1700; and Sunday, 1000–1600 during the summer (April 1 through the first Sunday of October).
>
> The main tourist information office is within walking distance of the train station (there also is an office in the station). But if your time is limited, hail a cab at the station and save some time as well as your shoe leather. Otherwise, take Carrington Street on your right, leaving the station to where it intersects Canal Street. A left turn at this point, followed by a right turn onto Maid Marian Way, will have you pointed in the right direction. When you reach Friar Lane, turn right again and walk to where Friar Lane meets Wheeler Gate and South Parade. The Old Market Square will be on your left. You can't miss it—but if you do, just inquire at one of the taxi queues in that area. Stop by and see the complimentary film *The Nottingham Story* for a brief overview of the city before venturing about.

Nottingham is famous for many things, among them the legend of Robin Hood. Many tales of Robin and his band of merry men have been passed down through the ages by ballad and legend, though only scattered fragments remain of his origin. It appears that one Robert Fitzooth, reputed to be the Earl of Huntingdon, was born in 1160 during the reign of Henry II. Of noble birth, he squandered his inheritance at an early age; so either by necessity or by choice, he sought refuge in the forest. Here he was joined by men in similar circumstances, such as Little John, Will Scarlet, Friar Tuck, and—to add the love-interest angle to the legend— Maid Marian.

Robin Hood reigned in the forest, defying the powers of government, protecting the poor, and giving to the needy. The king's deer provided food and the king's forest provided fuel. Other necessities were obtained through barter. Taking the king's property was, of course, illegal and it drove the Sheriff of Nottingham "bananas," to the point where he offered a substantial reward for Robin's capture—dead or alive. Robin Hood eluded capture and supposedly lived to be eighty-seven years old. Records show his death occurred on November 18, 1247. This man, who lived in an age of feudal tyranny, endeared himself to countless generations and became the legendary hero of Nottingham. A fine statue to his memory stands in the courtyard of Nottingham Castle. Perhaps in the future there will be one of Kevin Costner, too.

The castle was built as a fortress in 1068 by William the Conqueror. It was destroyed during the English civil war, rebuilt, and again destroyed by an angry mob in 1831. Following its second restoration, the castle was transformed into a museum and art gallery late in the nineteenth century. There is a series of underground passages beneath the castle. Naturally, there are many tales of intrigue relating to their purpose. The castle is open to the public daily; the underground passages can be seen only on conducted tours. Don't miss the *Story of Nottingham* at the Castle Museum and Art Gallery.

For centuries, Nottingham has been famous for its lace. Visit the Lace Centre on Castle Road for demonstrations and the history of lace making. The center also has a lace shop.

If your time in Nottingham is limited, no doubt you should first see the historic castle area and return another day to see modern downtown Nottingham. To visit the castle, turn right as you exit the rail station onto Carrington Street. Turn left onto Canal Street, and three blocks farther along in the same direction, you will come to Castle Road running up the hill to your right. Following it a short distance brings you to England's

London–Nottingham

DEPART ST. PANCRAS STATION	ARRIVE NOTTINGHAM STATION	NOTES
0700	0851	M–F
0730	0926	Sa
0800	0951	M–F
0900	1049	M–F
0915	1102	Sa
1000	1147	M–F
1030	1241	Su
1045	1232	Sa
1100	1255	M–F
1130	1331	Su
1200	1346	M–F
1215	1400	Sa

DEPART NOTTINGHAM STATION	ARRIVE ST. PANCRAS STATION	NOTES
1424	1612	Sa
1433	1624	M–F
1504	1703	Su
1533	1723	M–F
1554	1741	Sa
1633	1821	M–F
1638	1826	Su
1724	1913	Sa
1733	1926	M–F
1800	1958	Su
1903	2100 (2101 Sa)	M–Sa
1932	2131	Su
2133	2329	M–F

oldest inn, Ye Olde Trip to Jerusalem, where we suggest you rest before continuing up Castle Road to the Nottingham Castle entrance, just off Castle Place. Built in 1189, a portion of the inn was dug into the almost vertical rock formation supporting Nottingham Castle above. Legend has it that Robin Hood scaled this rock in his invasions of Nottingham

Castle. The pub's "grub" isn't bad—in fact, it's downright good—so you might want to arrive there about lunchtime. Books about Nottingham and the lore of Robin Hood are on sale in the Ye Olde Trip to Jerusalem pub and in Nottingham Castle.

The train trip from London's St. Pancras Station passes through England's Midlands en route to Nottingham, passing St. Albans, where Britain's first Christian martyr was executed, and Bedford, where John Bunyan wrote *Pilgrim's Progress*. For variety, you might want to return to London via Peterborough, transferring there to a train for King's Cross Station. Consult the train information office in Nottingham's station. It is open Monday through Saturday 0800–1830, and Sunday 1000–1900.

Nottingham's main tourist information center lies astride the city's two huge shopping centers—the Victoria and the Broad Marsh. Both are somewhat mind-boggling in size, and they are linked together by wide pedestrian avenues as well as a bus service (nos. 71 and 91) running between the two establishments every eight minutes throughout the day, Monday through Saturday (price: 35p). The young modern shopper must not miss the Hockley area of shops to catch up on the latest craze. And we would not forget that antique aficionados would enjoy the abundance of shops along Derby Road.

A new site for crime and punishment fans is *"Condemned!"* at the Galleries of Justice. Be prepared as you visit the nineteenth century Shire Hall to assume the identity of a criminal, experience a public trial, and be taken off to the hangman's gallows.

If your trip permits being in Nottingham on a Friday or Saturday evening, we suggest you "eat, drink, and be merry" by enjoying the five-course medieval meal at the Sherriff's Lodge Medieval Banqueting Hall. Ale, of course, and entertainment are included. Book in advance by calling (0115) 924–0088.

Meanwhile, back at the Old Market Square, the tourist information center has a wide selection of literature, souvenirs, and details of walking tours of Nottingham that take you, among other places, along one of the city's main thoroughfares, Maid Marian Way. You may also wish to inquire about the new Explorer Pass that gives the Nottingham visitor access to five of the top attractions of the city at a great price.

Day Excursion to

Oxford

Depart from Paddington Station

Distance by train: 63 miles (102 km)

Average train time: 1 hour

Train information and InterCity services: (034) 548–4950

Oxford Tourist Information Centre: Gloucester Green; *Tel:* (0186) 572–6871; *Fax:* (0186) 524–0045

> *Hours:* Open during the summer months, Monday through Saturday, 0930–1700; Sunday and summer Bank Holidays, 1000–1300 and 1330–1530.
>
> The Oxford Tourist Information Centre is located behind the bus bars on Gloucester Green, a short walk from the rail station. Just follow the black-and gold-pedestrian signs via either Hythe Bridge Street or Park End Street.

The first glimpse of Oxford as you approach it by train from London confirms its title, "the city of dreaming spires." Towers, domes, and pinnacles soar on its skyline as an impressive preview of one of the great architectural centers of the world. For here in this small and compact city center are some 900 "listed" buildings, illustrating practically every style of architecture from the eleventh century to the present day.

Oxford has the oldest university in Great Britain. It had its beginnings in the twelfth century. Between the thirteenth and fifteenth centuries, it became an established national institution and now has a history of 800 years of continuous existence. Oxford's student body has doubled in the past thirty years to about 16,000 students, of which the majority are undergraduates. There is not a separate campus; most of its buildings lie within the center of the city. The university is a federation of independent colleges. Visitors coming to Oxford during the summer may miss the normal sight of students passing between classes and the student sporting activities, but the buildings alone are worth the trip.

Apparently, there is no single explanation as to exactly how and when the university actually began. One theory claims that it was founded by English students who were expelled from the University of Paris in 1167. Others claim it came about from a gathering of various groups of students from monastic institutions in and around the growing city. From whatever origins, by the end of the twelfth century, Oxford was the established home of the first center of learning in England.

London–Oxford

Very frequent service is available from London Paddington Station to Oxford, with journeys taking from 44 to 90 min. Departure times given here are for trips taking 70 min or less. London departures and arrivals are from and at Paddington Station.

LONDON PADDINGTON TO OXFORD.

M–F: Depart Paddington Station at 0748, 0818, 0848, 0906, 0918, 0948, and every 30 min until 1648.

Sa: Depart Paddington Station at 0748, 0818, and every 30 min until 1748.

Su: Depart Paddington Station at 0845, 0851, 0945, 1045, 1145, 1206, 1245, and then hourly until 2145.

OXFORD TO LONDON PADDINGTON.

M–F: Depart Oxford Station at 1345, 1415, and every 30 min until 1615; then at 1635, 1655, 1715, 1745, 1815, 1845, 1915, 2015, 2025, 2115, 2125, 2215, 2224, and 2315.

Sa: Depart Oxford Station at 1345, 1415, and every 30 min until 1915, then 2015, 2025, 2102, 2115, 2215, and 2315.

Su: Depart from Oxford Station at 1345, 1445, and hourly until 1745, then 1831, 1905, 1933, 2020, 2115, 2204, and 2359.

Fewer than half the students come to Oxford University from such exclusive schools as Eton, which was founded by Henry VI in 1440. Students are only required to meet their tutor once or twice a week, either individually or with one other student. This seemingly free and easy system, which builds on individuality and confidence, is the hallmark of an Oxford education. All students live in the college for their first year and one other year prior to graduation. Students are usually housed in single rooms; the restrictions on coming and going or on having guests are few.

A renaissance of reconstruction and rebuilding in Oxford during the eighteenth century destroyed much of the old street system and the houses inhabited by many religious groups. From this, the city that emerged was more spacious than before. Notwithstanding this urban renewal program, Oxford still has a certain organized clutter about it that becomes readily discernible as you move from the rail station to the city center.

In addition to being a seat of learning, Oxford—unlike Cambridge—has a strong industrial background. It was here that William Morris founded his automobile empire, now Rover Group. The commercial and academic worlds have combined to create other flourishing industries such as publishing, research and development, and tourism. Oxford is also famous as the home of several distinguished hospitals.

Today the use of cars is discouraged in the city center, with visitors making the most instead of Oxford's excellent train services, supplemented by an extremely efficient Park-and-Ride System for motorists. The city fathers also urge everyone to return to the traditional Oxford method of propulsion, the bicycle. By the way, be on the lookout for bicycles propelled by students pedaling themselves to lectures or laboratories.

You can also buy your ticket here for the Official Walking Tours, which leave the information center daily throughout the year at 1100 and 1400. The tours, which last two hours, will take you around the most interesting parts of the city and into those colleges open to the guides on that day.

From this beginning, build your own plan of activities, perhaps to include the Oxford Story Exhibition, punting and cruising on the Thames or Cherwell, an open bus tour, or a visit to the ancient Bodleian Library or one of the university's five excellent museums, all of which are free.

Day Excursion to

Portsmouth BRITAIN'S NAVAL PORT

From London: Depart from Waterloo Station

Distance by train: 74 miles (119 km)
Average train time: 1 hour, 30 minutes
Train information and InterCity services: (034) 548–4950
Portsmouth Tourist Information Centre: The Hard; *Tel:* (0170) 582–6722; *Fax:* (0170) 582–2693
  Hours: Open daily (except December 25 and 26) from 0930 to 1745 during the summer and 0930 to 1715 during winter.
  Trains call first at the Portsmouth and Southsea Station, so stay aboard to the end of the line. Then, instead of moving straight ahead to the ferry dock, exit the station on the right-hand side of the platform to the main street, The Hard, right next to the Portsmouth Naval Base and the Harbor Rail Station. The Hard Information Centre, from where you will be able to see the gate of the naval base, is to your left.

Other centers are located outside the Sea Life Centre, the Civic Offices, and Commercial Road. The Hard Centre can direct you should you need their services.

A visit to Portsmouth requires prioritizing what to see there. The city abounds in vast quantities of history, architecture, amusements, and literature. Portsmouth has variety, contrasts, and veneration. Here are a few choices:

Old Portsmouth is for those who relish fine buildings. Lombard Street is flanked by natural harbors, east and west, and is the home of one of the world's greatest naval bases, Portsmouth Naval Base. The resort area, Southsea, offers the largest amusement complex on England's south coast plus 4 miles of beaches, promenades, and gardens that boast splendid seventeenth- and eighteenth-century houses, many with distinctive Dutch gables. On adjoining High Street, the primarily eighteenth-century motif gives way the ultramodern "new" Portsmouth, with its traffic-free shopping precinct, "Cascades," on Commercial Road.

The literary greats of Portsmouth—Charles Dickens, H. G. Wells, Conan Doyle, Rudyard Kipling, and Neville Shute, to name a few—have left their mark on the city in birthplaces, residences, and museums. Resting in the world's oldest dry dock in Portsmouth Dockyard is Lord Horatio Nelson's flagship, *H.M.S. Victory.* Alongside the ship stands the Royal Naval Museum with relics of England's naval hero, ship models, and an outstanding collection of marine paintings. For priority, our first selection is *H.M.S Victory.* It has been described as the proudest sight in Britain, and well it is! Meticulously preserved, it stirs the imagination as you relive the events of the Battle of Trafalgar that "made all England weep."

Some vital statistics in history regarding *H.M.S. Victory* may be beneficial while you are waiting to go aboard. The ship was launched on May 7, 1765. (Lord Nelson was a mere child of six on that date.) She is a vessel of 3,500 tons with an overall length of 226½ feet. All totaled, *Victory* carried 104 guns and a complement of 850 officers and men. In 1801, the ship was rebuilt extensively and given the appearance she has today. Recommissioned in April 1803, she became Nelson's flagship. On October 21, 1805, the English fleet under Nelson's command vanquished the combined fleets of France and Spain off Cape Trafalgar. Lord Nelson was killed aboard *Victory* in the final moments of what has been called the most decisive battle ever fought at sea.

Portsmouth also features the Victorian ironclad *H.M.S. Warrior 1860*. Launched in 1860, she was the largest, fastest, and best-armored warship of her time. She has been restored throughout to her appearance during her first commission of 1861–64; when you step aboard you can catch a unique glimpse of life as it was experienced on a nineteenth-century British warship.

The Royal Naval Museum supports these famous ships with displays that set them in their historic context and continues the story of the British Navy into the twentieth century, up to the Falklands Campaign of 1982.

You may also inspect the hull of Henry VIII's *Mary Rose,* which is undergoing restoration in a special dry-dock workshop. Launched in 1510, *Mary Rose* went down while sailing against a French invasion fleet in 1545; the remains were raised in 1982. The story of the Mary Rose—her loss and her dramatic recovery—is related in an audiovisual presentation, and the objects salvaged from the ship are on exhibit.

In the resort department, Portsmouth offers the Pyramids Centre, a giant leisure attraction built by the sea next to King Henry VIII's Southsea Castle. A true tropical paradise, where the temperature never drops below 84°F., the center features four areas of entertainment, ranging from swimming pools, top-name entertainment, and a patio bar to a supervised "Fun Factory" where Mom and Dad can park the kids. Another great place for the family is the Sealife Center, featuring marine life along the South Coast.

Close by the Southsea Castle and the Pyramids Centre, Portsmouth's D-Day Museum and Overlord Embroidery tells the story of that historic event through pictures, plans, and the re-creation of wartime scenes, along with exhibits of various weapons and vehicles. A special audiovisual presentation relates the events leading to the recapture of Normandy. More history unfolds in the castle, where an audiovisual show reconstructs scenes of "Life in the Castle."

Portsmouth bears the title, "The South's Historic Maritime Resort City." We are certain that you will agree with this.

Among other developments to watch out for is the Millenium Project, a large undertaking that will link Portsmouth Dockyard to Southsea via Old Portsmouth.

London–Portsmouth

Schedules shown are for direct trains that operate from and to London Waterloo Station. Other service is available from London Victoria Station via Gatwick Airport Station and/or Brighton; some schedules on these routes may require a change of trains. There are two stations in Portsmouth; the Portsmouth and Southsea Station near the center of the city, and the Portsmouth Harbour Station, which serves the Portsmouth Royal Navy base (*H.M.S Victory*, the *Mary Rose,* and other historic ships) and ferries to the Isle of Wight.

DEPART WATERLOO STATION	ARRIVE PORTSMOUTH HARBOR STATION	NOTES
0720	0907	Sa
0722	0848	M–F
0745	0941	Su
0800	0935 (0931 Sa)	M–Sa
0815	0953	Su
0840	1012	M–F
0845	1041	Su
0900	1029 (1031 Sa)	M–Sa
0915	1053	Su
0940	1106	M–Sa

M–Sa service continues after 0940 on the hour and at 40 minutes after the hour until mid- to late afternoon. Su service continues after 0915 every 30 minutes until midafternoon.

DEPART PORTSMOUTH HARBOR STATION	ARRIVE WATERLOO STATION	NOTES
1450	1623	M–Sa
1515	1645	M–Sa
1520	1654	Su
1531	1721	Su
1550	1723	M–Sa

M–Sa services continue after 1550 at 15 and 50 minutes after the hour until 1850, then at 1921, 1950, 2021, 2121, and 2221. Su service continues after 1531 at 20 and 31 minutes after the hour until 2131, then at 2237.

Day Excursion to

Ramsgate

SEASIDE RESORT

Depart from Victoria Station

Distance by train: 79 miles (127 km)
Average train time: 1 hour, 50 minutes
Train information and InterCity services: (034) 548–4950
Ramsgate Tourist Information Centre: 19–21 Harbour Street CT11 8HA; *Tel:* (0184) 358–3333; *Fax:* (0184) 359–1086
  Hours: All three centers operate on similar schedules: Monday through Thursday, 0900–1730; Friday, 0900–1700. During summer periods, they also are open on Saturday and Sunday, 1000–1600.

This day excursion to Ramsgate encompasses the northeast tip of England's Kent County, which is called Thanet. There are tourist information centers in all three Thanet towns touched by rail service—Margate, Broadstairs, and Ramsgate.

The *Margate Tourist Information Centre* is north-east of the railway station near the harbor at 22 High Street. The *Broadstairs Tourist Information Centre* is near the railway station at the foot of the hill at 6B High Street. *Tel:* (0184) 386–2242; *Internet:* http://www.broadstairs.gov.uk

Ramsgate Tourist Information Centre is some distance from the railway station in the town center on Harbour Street. Buses from the station will take you near there, or hail a taxi.

Although the sea inlets have almost been drained, Thanet still bears the semblance of an island with clusters of seaside towns—Margate, Broadstairs, and Ramsgate, each with its own character. Londoners were attracted to Thanet early in the nineteenth century, and it has been a thriving resort area ever since. The attraction of sandy beaches, safe bathing, and entertainment are the assets the area has to offer.

Ramsgate has been selected as the primary point for the day excursion, for it is the terminal stop for trains departing London's Victoria Station on the North Kent line. En route stops at other Thanet towns are made on this rail line at Margate and Broadstairs. It should be noted that it is possible to return to Victoria Station via another rail route from Ramsgate through Ashford, or yet another route calling at Dover and Folkestone. With so many possibilities, you should consult the timetables posted in all three of the Thanet towns for possible variations of your own itinerary. The

London–Ramsgate

Note: Some trains on this route split at Faversham, part of the train continuing to Ramsgate and other cars going to Dover. Passengers going to Ramsgate must ensure that they are in one of the proper coaches before the train reaches Faversham.

DEPART VICTORIA STATION	ARRIVE RAMSGATE STATION	NOTES
0735	0929	M–F
0805	0949 (0952 Su)	Daily
0835	1029	M–Sa (1)
0905	1048 (1052 Su)	Daily
0935	1129	M–Sa (1)

M–Sa service continues after 0935 at 5 and 35 minutes after the hour until midafternoon; Su service is hourly at 5 minutes after the hour until 2205.

DEPART RAMSGATE STATION	ARRIVE VICTORIA STATION	NOTES
1435 (1430 Su)	1617	Daily
1452	1647	M–Sa (1)
1535 (1530 Su)	1723 (1717 Sa, Su)	Daily
1552	1747	Sa (1)
1625 (1635 Sa, 1630 Su)	1817	Daily
1652	1848 (1847 Sa)	M–Sa (1)
1727 (1725 Su, 1729 Sa)	1917	Daily
1752	1947	M–Sa (1)
1825 (1829 Sa)	2017	Daily
1852 (1855 Sa)	2047	M–Sa
1925	2117	Su
1952	2147	M–Sa
2025	2217	Su
2055	2247	M–Sa
2125	2317	Su
2155	2347	Daily

(1) train splits or merges at Faversham

train schedule shown here gives details for the London Victoria Station–Chatam–Faversham–Margate–Ramsgate rail line only.

This frequent train service departs from the first bay (platforms 1–8) of London's Victoria Station. A word of caution: The first cars (usually four) closest to the ticket barrier will go to Dover. The balance of the cars (usually eight) at the head of the train will terminate in Ramsgate. The train "splits" at Faversham. You will be reminded of this by a train announcement when the train stops briefly in the Bromley South Station after leaving Victoria Station and crossing the Thames. Stay alert and board one of the proper cars.

Margate is the Thanet town that has been conjuring up visions of holidays for years. Its biggest drawing card is the famous amusement park Dreamland Fun Park, set on a twenty-acre complex. The municipality of Margate owns 9 miles of seafront with sandy beaches and promenades running practically its full distance. The atmosphere of the area differs somewhat from that of England's south coast in that it is more sedate in mood and tempo. Perhaps the presence of the North Sea is one of the contributing factors.

Arriving at Margate Station, the first sight to greet you is the golden sand of the beach. The promenade paralleling the beach is a length of souvenir shops, restaurants, confectioneries, and amusement halls. Beyond the Dreamland Fun Park lies Margate's main shopping center, where courteous Kentish clerks are most eager to assist you in your shopping. Extending from the promenade, Margate's Old Town of narrow streets and houses clusters around the town's harbor.

Broadstairs, known as "Kent's Best-Kept Secret," has a Victorian atmosphere about it and became a fashionable watering hole during the regency of King George IV. Victorians, one of the most eminent being Charles Dickens, favored holidays in Broadstairs. A leaflet from the information center will permit you to follow in his footsteps and see many interesting points within the town. Every June, townspeople remember Dickens by appearing in costume while attending a series of plays, readings, parades, and parties set against the backdrop of Victorian Broadstairs.

Ramsgate, being strong on regency flavor, centers its activities around the royal harbor and marina. Annual events include the May Spring Festival, August Harbor Heritage celebrations, and September Model Ship Rally. The harbor is a source of constant interest, as is the model village at West Cliff, a charming miniature of England's Tudor countryside.

Permanently moored on the cliff tops at Pegwell Bay in Ramsgate is a Viking ship commemorating the original Viking landing in A.D. 449.

Ramsgate harbor has seen Wellington's troops embark for the Continent, where they continued on to defeat Napoleon at Waterloo. The harbor also received thousands of battered British troops during the evacuation from Dunkerque in 1940.

Many recall memories of their travels through their senses of sight and sound. In the case of Ramsgate, we recall our visits there by our sense of taste. Most memorable was our dining experience at Harvey's Crab & Oyster House located on Harbour Parade. Walk down to the harbor area—you can't miss it. As the name indicates, seafood is the house specialty. The restaurant's card states "Open 12–2:30 p.m. & 8 p.m. till late. Booking advisable. Tel: (0184) 359–1110."

Day Excursion to

St. Albans
FROM ROMANS TO ROSES

Depart from King's Cross Thameslink

Distance by train: 20 miles (32 km)

Average train time: 25 minutes

Train information and InterCity services: (034) 548–4950

St. Albans Tourist Information Centre: The Town Hall, Market Place, Herts AL3 5DJ; *Tel:* (0172) 786–4511; *Fax:* (0172) 786–3533

> *Hours:* Office hours are 0930–1730 Monday through Saturday from Easter to October. From mid-July to mid–September it is also open Sundays from 1030–1630. Between November and Easter hours are 1000–1600 Monday through Saturday.

> Arriving in St. Albans, leave the train station by walking uphill toward the city center on Victoria Street. At the junction of St. Peters and Chequer streets, the tourist information center can be seen opposite, in the Town Hall. The uphill walk takes about fifteen minutes. The alternative is city bus transportation, which departs from a bus shelter in the station area. The bus stop for returning to the station is at the top of Victoria Street.

St. Albans takes its name from Britain's first Christian martyr, a Romano-British citizen who was beheaded for his faith on a hilltop outside Verulamium, one of the most important towns at that time in the western Roman Empire. A magnificent fifteenth-century Norman cathedral now stands on the hilltop, and Verulamium has become a parkland on the western side of the city.

London–St. Albans

This is a very heavily traveled route, often crammed with commuters. Typically, on M–Sa there are 3 or 4 or more trains each hour in either direction, and on Su usually 2 trains per hour. Rather than show some schedules (and to save space on the printed page), the best advice is that you make your way to the appropriate station, where you can be assured you won't have to wait more than 15 minutes to catch your train.

Note: King's Cross Thameslink Station is *not* the same as King's Cross Station. King's Cross Thameslink station can be reached from the King's Cross underground station and from the King's Cross train station by following the appropriate signs. King's Cross Thameslink Station is approximately 300 meters from King's Cross train station. The Thameslink trains also operate from London Bridge Station, Blackfriars Station, and other stations in Central London. Information and a complete timetable may be obtained at most London train station information offices.

DEPART KING'S CROSS THAMESLINK	ARRIVE ST. ALBANS STATION	NOTES
0804 (0800 Su)	0836 (0835 Su)	Daily
0845 (0830 Su)	0904 (0905 Su)	Daily
0914 (0900 Su)	0939 (0935 Su)	Daily
1005	1024 (1035 Su)	Daily
1035	1054 (1056 Su)	Daily
1105	1124 (1126 Su)	Daily
1135	1154 (1156 Su)	Daily

(Plus other frequent service)

DEPART ST. ALBANS STATION	ARRIVE KING'S CROSS THAMESLINK	NOTES
1435 (1428 Su)	1454 (1457 Su)	Daily
1535 (1528 Su)	1554 (1557 Su)	Daily
1614	1636	M–F
1615	1638	Sa
1632	1657	Su
1712	1735	M–F
1715	1738	Sa
1732	1757	Su

(Plus other frequent service)

Note: To reach King's Cross Thameslink, follow directions to the underground Piccadilly Line from King's Cross.

St. Albans has much to offer its visitors. Tucked away in various corners of the city are old coach inns, many with a fascinating history. The White Hart Inn, built in the fifteenth century, was restored in 1930. The Fleur-de-Lys Inn on French Row was erected between 1420 and 1440 on the site where King John of France was held prisoner after the Battle of Poitiers. Another inn, the Fighting Cocks, claims to be the oldest licensed house in England. It derived its name from the cockfights that were held there for many years. All three of these ancient "watering holes" are open to the public during licensed hours. St. Albans has always had an open mind concerning alcoholic beverages; Elizabeth I granted the city permission to issue wine licenses in 1560.

French Row in St. Albans, a narrow street of medieval appearance, is fronted by a clock tower built between 1402 and 1411 from the flint and rubble of Verulamium. Its original curfew bell was cast in 1335. Across from the bell tower stands the Wax House Gate, where once candles and tapers were made and sold to pilgrims visiting the shrine of Saint Albans. The path through the gate is still the shortest route for pedestrians en route to the cathedral, proving that the ancients had a sharp eye for customer traffic flow. The St. Albans Cathedral contains traces of an eighth-century Saxon church. It has one of the largest Gothic naves in Europe. The cathedral tower was built largely of stone from Verulamium.

Many of the points of interest in St. Albans must be reached on foot. The information center has a pamphlet describing a walking tour, St. Albans's Town Trail, which includes the cathedral and the abbey. The tour (2½ miles) may prove a bit too ambitious for the less-experienced, less-conditioned walker, but both lead past one or more of the previously described inns, where a libation will probably instill a desire to press on— or stay at the inn until "time" is called.

Helpful publications to take on the trails are *A Historical Map of St. Albans* and *Mini Guide*. The center has them available for a small fee. The information center is close to the marketplace. Markets are held in St. Albans every Wednesday and Saturday. If you are in town on these days, be sure to "go to market" and enjoy the opportunity of watching the locals barter back and forth with the tradesmen. Everything from apples to zinnias, including the weather and current prices, will become subjects of discussion.

The Roman city of Verulamium is engrossing. You can spend an entire day at the site visiting its 200-acre grounds, which include a temple, forum, museum, hypocaust, and theater. The museum houses an impressive collection of Roman antiquities. From the center of St. Albans, you can reach Verulamium in about twenty minutes on foot, or you can opt for a local bus. The tourist information office will give you the directions.

At the Verulamium Museum, artifacts taken from the ruins are displayed in an environment of natural surroundings. The small items from the houses and shops range from iron hinges, latches, and locks to personal ornaments worn by the inhabitants. A full range of pottery and glassware, for both table and kitchen use, is on exhibit.

Exploratory excavations of the site have taken place from time to time, but experts estimate that only one-third of the area within the Roman town walls has been uncovered. Modern techniques such as aerial photography continue to reveal additional features.

The gardens of the Royal National Rose Society are in St. Albans. The society made its first award for a new rose in 1883 and subsequently established its own trial grounds, where you can see the future "greats" of the rose world. New varieties from all over the world are sent to St. Albans to undergo a comprehensive, three-year assessment. The twelve acres of gardens, a spectacle for the casual visitor, are a total fascination to rose enthusiasts. Now open in the spring from mid-April through early June and for the summer from mid-June to late September; the gardens are accessible to the public during varying hours daily; group discounts are offered. *Tel:* (0172) 785–0461 for details.

The range of history in St. Albans extends from A.D. 43, with the first evidences of the Roman enclosure at Verulamium to the moment you arrive to enjoy the vitality of this timeless city. To step over St. Albans's threshold is to step into a land of enchantment and history.

Day Excursion to

Salisbury

MAGNA CARTA ARCHIVE

Depart from Waterloo Station

Distance by train: 84 miles (135 km)
Average train time: 1 hour, 25 minutes
Train information and InterCity services: (034) 548–4950
Salisbury Tourist Information Centre: Fish Row, Wiltshire SP1 1EJ; *Tel:* (0172) 233–4956; *Fax:* (0172) 242–2059

> *Hours:* Monday to Saturday 0930–1700 year-round, with extended opening hours and Sundays during the summer. The center operates a booking service for local hotel accommodations as well as the popular Book-A-Bed-Ahead program.
>
> Salisbury's Tourist Information Centre is situated at the rear of the Town Guildhall where Market Square corners on Fish Row. Proceed on foot down Fisherton Street, which you will find to your far left as you exit the station. After crossing the River Avon, the street will narrow and change names several times until it becomes Fish Row. The tourist information center at the rail station is open April–September on Monday through Saturday from 0930–1630.

Salisbury holds the distinction of being one of the few English cities not originally founded by the Romans. The old town, Old Sarum, had been in existence since the Iron Age. The Romans fortified it, and the Saxons later developed it into an industrial town. All went well in Old Sarum until arguments between the occupants of the church and the castle caused a new church to be built in the valley below the original town site. This new location proved to be more popular than the old. Consequently, although known as Salisbury, the town's official name is New Sarum.

The center of Salisbury has traditionally been divided into two distinct areas: the cathedral and the marketplace. This tradition still exists, and the gates leading to the cathedral and the buildings in the "close" surrounding it are locked every night. Beautiful houses of medieval and Georgian architecture overlook the green.

The marketplace has a history all its own. In the original Charter of 1227, the town was authorized to hold a Tuesday market. This got out of hand and grew into almost a daily market until protests from nearby towns resulted in a reduction of market days in Salisbury to Tuesdays and Saturdays only. Today, Salisbury maintains those traditional market days.

Salisbury boasts a number of historic inns that have given rest and refreshment to travelers down through the centuries. The fireplaces in the

King's Arms Inn have the same stone as that used in the construction of the cathedral. The Haunch of Venison, an old English chop house, was built about 1320. The Red Lion Hotel, dating back to the same era, was the starting point for the Salisbury Flying Machine, the nightly horse-drawn coach to London.

In Salisbury, you will find many impressive examples of architectural styles, ranging from the town's thirteenth-century cathedral to a modern pedestrian shopping district known as the Old George Mall. The most unexpected structure is the foyer of the movie theater on New Canal Street. Once the banqueting hall of the merchant John Halle, four-time mayor of Salisbury, it is now a splendid example of fifteenth-century black-and-white timbering.

From April through September, you can join a daily guided walking tour of Salisbury at 1100 and 1800 from in front of the information center on Fish Row. The tour lasts approximately one and a half hours. On Friday night, the 1800 walking tour becomes a special ghost walk at 2000.

The cathedral has a unity of design that no doubt is attributable to the fact that, unlike most other cathedrals, which took centuries to complete, the Salisbury Cathedral was constructed in only thirty-eight years. In other words, it wasn't affected by several different periods of architecture. Foundation stones were laid in 1220, during the heyday of Gothic design. One of its greatest treasures is its ancient clock mechanism, which dates from 1386 and is one of the oldest pieces of operating machinery in the world. It originally stood in a detached belfry.

The cathedral contains a library founded at Old Sarum in 1078; seventy of the books installed in the library at that time are still there. The great treasure of the Cathedral, housed in Chapter House, is the Magna Carta, written at Runnymede on June 15, 1215. It was brought to Salisbury by William, Earl of Salisbury, who placed it in the cathedral for safekeeping. It remained there until World War II, when it was hidden for five years in a quarry.

Among its many historical achievements, Salisbury made its mark in the annals of medical care. Of the four hospitals currently in or near the city, the Trinity Hospital, on Trinity Street, has a rather interesting story concerning its founding in 1379 by Agnes Bottenham. Chronicles relate that Ms. Agnes ran a "house of ill repute" on the site, and when it prospered, she built a hospital and almshouse there as an act of penitence.

London–Salisbury

DEPART WATERLOO STATION	ARRIVE SALISBURY STATION	NOTES
0710	0837	M–Sa
0835	0954	M–Sa
0857	1027	Su
0935	1102 (1108 Sa)	M–Sa
1035	1154	M–Sa
1057	1233	Su
1135	1302	M–Sa
1235	1354	M–Sa
1257	1427	Su

DEPART SALISBURY STATION	ARRIVE WATERLOO STATION	NOTES
1425	1556	Sa
1429	1618	Su
1523 (1526 Sa)	1647	M–Sa
1543	1717	Su
1635	1811	Sa
1647	1818	M–F
1650	1816	Su
1726	1850	M–Sa
1750	1916 (1915 Su)	M–F, Su
1815	1947	M–Sa
1826	2002	Su
1953 (1958 Sa)	2119 (2120, 2132 Su)	Daily
2045	2225 (2224 Sa)	M–Sa
2106	2236	Su

Visitors interested in seeing Old Sarum, 1½ miles north of the new town, can do so by city bus or taxi. Excavations and reconstruction have been under way for some time. Oddly enough, even after the old city was abandoned, two representatives of Parliament continued to be sent, despite the fact that the city had no inhabitants. It was a case of representation without taxation.

Day Excursion to

Sheffield

TRADEMARK OF QUALITY

Depart from St. Pancras Station

Distance by train: 165 miles (265 km)

Average train time: 2 hours 10 minutes

Train information and InterCity services: (034) 548–4950

Sheffield Tourist Information Centre: Leader House, Surrey Street S1 2LH; *Tel:* (0114) 273–4671; *Fax:* (0114) 272–4225

Internet: http://www.sheffieldcity.co.uk

Hours: Open 0930 to 1715, Monday to Friday and 0930 to 1615 on Saturday

The Tourist Information Centre is about a ten-minute walk from the rail station. Cross the road by the traffic-light–controlled pedestrian crossing. Pass to the left of the Sheffield Hallam University Nelson Mandela Building and walk straight up steep Howard Street, passing the University's main entrance on your right. Cross the road straight ahead; at the other side turn right then go up the steps on your left, on to Surrey Street. When you see Hibberts Art Shop on your right (just past the end of Tudor Square, where the Crucible and Lyceum Theatres can be seen), turn left, and walk past the front of the modern Town Hall extension.

The Tourist Information Centre is at the far end, but is in the process of relocating to the city center next to Tudor Square. Double-check the location at the station before trekking out. Taxi service is also available from the station.

Sheffield, England's fourth largest city (population 529,000) is world famous for steelmaking, toolmaking, engineering, and cutlery. Surviving records show that cutlery was being made in Sheffield in 1297, and Chaucer referred to a Sheffield *thwitel* (knife) in his *Canterbury Tales.* By the late nineteenth century, Sheffield was regarded as the steel capital of the world, and in 1913 Harry Brearley made one of the great discoveries of our century, stainless steel, at Sheffield's Brown Firth Laboratories.

But forget images of smoke-belching chimneys. Present-day Sheffield is still England's greenest city. Built on seven hills and five river valleys (fast-flowing streams drove the waterwheels that powered the cutlery industry before the steam age), Sheffield has more than fifty parks and green spaces—and four trees to every person! It is surrounded by open countryside, and more than a third of the city lies within the beautiful Peak National Park. Slated for the twenty-first century is the unique *Heart of the City* development. This ambitious project will provide Sheffield with three new public squares, a winter garden to house hundreds of temperate plants, plus a millennium gallery.

London–Sheffield

DEPART ST. PANCRAS STATION	ARRIVE SHEFFIELD STATION	NOTES
0730	0950	M–F
0830	1051 (1058 Sa)	M–Sa
0930	1151 (1220 Su)	M–F, Su
1000	1225	Sa
1030	1248	M–F
1030	1345	Su
1130	1350 (1357 Sa)	M–Sa
1130	1424	Su

DEPART SHEFFIELD STATION	ARRIVE ST. PANCRAS STATION	NOTES
1424	1649 (1652 Sa)	M–Sa
1456	1718	Su
1524	1749	M–F
1554	1824	Sa
1624 (1625 Su)	1855 (1856 Su)	M–F, Su
1651	1922	Su
1724	1950 (1956 Sa)	M–Sa
1820	2055	Su
1924	2157 (2203 Sa)	M–Sa
1935	2218	Su
2030	2329	M–F

Sheffield has won a reputation for sporting excellence and in 1995 was the first city to be awarded the official title *National City of Sport*. The country's top teams in ice-hockey (Sheffield Steelers) and basketball (Sheffield Sharks) are based here, as is the national diving squad. The city has hosted more than 200 national and international sports events over the past five years and now is specially designated as the city for the United Kingdom Sports Institute.

With the Peak National Park nearby, outdoor sports are particularly popular. A completely unexpected attraction, set in the heart of the city, is Europe's largest artificial ski slope complex, Sheffield Ski Village. Just bring your gloves; you can rent everything else.

Another well-known export is music. Joe Cocker, Def Leppard, Pulp, and many other bands started here. This heritage is recognized at the National Centre for Popular Music, an exciting interactive "museum" with no static exhibits at all. Newly opened in the spring of 1998, this state-of-the-art attraction is expected to bring more than 400,000 visitors to Sheffield annually.

Two traditional museums, commemorating Sheffield's industrial heritage, are Kelham Island and Abbeydale Industrial Hamlet. At the former, the largest working steam engine in Europe can be seen in action. The latter museum displays scythe-producing, water-driven machinery, some of which date back to the seventeenth century. The City Museum, Weston Park, has excellent collections of Sheffield cutlery and Sheffield plates. Cutler's Hall, on Church Street, is the headquarters of the Cutler's Company, which was formed in 1642. The present Cutler's Hall dates from 1832 and houses the company's silver and cutlery collections, which can be viewed by appointment only (inquire at the Tourist Information Centre).

A heritage site is Victoria Quays, Sheffield's canal basin. The canal was built to ship in iron ore from Sweden and ship out steel products to England's east coast ports; now Victoria Quays is a waterside oasis in the heart of the city center, with its beautiful warehouse buildings, a cobbled waterfront and the Sheaf cutlery works, now a family pub and restaurant.

Another historic building in the city center is the Lyceum in Tudor Square, a magnificently restored Victorian theater that together with the modern Crucible Theatre forms the country's largest theatrical complex outside London. Nearby is the Ruskin Gallery, which displays the collection of the Guild of Saint George, left to the city by Victorian sage, artist, and critic John Ruskin. Next door, the Ruskin Craft Gallery displays contemporary craft products, many of them for sale.

A fifteen-minute journey from the city center on the new Supertram, Britain's largest and most advanced urban light rail transport system, will take you to one of Britain's most successful shopping malls, Meadowhall, with 270 shops, a food court, and cinemas. On the way you pass Britain's newest airport, Sheffield's business and short-haul airport.

The Tourist Information Centre offers an excellent city map. The centre also offers accommodation information and advance booking services. Helpful brochures, including *A City in My Pocket*, the *Mini-Guide*, the *Insider's Guide*, and a number of other visitor publications are available at no cost. With one of the largest student populations in the country (more than 40,000), Sheffield has a wide variety of nightlife choices for fun-loving tourists.

Shops highlighting the local steel-crafting trade include Osbournes Silversmiths, Ltd., Rivelin Cutlery Works, United Cutlers of Sheffield, George Butler Ltd., Hiram Wild Factory Shops, and Mortons of Sheffield. Other outlets include the Master Cutler and Don Alexander. The tourist office can supply addresses and hours.

Day Excursion to

Southampton AN IMPOSING HERITAGE

Depart from Waterloo Station

Distance by train: 79 miles (127 km)
Average train time: 1 hour, 10 minutes
Train information and InterCity services: (034) 548–4950
Southampton Leisure and Visitor Centre: Civic Centre Road SO14 7LP; *Tel:* (0170) 322–1106; *Fax:* (0170) 363–1437
  Accommodations: (0170) 322–1106
  Hours: Monday–Saturday, 0900 (1000 on Thursday) to 1700 throughout the year; closed on Sunday.
    From the railway station, you can board any "City Centre"-bound bus and ask the driver to "deposit" you at the Civic Centre, next to which you will find the Leisure and Visitor Centre. There is a map outside the Southampton railway station showing the route to the center.

In the minds of many, Southampton conjures visions of the great transatlantic ocean liners, for it is Britain's prime ocean-passenger port and home of many of the world's greatest passenger ships, including Britain's flagship, the Queen Elizabeth II (QE2). Many visitors, however, know little about Southampton's span of centuries, which has given it a rich heritage of England and of Europe. Southampton's museums, classic buildings, and ancient ruins help reveal this rich and interesting history.

Southampton is best seen on foot, with the possible assistance of a city bus now and then. Pick up the free *Southampton's Visitors Guide* at the Leisure and Visitor Centre—it contains suggestions for sightseeing. Visitors from the United States will take special interest in the sailing of the

Mayflower from Southampton in 1620. Persons proving descent from the original *Mayflower* passengers can have their names entered on the memorial. The center also can make hotel and bed-and-breakfast reservations in Southampton and its surroundings.

As mentioned in the official handbook, there are many places of interest within easy walking distance of the city information center. A visit to them will gradually unfold a picture of Southampton's past. To catch Southampton's seagoing flavor, a visit to the Ocean Village or the Town Quay Marina would be in order. Similar to the harbor renovation of Baltimore, Maryland, Southampton's Ocean Village has transformed some of its old docks into a cosmopolitan playground with a bevy of specialty shops and eateries overlooking a yacht basin. Quayside at Southampton's port, you stand in history. Four hundred years before the Pilgrim fathers departed on their journey to the new world, Richard the Lion-Hearted embarked on the Third Crusade. The Town Quay Marina plays host to the cream of the yacht-racing world. Both areas are close to the terminal used by the QE2. Check with the information centre concerning walking directions and the possibility of the QE2 being in the harbor.

Next in line is the Tudor House Museum, where the costumes, paintings, and furniture of centuries past are displayed against the oak beams and stone carvings of Tudor House itself. The Tudor House is one of the few surviving examples in Southampton of a large town house from the early Tudor period. It contains a banquet hall and is surrounded by an authentic Elizabethan herb garden. Don't miss the tunnel entrance to the remains of a twelfth-century merchant's home. The kids will love it.

Next on the agenda is Wool House, once a medieval warehouse and now a showplace for the city's involvement with the sea. Since early times, Southampton has been an important port of call. Docks were piled high with luxuries from the Mediterranean and the East, brought there by Genoan and Venetian fleets.

With all of the rekindled global interest in the 1912 sinking of the *Titanic* on her maiden voyage, one cannot miss visiting the "Story of the White Star Line" Exhibition. The *Titanic's* story is told through the voices of some of the actual survivors and the people of Southampton whose lives were affected by the tragedy.

If you never expected to see a marine museum in a wool house, you'll be equally surprised to find an archaeological collection in a museum bearing the name God's House Tower. It started out as a gun store, changed

London–Southampton

DEPART WATERLOO STATION	ARRIVE SOUTHAMPTON STATION	NOTES
0730	0849	M–F
0750	0916	M–Sa
0755	0931	Su
0810	0935	M–F
0830	0943 (0941 Sa)	M–Sa
0850	1016	M–Sa
0855	1031	Su
0910	1029	M–F
0930	1100	Su

M–F service continues after 0910 at hourly intervals until mid afternoon; M–Sa service continues after 0850 at 30 and 50 minute after the hour until mid afternoon; Su service continues after 0930 at 55 and 30 minute after the hour until 2155.

DEPART SOUTHAMPTON STATION	ARRIVE WATERLOO STATION	NOTES
1435	1605 (1603 Sa)	M–Sa
1452	1627	Su
1455	1621	M–F
1515	1629 (1628 Sa,1636 Su)	Daily
1535	1603	M–Sa
1552	1727	Su
1555	1718	M–F
1615	1729 (1728 Sa, 1736 Su)	Daily
1635	1805 (1803 Sa)	M–Sa
1652	1827	Su
1655	1821	M–F
1715	1831 (1828 Sa, 1836 Su)	Daily
1735	1903	Sa
1740	1908	M–F
1752	1927	Su
1755	1920	M–F
1815	1930 (1928 Sa, 1936 Su)	Daily
1835	2003	Sa
1842	2013	M–F
1852	2026	Su
1915	2030 (2028 Sa, 2036 Su)	Daily
1942 (1940 Sa)	2112 (2114 Sa)	M–Sa
1952	2126	Su
2015	2136	Su
2042	2211 (2216 Sa)	M–Sa
2051	2232	Su
2152	2325 (2332 Su)	Sa, Su
2250	0055	Sa
2252	0027	Su

its use many times, and finally opened as a museum in 1950. It currently houses the most extensive collection of post-Roman European pottery to be found in Europe.

Also in Southampton's repertoire is the Hall of Aviation on Albert Road. The museum is a memorial to R. J. Mitchell, Southampton's famous aircraft designer of the Spitfire, the fighter that valiantly defended the country during the Battle of Britain. The exhibits include a Spitfire Mark 24, possibly one of the last of 24,500 Spitfires produced by the Supermarine Aircraft Company in nearby Woolston, a quarter mile from the museum. The museum's collection also includes a Sandringham Flying Boat as well as hundreds of photographs, plans, and models connected with R. J. Mitchell and the Supermarine factory.

The route between the museums, by the way, is dotted with historic buildings, such as the Duke of Wellington Pub and the Red Lion Pub. Pausing for a pint may provide a pleasant period for pondering Southampton's past and present.

Free guided walks through medieval Southampton depart from the Bargate at varying times throughout the year. Ask for complete details at the Leisure and Visitor Centre.

Day Excursion to

Stonehenge
MYSTERIOUS PAGAN SHRINE

Depart from Waterloo Station

Distance by train: 84 miles (135 km)

Average train time: 1 hour, 45 minutes

Train information and InterCity services: (034) 548–4950

Salisbury Tourist Information Centre: Fish Row, Wiltshire SP1 1EJ; *Tel:* (0172) 233–4956; *Fax:* (0172) 242–2059

Hours: Stonehenge is open from 0930–1800 from March 16 to October 15; 0900–1900 from June 1 to August 31. The remainder of the year, hours are daily 0930–1600.

There are several means by which you can proceed to Stonehenge from the Salisbury railway station. (See below.) A gift shop, refreshments, and public toilets are available at the site and all facilities provide access for the disabled.

London–Stonehenge

No train service to Stonehenge; take a bus from Salisbury. Consult the London–Salisbury timetables, p. 161.

"Observatory, altar, temple, tomb, erected none knows when by none knows whom, to serve strange gods or watch familiar stars . . ." wrote the poet Sir John Squire about Stonehenge. Stonehenge is unmatched—truly one of the wonders of the world. There are many opinions regarding the use and purpose of the monument. Whatever the reason for its existence, however, Stonehenge remains an awe-inspiring reminder of the past

The landscape for a few miles around the Stonehenge monument reportedly contains more prehistoric remains than any other area of the same size in Britain. There are earthworks, burial sites, erected stones, and hill carvings. Because they belong to the prehistoric period, long before any written records were made, there are many questions about them all that we shall never be able to answer. Through technology, we have been able to tell *how* they were made and, in some cases, *when* and by *whom*. The unanswered question is *"Why?"*

Stonehenge sits on the Salisbury plain, an almost treeless, windswept plateau. With its origins dating from about 2950 to 1600 B.C. Stonehenge comprises a circular group of stones roughly 110 feet in diameter that stand in an area surrounded by a low earthen rampart and ditch approximately 330 feet in diameter. The largest stones, some weighing as much as fifty tons, were brought to the site from quarries some 20 miles distant. The stones are placed in such a manner as to reflect the position of the sun on the four main dates of the seasons, the solstices and equinoxes, possibly as an agricultural almanac or for spiritual purposes.

The monument stands on approximately 300 feet of solid chalk. Unfortunately, Stonehenge has been robbed constantly of its stone throughout the centuries. In Victorian times, it was common practice for visitors to bring hammers and chisels to carve their names and other graffiti and to chip off souvenir sections of the temple stones.

Diodorus Siculus, historian to Julius Caesar, described Stonehenge as a temple to the sun god Apollo. Modern Britons have marked the area with small clumps of trees to commemorate the Battle of Trafalgar in 1805.

If time is of the essence to get to Stonehenge, a taxi can get you there in about twenty minutes. Buses, operated by Wilts & Dorset, depart from the station for Stonehenge via Salisbury and Amesbury on a daily basis, Sundays and public holidays included. The adult round-trip fare is £4.60; admission to the Stonehenge site (£3.90) is not included. The Wilts & Dorset bus schedule is arranged so as to connect with all express trains to and from the Waterloo Station in London. If you plan to linger at the site, this will provide you with ample time to do so.

In conjunction with Wilts & Dorset, Guide Friday, one of Britain's leading operators of town and city tours, offers a tour of Stonehenge for an adult fare of £12.50 (senior citizens £10.50; children under the age of twelve, £6.00). Fares include entrance to Stonehenge, and you are accompanied by a guide throughout the tour. Tour time is just under two hours. For complete details and bus schedules, we suggest that you call ahead to the Wilts & Dorset travel office in Salisbury (0172) 233–6855.

Two tour companies, AS Tours and Days Out Tours, also offer excellent one-day tours from the rail station to Stonehenge. Check with the tourist information center for details.

Time permitting, upon arriving back in Salisbury, you may want to explore the city prior to boarding your London-bound train. If so, stay aboard the bus returning from Stonehenge until it arrives at the Salisbury bus terminal approximately five minutes after its arrival at the rail station.

Do use one of the special excursion buses. If you use the regular public bus system between Salisbury and Amesbury, you will have to walk or take a taxi for the 2 miles between Amesbury and the Stonehenge site.

A sad note: Because of damage to the monument, visitors are not permitted to enter the actual stone circle, but can view it only from a distance. Now visitors are required to remain behind a fence built around the Stonehenge temple to protect it. "TIME," as the announcement observes, "IS TAKING ITS TOLL."

Day Excursion to

Stratford-upon-Avon   SHAKESPEARE COUNTRY

Depart from Paddington Station

Distance by train: 121 miles (195 km)

Average train time: 2 hours, 30 minutes

Train information and InterCity services: (0121) 643–2711

Stratford-upon-Avon Tourist Information Centre: Bridgefoot Street, Warwickshire CV37 6GW; *Tel:* (0178) 929–3127; *Fax:* (0178) 929–5262

Hours: Monday–Saturday 0900–1800; Sunday 1100–1700

The tourist center is about a 15 minute walk or £1.50 taxi ride from the railroad station. If you decide to walk, turn left onto Alcester Street and follow to Greenhill Street. Turn left. Follow Greenhill to Wood Street, and continue to Bridge Street, which is a main road at the bottom of the hill. Cross over the canal bridge, you will see the center on the left side.

Guide Friday Tourism Centre: Civic Hall, 14 Rother Street, Warwickshire CV37 6LU; (0178) 929–4466; *Fax:* (0178) 941–4681

The Guide Friday Centre is a short walk from the rail station. Turn left out of the station and go towards the town center. Past the crossroad, you will see the American Fountain. At the second traffic light, turn right. Civic Hall is the large white building on the right.

William Shakespeare, the English poet and playwright recognized universally as the greatest of all dramatists, was born in Stratford-upon-Avon in 1564. His mother was the daughter of a local farmer; his father was a glove maker and a wool merchant who entered politics to become mayor of Stratford. Although Shakespeare lived throughout his professional career in London, he kept his home ties with Stratford. In 1597 he purchased New Place, one of Stratford's largest houses. He died there in 1616 and was buried in Stratford's parish church.

Rail travelers can travel from London's Paddington Station to Stratford-upon-Avon via the Thames Trains, Ltd., Turbo Express trains. Trains depart from Paddington beginning at 0918 and at regular intervals throughout the day, Monday through Friday. There are four direct return services from Stratford-upon-Avon to London, including a late train especially for theatergoers. For more detailed information on these services, telephone (0171) 262–6767 or (0129) 526–2256 or (0186) 572–2333. Saturday and Sunday departures on this route, however, are limited. InterCity services also are available to Leamington Spa or Birmingham, with connecting services to Stratford *Tel:* (0178) 856–0116 or (0121) 643–2711.

London–Stratford-upon-Avon

Schedules shown are for direct trains from and to London Paddington Station. Other service is possible by changing trains in Reading or in Leamington Spa.

DEPART PADDINGTON	ARRIVE STRATFORD-UPON-AVON	NOTES
0918	1127 (1130 Sa)	M–Sa
0945	1156	Su
1118	1325	M–Sa
1145	1400	Su
1348	1600	M–Sa

DEPART STRATFORD-UPON-AVON	ARRIVE PADDINGTON	NOTES
1410	1614 (1617 Sa)	M–Sa
1438	1645	Su
1732	1943 (1945 Sa)	M–Sa
1755	2013	Su
1931	2207	Sa
2000	2215	M–F
2315	0125	M–F

Our advice is to take a guided tour of Stratford-upon-Avon. The popular "Stratford and Shakespeare Story Tour" is operated by the Guide Friday Tourism Centre. The open-top bus tours stop at each of the Shakespearean properties: Shakespeare's birthplace on Henley Street; Anne Hathaway's Cottage; Mary Arden's House, where Shakespeare's mother grew up; New Place/Nash's House, in which Shakespeare spent his retirement years before his death in 1616; and Hall's Croft, home of Shakespeare's daughter, Susanna. Visitors have the freedom to get on and off the bus as frequently as they wish since the ticket is valid all day.

From May to September, tours depart every fifteen minutes; March to mid-May and October to November, every half hour; December and January, every hour. You can join the tours at any of the Shakespearean properties, as well as the Pen & Parchment Inn on Bridgefoot Street, Evesham Place, or on Windsor or Meer Streets. A Guide Friday Bus Tour ticket allows holders to visit any three of the Shakespeare Houses, if purchase and visit are on the same day. The tour tickets are available at all the Shakespeare Houses and priced at: Adults £8.00, Child £4.00, Family £21.00, Senior Citizen and Student £7.00.

Other tour highlights include the Royal Shakespeare Theatre, the Swan and Other Place Theatres, the Holy Trinity Church where Shakespeare is buried and protected by a purportedly cursed tombstone, the Old Fifteenth-Century Grammar School, which Shakespeare attended, and Harvard House, home of Katherine Rogers, whose son founded the library in the United States that became Harvard University.

A visit to the Royal Shakespeare Theatre is a must. Reserve theater seats as far in advance as possible. Telephone (0178) 926–9191 for 24-hour information on program and seat availability. To book seats, telephone the theater box office direct at (0178) 929–5623 or fax (0178) 926–1974. The theater has several restaurant/bar facilities. Telephone (0178) 941–4999 for more information and reservations for special restaurant/theater packages.

The Box Tree is a luxuriously appointed restaurant overlooking the Avon River and serves classical cuisine (closed on Sunday). The River Terrace is a modern restaurant/coffee shop/wine bar serving light international dishes. You can even "Pick-up-a-Picnic" by placing your order with the cashier at the River Terrace Restaurant two hours in advance.

Day Excursion to

Windsor

THE ROYAL CASTLE

Depart from Waterloo Station

Distance by train: 25 miles (41 km)
Average train time: 50 minutes
Train information and InterCity services: (034) 548–4950
Windsor Tourist Information Centre: No. 24 High Street SL4 1LH; *Tel:* (0175) 385–2010; *Fax:* (0175) 383–3450
   Hours: 0930–1800 in summer, Sundays 1000–1800; and 0930–1600 in winter.
     The traditional "**i**" will lead the way to the tourist information center from either arrival point, Windsor Riverside Station or Windsor Central Station. The grounds of Windsor Castle are immediately across the street from the information center.

You have a choice of two rail routes from London to Windsor. For the schedule given here, we have selected the route from Waterloo Station in

London to Windsor Riverside Station. This line does not require changing trains en route. The alternate route, which departs Paddington Station in London, requires a change at Slough to a shuttle train before arriving at Windsor Central Station. If you take the Paddington-Slough route, the shuttle train arrives and departs in Slough from track 1. Either route gives you a magnificent view approaching Windsor Castle. On either train, sit on the left-hand side (outbound) to take full advantage of the scenery. Be sure to purchase an illustrated guidebook on Windsor Castle—it will become a fond reminder of your visit.

Historic Windsor Castle is the official home of English royalty. William the Conqueror built the first structure on this site, a wooden fort that doubled as a royal hunting lodge. Other English kings added to the castle during their reigns, but despite the multiplicity of royalty and architects, the castle has managed to retain a unity of style all its own. It's the largest inhabited castle in the world.

Queen Elizabeth II uses the castle far more than any of her predecessors. For this reason, it is wise to inquire if the queen is in official residence before going to Windsor. When she is, which is usually during the months of April, June, and December, her Royal Standard will be flying atop the Round Tower's flagpole, and the state apartments will be closed to the public. There will still be many areas of Windsor Castle open to the public; however, you will miss seeing the splendor of the various rooms contained within the state apartments. Chances of seeing Her Majesty, should she be in residence, are slim. Nevertheless, during that time you may find Prince Philip watching his son Charles, the Prince of Wales, and his polo team bashing about in the Great Windsor Park. Again, it may be difficult to find the princes, for although the castle itself occupies a mere thirteen acres, the park stretches over 4,000 acres below the battlements of the castle.

The £50 million restoration effort after the devastating fire in the castle on November 20, 1992, was completed in 1998. Refurbishment of the Queen's Private Chapel, St. George's Hall, and the State Dining Room have been painstakingly replicated and updated, although we thought we could still smell a slight odor of burning timbers.

While in St. George's Chapel, dedicated to Britain's highest order of chivalry, *The Most Noble Order of the Garter,* ask the guards about the knights' shields. Some of the shields are totally covered up and the reason is ... well, you'll find out. Perhaps they had forgotten their royal oath! The chapel also is home of the *King's Champion,* a full-armored statue

London–Windsor

There are two train stations in Windsor–Eton: the Windsor & Eton Riverside Station and the Windsor & Eton Central Station. Direct service to Windsor & Eton Riverside station is available from and to London Waterloo Station; service from and to Windsor & Eton Central Station requires a change of trains at Slough. Schedules shown here are direct trains from and to Windsor & Eton Riverside Station.

DEPART WATERLOO STATION	ARRIVE WINDSOR RIVERSIDE STATION	NOTES
0742	0833	M–F
0750	0846	Su
0758	0847	Sa
0812	0904	M–F
0828	0919	Sa
0842	0934	M–F
0850	0946	Su
0858	0947	M–Sa

M–Sa service continues after 0858 at 30-minute intervals until late afternoon; Su service continues after 0850 at hourly intervals until late afternoon.

DEPART WINDSOR RIVERSIDE STATION	ARRIVE WATERLOO STATION	NOTES
1355	1447	M–Sa
1402	1458	Su
1427	1517	M–Sa
1455	1547	M–Sa
1502	1558	Su
1527	1617	M–Sa
1555	1647	M–Sa

and continuing very frequent service with a similar pattern until late P.M.

commemorating the throwing down of the gauntlet in defense of the sovereign. Directly to the right of the King's Champion begins the wood paneling engraved with the names of the original members of the Order. The next three walls contain a chronological listing of all those who have been knighted, to the present day—and including the women who have been added to this order in recent decades.

Rare state occasions such as the Investiture of the Garter, when the queen proceeds down the walks of Windsor Castle accompanied by a full entourage of castle guards and Knights of the Garter, are difficult for the general public to view. The changing of the castle guard, however, is an event conducted in a manner in which the general public can participate. The new guard leaves the Victoria Barracks precisely at 1055, then marches along High Street to the castle. The guard changing takes place at 1100 and the old guard returns by the same route at 1130. By positioning yourself along High Street or Castle Hill, you will have a good view of the pageantry as it unfolds.

From the battlements of Windsor Castle, you may look down and across the stately River Thames onto the playing fields of Eton College, where "how the game is played" has always been more important than the final score. The importance of Eton lies less in what it is than in what it stands for. The schoolyard and cloisters are open 1400–1630 except during school holidays, when they are open 1030–1630 April to September.

Your initial entry into the single-street town of Eton may be a bit frightening at first, for you will probably find yourself surrounded by a group of young gentlemen uniformed in pin-striped trousers, white bow ties, and formal black coats with tails. You have not been thrust among a flock of penguins. What you are surrounded by are the fellow students of Prince William from Eton College. This school for kings is one of Britain's most exclusive educational institutions and a strong reminder that the British on occasion can cling fiercely to their traditions.

A respite from pageantry and tradition during your visit to Windsor may be taken by cruising on the River Thames. At the bottom of High Street, at its intersection with Barry Avenue, the Windsor Boat Pier offers two cruises. The first is a thirty-five-minute trip upstream, and the other is a full two-hour trip with light refreshments and a licensed bar aboard.

Kids of all ages will enjoy a visit to LEGOLAND Windsor, located just 2 miles from Windsor town center (Internet: http://www.lego.com/legoland/windsor). Take the LEGOLAND shuttle bus from either of the Windsor rail stations. The theme park is open daily from March 19–September 26 from 1000–1800; during August, it's open until 2000. Learn to drive your own LEGO car on a real road system with traffic lights and roundabouts. At the Waterworks, fire water cannons and make water flow uphill or squirt from fountains. Cruise down Fairy Tale Brook in a boat or whirl around on the Whirly Birds Helicopter. In *My Town,* you don't just watch the circus—you're part of the show. Entrance fees for Little Kids (ages 3–15), £12; Adult Kids (ages 16–59), £15; and Senior Kids (age 60 plus), £11. Have fun!

If you have not yet been introduced to the British public house (pub), there is no better time than now. The Royal Oak, directly across the street from Windsor Riverside Station, is highly recommended for a relaxing break prior to trekking uphill to the castle entrance, and as a resting spot to royally reminisce before boarding the train back to London Town. No more prim a pub can you find in all of England. Its impeccable oaken interior matches the high quality of its food and service. The inn was constructed as an ale house in 1736 and restored in 1937. Should we meet you there, we'll buy the first round!

Day Excursion to

York

FINE MEDIEVAL CITY

Depart from King's Cross Station

Distance by train: 188 miles (302 km)

Average train time: 1 hour, 57 minutes

Train information and InterCity services: (034) 548–4950

York Tourist Information Centre: De Grey Rooms, Exhibition Square, Y01 2HB; *Tel:* (0190) 462–1756; *Fax:* (0190) 462–5618

> *Hours:* Open September through June, Monday–Saturday 0900–1800; July and August, Monday–Saturday 0900–1900; year-round on Sunday 0930–1800. Office in the railway station open 0900–2000 Monday–Saturday, Sunday 1000–1700.

> Check in with the York Tourist Information Centre in the rail station, then turn left leaving the train station and proceed along the city wall toward the tower of the York Minster. After crossing the River Ouse, at the intersection of Duncombe Place and St. Leonard's Place, you will see the Minster straight ahead. York's main tourist office is nearby in Exhibition Square.

While in York station stop by the ticket office and request the *First Stop York* free booklet that offers half-price vouchers to many attractions in the town; or call (800) 722–7151 or visit http://www.railpass.com/guides/otherguides.com to purchase *York For Less,* a wonderful discount book full of valuable savings.

"The history of York," according to King George VI, "is the history of England." The Romans took it from a Celtic tribe, the Brigantes, in A.D. 71. According to legend, King Arthur captured the city sometime after the Roman legions retreated in A.D 406. The Saxons took charge in the seventh century, and the Danes ran the Saxons off in 867, only to get their comeuppance from the Anglo-Saxons in 944. In 1066, York saw the fastest turnaround ever when King Harold of England defeated the King of Norway at Stamford Bridge, 6 miles from York. Nineteen days later, York (and all of England, in fact) passed to the Normans when Harold was killed in the Battle of Hastings.

William the Conqueror, following his victory at Hastings, came north to quell a rebellion, which he accomplished through his version of urban renewal—the "scorched-earth" policy. The ruins and rubble of the Romans, the Saxons, the Vikings, and the Anglo-Saxons, however, remain today.

Charles I, fleeing the fermenting civil war, left London in 1639 to take residence in York. Cromwell's troops finally took York in July 1644. A condition of surrender was that there would be no pillaging; thus, the fine medieval stained glass of York Minster was saved. It is estimated that the Minster contains more than half of all the medieval stained glass in England.

York, similar to Chester, has retained most of its fourteenth-century city walls. You will see part of them as you exit from York's railway station. The city of York is best explored on foot. Once you are armed with a map from the tourist information center, proceed on foot into the city. Although it's a ten- to fifteen-minute walk, you'll see a lot of history en route. While at the tourist office, ask for the York City Council's parents folder for those traveling with youngsters. York is considered to be "the child-friendly city." And if during your journey you start to think, "I wish I could spend more time here in York," as is often heard by the tourist officials, inquire about overnight accommodations.

The York Association of Voluntary Guides provides excellent free tours that depart from Exhibition Square daily at 1015 throughout the year, with an additional tour at 1415 from April to the end of October, and an evening tour at 1900 in June, July, and August The tour lasts about two hours. To request special theme tours or private tours, write to: The Hon. Secretary, Tourist Information Centre, De Grey Rooms, Exhibition Square

London–York

DEPART KING'S CROSS STATION	ARRIVE YORK STATION	NOTES
0700	0854 (0906 Sa)	M–Sa
0730	0927	M–F
0800	0953 (1002 Sa)	M–Sa
0830	1039 (1040 Sa, 1045 Su)	Daily
0900	1054 (1059 Sa, 1116 Su)	Daily
0930	1133 (1136 Sa, 1130 Su)	Daily
0940	1127	Sa
1000	1152 (1200 Sa, 1205 Su)	Daily

and continuing every half hour until mid- or late afternoon

YORK TO KINGS CROSS

M–F: Depart York Station at 1429, 1436, 1451 (nonstop to King's Cross), 1509, 1531, 1555, 1628, 1654, 1720 (nonstop to King's Cross), 1749, 1826, 1936, 2002, 2133, and 2358; journey time approximately 2 hours.

Sa: Depart York Station 1432, 1451 (nonstop to King's Cross), 1526, 1550, 1631, 1654, 1726, 1827, 1935, and 2002; journey time approximately 2 hours.

Su: Depart York Station at 1415 (nonstop to King's Cross), 1426, 1453, 1518 (nonstop to King's Cross), 1551, 1601, 1635, 1701, 1727, 1759, 1816, 1845, 1908, 1935, 2002, and 2045; journey time approximately 2 hours.

York, Y01 7HB, or telephone (0190) 464–0780 between 0930 and 1130 Monday to Friday.

Another tour, The Complete York Tour, offers a reduction for holders of BritRail Passes and railway tickets to York. The tour covers the York Minster and direct admission (no queuing) to the Jorvik Viking Centre. The price is £10.00 for adults, £9.00 for seniors and students, and £5.00 for children. Tours start daily at 1000 (Sundays arrangement only) by the tree in front of the West End of the Minster and finish at 1400. By previous arrangement, visitors arriving on a train before 0930 may be met at the railway station for no extra charge. For information call (0190) 470–6643. A horse-and-carriage service operates outside the York Minster during good weather for those who are too tired or unable to walk. Hour-long, open-top bus tours depart from the railway station and travel different routes as well.

Among its points of interest, York Minster draws first choice. Built between 1220 and 1472, the Minster is England's largest Gothic cathedral. As the mother church of the Church of England's northern province, it is outranked in religious importance only by Canterbury Cathedral. A superb view can be had from the tower top… 275 steps above! No sight seeing is allowed on Sundays or other times of religious service.

Also be certain to visit the National Railway Museum on Leeman Road, a ten-minute walk from the York railway station. The Great Railway Show at the museum commemorates the Railway Age from the 1820s to the present day. Visitors walk down station platforms and, in imagination, become passengers on an Edwardian Express or on a boat train to Paris. The museum's National Railway Collection ranges from a lock of Robert Stephenson's hair to the splendor of the Royal Train.

The new Road Train, recommended to those visiting both York Minster and the National Railway Museum, allows visitors to put their feet up between the two sites.

York has one of the most interesting folk museums in the world, the Castle Museum. Famous streets of York have been reconstructed to depict the daily life and occupations of various periods from Tudor to Edwardian times. The museum also contains an eighteenth-century water mill that operates throughout the summer. Other sections are devoted to Yorkshire crafts, costumes, and military history; the Tea Room has 1960s decor and style of music. Whoa, man! Flashback!

While walking, you'll find the narrow, winding streets of York the most fascinating of all the city's attractions. The streets developed from the original Roman street plans. In turn, each century added a bit more color—and perhaps confusion. The Vikings left their mark in the use of street names ending in "gate," such as Stonegate and Petergate. The medieval citizens following the Vikings gave York its winding streets. One of these streets, The Shambles, is reputed to be one of the best-preserved medieval streets in Europe. Originally the street was crammed with butcher shops in half-timbered overhanging buildings. The east-west line of the street kept the meat in cool shade for most of the day and now houses an interesting assortment of stores and bookshops, where the meat hooks still hang.

Scotland

Internet: http://www.scotland.gov.uk
http://www.holiday.scotland.net

"The pipes, the pipes are calling . . . " They are calling you to Scotland, a country where there is much more to it than first meets the eye. Come to Scotland with an open mind, a keen eye, and a sense of adventure. It is a land of contrasts—friendly, bustling towns and cities but with easy escape to solitude. It has some of the least populated parts of Europe and yet one of the largest arts festivals.

Scotland forms the northern part of the island of Great Britain and is divided into three main regions: the Southern Uplands, the Midland Valley, and the Highlands. Filled with patriotic pride, many Scots consider themselves to be the "true Brits." With more than 5,000 years of history, they predate their Anglo-Saxon cousins by several centuries. You can visit ancient towns that were built before the pyramids of Egypt.

Although Scotland has been part of the U.K. since the formal Act of Union in 1707, it still issues its own banknotes and maintains its own legal and educational systems as well as its own culture and traditions. From bagpipes and kilts to fine Scotch whiskey and that mysterious food known as haggis, Scotland is unique.

Scotland has produced some of the world's most talented people. Alexander Graham Bell, inventor of the telephone, was originally from Scotland, as is the famous actor Sean Connery, best known for his role as James Bond in 007 movies. Robert Burns, from Ayr, wrote "Auld Lang Syne," and John Paul Jones, who established the U.S. Navy, was born in Dumfriesshire. Other famous Scots include Robert Lewis Stevenson, author of *Kidnapped* and *Treasure Island;* and Sir Arthur Conan Doyle, creator of the detective Sherlock Holmes.

Rail Travel in Scotland

What better way to visit a country famous for its hospitality, scenery and history than by train? ScotRail provides a variety of ways to discover Scotland. Any BritRail Pass is valid, of course, in Scotland. ScotRail, however, also has rail passes available for travel only in Scotland.

The Freedom of Scotland Travelpass is valid for travel any four days within an eight-day period, any eight days within a fifteen-day period, and any twelve days within in a fifteen-day period. See the Appendix for current prices, or in North America, call toll-free (800) 722–7151 to order or for more information.

The Travelpass includes unlimited standard-class rail travel on all ScotRail and Strathclyde Passenger Transport services and all scheduled Great North Eastern Railway and Virgin Trains operating wholly within Scotland, including Carlisle and Berwick-upon-Tweed. The pass also includes all Caledonian MacBryne and Strathclyde ferry services within Scotland, a 33 percent discount on P&O Ferries on the Scabster to Stromness (Orkney) route and a 20 percent discount on the Aberdeen–Orkney–Shetland routes (including between Orkney and Shetland). The discounts are available on reclining-seat fares only and do not apply to cabins. Some bus services between cities and all Glasgow Underground services are also included.

ScotRail Short Breaks will help you discover Scotland's breathtaking beauty, hospitality, and some of the world's most romantic rail journeys on its famous railway lines, including the West Highland Line, the Kyle Line, and the North Line. Call ScotRail for the most current listings—telephone numbers are listed below.

We have selected the two Base Cities of Edinburgh, Scotland's capital, and Glasgow, Scotland's largest city. The day excursions listed can be visited from either base city; our rail schedules include departures from both Edinburgh and Glasgow. So sit back, relax, and enjoy the ride.

ScotRail, Brunel House, 36 Station Road, Chinnor, Oxfordshire, OX9 4GW.

International telephone: (1844) 353–077; in the U.K.: (0870) 161–0161; *Fax:* (0184) 435–2492.

Internet: http://www.scotrail.co.uk

E-mail: meenanf.scotrail@ems.rail.co.uk

Base City . . .

Edinburgh

Internet: http://www.edinburgh.org

"This profusion of eccentricities, this dream in masonry and living rock is not a drop-scene in a theater, but a city in a world of everyday reality!"

—Robert Louis Stevenson

There is an understandable feeling of rocklike perpetuity enveloping Edinburgh. Formed by volcanic heat, scoured and shaped by ice-age glaciers in a valley punctuating its skyline with upward-thrusting crags, the setting of Scotland's capital city of Edinburgh is nothing short of dramatic.

Edinburgh's exact origins are lost in antiquity. Although dissenting opinions exist, it seems that a primitive fortress was established around A.D. 452 by the Picts on the sloping ground leading from the great Castle Rock on which Edinburgh Castle stands today. There have been fortresses on Castle Rock since that time, each in turn razed by a challenger and then rebuilt only to be razed again. By the eleventh century, however, events around Edinburgh began to calm down and the town got on with the task of becoming civilized and prosperous. From its earliest days, Edinburgh offered a stern, almost aloof countenance to the world and inspired great individuals to great achievements.

Edinburgh is actually two cities. The Old Town, built on a rocky ledge running from Edinburgh Castle to the Royal Palace of Holyroodhouse, is steeped in ancient history. It huddles on high ground in typical medieval fear of attack. The New Town, formed on the lower side of Nor' Loch, a lake created from a swamp and eventually drained in 1816, spreads serenely in a succession of streets and avenues, reflecting the optimism of later centuries. The New Town was conceived in 1767 when the Scottish Parliament approved an extension of the city and the Town Council lost no time in proceeding with the work. The city planning that followed made possible Edinburgh's present wide streets and spacious squares.

The two cities within a city further reflect two great attributes: on the one hand Edinburgh's reserved exterior, and on the other its ability to express great warmth and even, on occasion, a high degree of gaiety. Edinburgh has been called one of the most attractive capital cities in the world. As Oliver Wendell Holmes aptly put it, "Edinburgh is a city of incomparable loveliness."

From the beauty of its setting, enhanced by its architecture, to the turbulence of its history and the stalward qualities of its citizens, Edinburgh is a city of inexhaustible delight. Edinburgh Castle, the Palace of Holyroodhouse, the Royal Mile, and Princes Street await you. Welcome to Scotland's capital.

Arriving by Air

Though Edinburgh has its own international airport, direct service to or from North America is not available. Travelers arriving in Britain via London (Gatwick or Heathrow) or Manchester airports can either take a connecting flight to Edinburgh or the train. International air service is provided to Edinburgh from most European cities.

Glasgow is a convenient port of entry for visitors arriving in Scotland from overseas. Scotland's international airport is located 10 miles west of Glasgow. The airport is situated in an area that is relatively fog-free during most of the year, for the wind moving across the Irish Sea has few natural obstructions to interrupt its flow. Prestwick Airport (29 miles southwest of Glasgow), which for years served as the international airport for the area, is the most fog-free airport on the British Isles.

Arriving by Train

Waverley Station is the main train station in Edinburgh. Some InterCity trains from London go on to Aberdeen after a brief station stop in Edinburgh. If you are aboard one of these trains, be prepared to "set down" in the Waverley Station as quickly as possible following your arrival. Edinburgh's other station, Haymarket, is where all trains halt en route to Glasgow or Aberdeen. Trains arriving from England via Newcastle and York, however, bypass Haymarket Station.

Waverley Station in Edinburgh appears to be completely immersed in an open ravine. The area was once a swamp that was converted into a lake as a northern defense for Edinburgh Castle during the reign of King James II (1437–1460). The lake was drained in 1816 to become the site of the Princes Street Gardens which separate the Old Town and New Town in Edinburgh.

In 1847, rail lines were laid through the middle of the Princes Street Gardens to the east end, where Waverley Station was constructed. The tracks are now all but concealed by landscaping. Today's Waverley Station complex is the second largest in Britain.

Waverley Station has twenty-one tracks strewn about in a labyrinth of steps and passageways that could easily drive a laboratory rat berserk. But plenty of signs and the helpful presence of Edinburghers (who appear to be specially trained to assist visitors) will help you put it all together.

Basically there are three accesses to Waverley Station. The first is a set of rather steep steps, the Waverley Steps, connecting the north side of the station (the trackage runs east and west) with Princes Street, the city's main artery. The second and third approaches are ramps leading from the main floor of the station to the Waverley Bridge, which runs between the Old Town and New Town. Both ramps have pedestrian walkways. The northern ramp serves incoming vehicles; the one to the south is for outgoing vehicles.

Tracks 12 to 18 form the backbone, or center, of the Waverley Station. At the entrance to these tracks is a digital-display bulletin board for train arrivals, departures, and special announcements. If your train is departing from tracks other than 12 to 18, ask the railroad personnel at the ticket barriers for directions; otherwise, you may end up in some dark corner.

Pay special attention to multiple train departures from the same track. A line of coaches on a single train track can actually be two trains departing for two separate destinations. They are announced with red-bannered front train or rear train signs. It pays to ask questions—one advantage you have over the lab rat!

The Rail Travel Centre (train information center) is located in the waiting room area of the station. It is open 0700-2300 daily. Covered by a huge glass dome, the waiting area also contains digital arrival/departure information and a series of facilities, including rest rooms, a magazine kiosk, and eateries. The principal entrance to this area is located across the main-station concourse from the stub ends of tracks 16 and 17. Train reservations may be made at any of the counters.

Money exchange (Bureau de Change) is available from the Edinburgh & Scotland Information Centre.

Hotel accommodations are provided by the Edinburgh & Scotland Information Centre.

The Balmoral Hotel at Waverley Station is a five-star hotel that has been a landmark for Waverley Station, and the city of Edinburgh, since 1902 when it was known as the North British Hotel. The Balmoral is located between the station and Princes Street. Topped by a mammoth 200-foot Gothic clock tower, the hotel serves as a transition between the hustle of commerce on Princes Street and the bustle of the passengers arriving at and departing from the station. Erected during the Age of Steam, the hotel's spacious foyer and well-appointed lounges provides a brief but necessary respite for weary travelers.

Victorian throughout, the hotel has undergone a £23 million restoration. Undoubtedly, the Balmoral is one of Edinburgh's most familiar and most elegant landmarks, commanding an important position at the east end of Princes Street.

Edinburgh and Scotland Information Centre, 3 Princes Street EH2 2QP; *Tel:* (0131) 557–1700; *Fax:* (0131) 473–3881. *Hours:* July and August 0900–2000 Monday-Saturday, 1000–2000 Sunday; May, June, and September 0900–1900 Monday-Saturday, 1100–1900 Sunday. April and October 0900–1800 Monday-Saturday, 1100–1800 Sunday. November-March 0900–1800 Monday–Saturday, closed Sunday.

The center is located on the rooftop of Waverley Station beyond the north end of Waverley Bridge at the corner of Waverley Bridge and Princes Streets. Use the pedestrian ramp on the north side of the station, turning right as you reach the Waverley Bridge level. There are several tourist information signs to help guide the way.

Many of the facilities sought by incoming passengers—such as banking, city information, and hotel accommodations—may be found in the Edinburgh and Scotland Information Centre. The first section has information on Edinburgh and all of Scotland. Go straight ahead as you enter for self-service; go to the right for counter service. For entertainment information, proceed through the shopping section, where Scottish books, maps, and posters are available at the ticket desk; telephone (0131) 558–1072.

Hotel accommodations may be made here. The reservation fee is £3 per booking. Money exchange is available here as well.

Getting Around in Edinburgh

Two bus departure points serve the area surrounding the Waverley Street rail station. The first, at Waverley Bridge, is located immediately up the ramps leading out of the rail station. This departure point serves the city bus system and the sightseeing buses. Coach service for the Glasgow Airport and other main destinations utilizes the bus terminal on St. Andrew Square. To reach it, cross Princes Street where it intersects with Waverley Bridge. Then, walk north one block to St. Andrew Square.

Guide Friday Tourism Centre, Platform 1, Waverley Railway Station; *Tel:* (0131) 556–2244; *Fax:* (0131) 557–4083

E-mail: guidefriday@bt.co.uk

For bus tours of Edinburgh, go to the tourist information office and its selection of bus tour brochures. We have found that the Guide Friday bus tour of the city is complete and the commentary of their guides accurate and amusing. You can readily recognize the green and cream-colored open-top double-decker buses. You can get on and off at your leisure. Tours depart a minimum of every fifteen minutes and include Edinburgh Castle, Palace of Holyroodhouse, Princes Street, the Royal Mile, and New Town. Purchase your tickets from the bus driver, the Guide Friday Tourism Centre at Platform 1 in Waverley Station, or from the Tourist Information Centre. Fares: £7.50 adults, £6 students/seniors, £2.50 children.

Guided walking tours (Robin's Walking Tours) depart daily from outside the tourist information center. There are several to choose from: The Grand Tour of the City departs at 1000, then explore the Royal Mile at 1100, and at 1900 see Ghosts and Witches.

Mercat Tours, Mercat Cross, Royal Mile; *Tel* and *Fax:* (0131) 661–4541

Explore where the history of the old underground city meets the supernatural in the **Mary Kings Close** tour, presented by Mercat Tours and the City of Edinburgh. Dramatic guides, who are graduate historians, will lead you from the Mercat Cross, where the "entertainment" of the ages occurred (criminals were hung, flogged, tortured, and dismembered) down through the deserted, dark, and ghostly places of Old Town Edinburgh. Paranormal activity is logged on record, so don't be surprised if you happen to see or feel something from beyond. Tours depart daily, except Sunday, from 1030 through 2130. They take about ninety minutes and cost £5; group discounts are offered. Buffet, refreshment, and specialty combination tours are also available. We heard of one brave group actually spending the night in one of the bridge caverns among the spirits. Be sure to ask the guide about the most haunted pub in Edinburgh; you may need a stiff one after this tour.

Witchery Tours, 352 Castlehill, The Royal Mile, EH1 2NF; *Tel:* (0131) 225–6745; *Fax:* (0131) 220–2086

Internet: http://www.clan.com/edinburgh/witchery

E-mail: lyal@witcherytours/demon.co.uk

The Witchery Tours brochure states, "We are not for the faint-hearted." You are requested to dress appropriately for the weather and wear comfortable shoes. For some ghastly times blending history with humor and facts with fables, try the Ghosts & Gore Tour departing at 1900 and 2000 nightly from May through August. Duration is 1½ hours. Cost: £7 adults; £4 children.

The Murder & Mystery Tour is scheduled at 2100 and 2200 throughout the year, although the tour departure times may vary. Duration of the tour is 1¼ hours. Cost: £7 per person. Both tours include a copy of the *Witchery Tales* book. If you're up to braving the ghosts and goblins, the murders and mysteries, book your tickets in advance and meet your guide outside the Witchery Restaurant, Castlehill, Royal Mile (by Edinburgh Castle). We hope you return.

Enticing Edinburgh

Magnificent Edinburgh Castle is the national symbol of Scotland and one of its top attractions. The castle radiantly crowns an ancient volcanic mount above Edinburgh proper. Guided tours of Edinburgh Castle are available, or you can pick up a free headset and tour at your own pace. Following numbered plaques throughout the castle, your headset will provide you with its fascinating story. Stand in the oldest building in Edinburgh, St. Margaret's Chapel, just as the Queen of Scotland did more than 900 years ago. A beautiful stained-glass memorial to Sir William Wallace faces the altar. You can also see the Crown Jewels of Scotland, the Scottish National War Memorial, and the Stone of Destiny.

The castle is still garrisoned and every day (except Sunday) a cannon is fired at 1300. It makes a rather dramatic time check for unsuspecting visitors who end up doing the "One O'clock Jump."

During the annual Edinburgh Military Tattoo, the castle provides a most provocative backdrop for this dazzling celebration of music, theater, dance, and traditional Scottish pipes and pipers, drums and drummers marching on the castle esplanade. Undoubtedly, one of the world's greatest shows, each tattoo has overseas contingents as well as traditional Scottish, but it always closes with the appearance of the lone piper on the castle battlements, a very touching moment.

Originated in the seventeenth and eighteenth centuries in the Low Countries, "tattoo" was derived from the cry of the innkeepers at closing time. Local regiments would then march through the street playing fife and drums to signal a return to quarters, and the shout would go up *"Doe den tap toe"* (turn off the taps). This became the basis for many marvelous massed military bands performances given around the globe, with the Edinburgh Military Tattoo being the leader.

The Tattoo occurs every August; the1999 Edinburgh Tattoo will be held August 6–28. Contact the Edinburgh Military Tattoo Box Office, 32 Market Street, Edinburgh EH1 1QB; *Tel:* (0131) 225–1188; *Fax:* (0131) 225–8627. The Tattoo also has a marvelous Internet site at http://www.edintattoo.co.uk, packed full of history, wonderful descriptions, and photos, plus ordering information. Tickets range from £8.50 to £20. Please order well in advance as this is an extremely popular event worldwide.

Amid the contrasting charms of its Old Town and New Town, Edinburgh takes its place among an elite group of European cities conspicuous for their romance and physical attributes. As more and more enclosures were built during the post-medieval period, the term "close" came into existence in old Edinburgh to describe the narrow passageways giving access or right-of-way to the buildings in the rear of others. There are well over one hundred closes in Old Town, many of which have brass tablets at their entrances to explain their historical significance.

There are many aspects of Edinburgh to see on conducted tours, but the city's real beauty is best seen by exploring it on foot at your own pace. Walk the Royal Mile in Old Town from Edinburgh Castle to the Palace of Holyroodhouse. En route, you'll pass a fantastic assembly of picturesque old buildings, such as Brodie's Close, the John Knox House, the Cannonball House, Anchor Close, and the Canongate Tolbooth.

Brodie's Close housed Deacon Brodie, a respectable town councillor by day and a burglar by night. Brodie's lifestyle supposedly provided the basis for Robert Louis Stevenson's *Dr. Jekyll and Mr. Hyde.* The John Knox

House dates from the sixteenth century. It's traditionally connected with both John Mossman, Keeper of the Royal Mint to Mary, Queen of Scots, and John Knox, Scotland's religious reformer. A brief video presentation amid original timber-framed galleries and oak paneling will take you back to the sixteenth century. The John Knox House is located at the halfway mark of the Royal Mile in the Netherbow. Admission is £1.75.

The Cannonball House, dating from 1630, got its name from a cannonball lodged in its gable, ostensibly fired from the castle by an errant cannoneer during the blockade of 1745. Anchor Close is the site where the first edition of the *Encyclopedia Britannica* was printed as well as the Edinburgh edition of Robert Burns's poems. Reportedly, Burns himself read the proofs on the premises. Last renovated in 1591, the Canongate Tolbooth has been used as the Town Council House and a prison for the ancient village of Canongate, now incorporated into the city of Edinburgh. The Canongate Tolbooth now houses the People's Story Museum, which relates the life and work of ordinary people in Edinburgh from the late eighteenth century to the present.

Although the Palace of Holyroodhouse originated as a guest house for the Abbey of Holyrood, most of the palace we see today was built for Charles II in 1671. The most famous figure associated with the palace, however, was Mary, Queen of Scots, who spent six years of her tragic reign there. On the palace grounds, you can view Queen Mary's Bath House where, according to today's Scottish tour guides, she bathed daily. The guides also explain that her cousin, Queen Elizabeth I, bathed once a month—whether she needed it or not.

The Royal Mile was for many centuries the center of Edinburgh life. Its citizens lived and conducted their affairs on this busy, crowded street. At the entrance to the Palace of Holyroodhouse, you will find a line of the letter "S" embedded in the pavement. Until 1880, it marked the limits of sanctuary extended by Holyrood Abbey. It is said that debtors were often seen running toward the line with creditors in hot pursuit and bystanders wagering on the outcome.

Greyfriars Bobby. On Candlemaker Row, a short distance from Edinburgh's Royal Mile, stands a statue in tribute to a small dog's affection and fidelity to his master. In 1858, a wee Skye terrier followed the remains of his master, Auld Jock, to Greyfriars churchyard, where the dog lingered and slept on his master's grave for fourteen years until his death in 1872.

People tried to take Bobby away. They even found a home for him in the country. Still, Bobby returned to the churchyard, where friends began bringing food to sustain him during his vigil. The story of Greyfriars Bobby spread throughout Edinburgh, and soon Bobby's tale of devotion reached Queen Victoria in London. She sent a special envoy, Lady Burdett-Coutts, to investigate this unusual story.

Bobby, in the meantime, had made friends with children in a nearby orphanage. The terrier brought joy and love to the children, particularly to Tammy, a crippled boy with whom Bobby would play by the hour. Bobby lived his own life, however, and returned nightly to his master's grave—at first secretly, for the presence of a dog in a churchyard was unthinkable in those times. But as Bobby won hearts, he gained privileges, too. He even won the heart of the Lord Provost of Edinburgh, who had a collar made for the dog in 1867 and paid Bobby's licensing fee. (The collar can be seen today in the Canongate on the Royal Mile.)

Bobby never went to London to see the queen, but royal annals reflect that the queen actually was planning to pay him a visit at Greyfriars. Bobby died, however, before that honor became a reality.

The dog's body was buried alongside that of his master. Although Bobby is no longer visible, his presence is felt so strongly by the residents of the area that they frankly admit to opening their doors briefly before retiring at night, just in case. Perhaps when the door to heaven is opened for them, they will see Bobby again, running on the green pastures at the heels of his master, beside the still waters.

Bobby's statue stands close to the iron gates of Greyfriars churchyard, where Auld Jock and his faithful dog are interred. The story of Greyfriars Bobby was filmed by Walt Disney. We think it's worth your while to visit Greyfriars, just as we do each time we return to Edinburgh.

Shopping in Edinburgh. The city of Edinburgh is well known for its fine boutiques, shops, and department stores. You can still find bargains in the famous Harris tweeds, Fair Isle sweaters, and tartan plaids. Princes Street is lined with shops displaying a variety of Scottish wares, from argyles and bagpipes to whiskey. And when you run out of stores and shops to visit on Princes Street, turn north 2 blocks to George Street and continue your shopping there. (You may need to stop by the bank on the way.)

Shoppers' havens on Princes Street include Jenners, the largest and oldest independently owned department store in the world, and C & A, both opposite the Scott Monument in the Waverley Street Station area. If you've never been in a store 180 years old, try Romanes & Paterson, Ltd., at 62

Princes Street. You will find traditional Scottish tweed, exquisite Edinburgh crystal, Caithness glass, knitwear from the borders, and, of course, tartans.

Still not tired of shopping? The Scotch House nearby contains more than 300 tartans available by the meter, along with Shetland knitwear and original gifts. If you know a wee one, check out Hop Scotch, The Scotch House's special department for children.

Food, foam, and fun. With all that shopping, you may be ready for a snack and a libation. You don't have far to go—between and parallel to Princes Street and George Street is Rose Street, which probably has more convivial pubs to the meter than any other street in the world. In fact, Edinburgh was voted Britain's "Best City for Pubs." You'll have no problem finding food, foaming pints, and fun at more than 700 pubs ranging from traditional neighborhood bars to chic wine stubes.

For a real taste of Scotland, dine at Jacksons Restaurant, 209/213 High Street, The Royal Mile; *Tel:* (0131) 225–1793. It's located by Jackson's Close in a 300-year-old building that was formerly a stable. Traditional Scottish fare such as salmon, lamb, venison, and even haggis is served with the lighter touch of more modern cooking from Head Chef Andrew Smith. Manager John Anderson has graciously agreed to provide a free bottle of house wine per table to readers of *Britain by BritRail*—just show him this page in the book. To your health!

Day Excursions

A baker's dozen—thirteen exciting day excursions—have been selected for our readers. All were chosen so that those who prefer staying in Glasgow rather than in Edinburgh can enjoy them as well.

Scotland is known as "the land that likes to be visited." To ensure that your opportunity to visit this marvelous country by rail includes seeing as many of its features as possible, we have divided the selected day excursions into Scotland's four geographic areas: the east coast, central region, west coast, and Highlands.

East Coast. Along the east coast of Scotland, starting at the harbor of Dunbar near the English border, we then swing north from Edinburgh through Dundee, Montrose, and Aberdeen—not overlooking a stop en route at the golf capital of the world, St. Andrews.

Central Region. In the central part of the country, we have selected excursions to two of Scotland's most historic cities—Perth and Stirling—plus a visit to Andrew Carnegie's birthplace, Dunfermline, and a visit to Linlithgow to view the palace where Mary, Queen of Scots was born.

West Coast. For our forays to the western coast, we delve deep into the heart of Robert Burns's country by a visit to Ayr, the poet's favorite town. Further south, we call at Stranraer, the gateway to the Irish Sea and the Emerald Isle.

Highlands. North in the Highlands, Inverness serves as a gateway to explorations of Loch Ness, with its legendary monster, "Nessie," and as a base city for a dash to the west to Kyle of Lochalsh and the Isle of Skye.

Day Excursion to

Aberdeen
THE GRANITE CITY

Depart from Waverley Station

Distance by train: 131 miles (211 km)

Average train time: 2 hours, 30 minutes

Train information and InterCity services: (034) 548–4950

Aberdeen Tourist Information Centre: St. Nicholas House, Broad Street AB1 1RJ; *Tel:* (0122) 463–2727; *Fax:* (0122) 484–8805

Hours: Open daily throughout the year except on Sundays from October through May. Open Monday through Friday 0900–1700 and Saturday 1000–1400; in June and September, Monday through Saturday 0900–1700 and Sunday 1000–1600; in July and August, Monday through Friday 0900–1900, Saturday 0900–1700 and Sunday 1000–1400. On public and local holidays, with the exception of Christmas and New Year's Day, the center is normally open 0900–1700.

The main tourist information center is in St. Nicholas House on Broad Street. When leaving the station (there also is a center in the rail station), turn right onto Guild Street and walk until you arrive at Market Street, where the docks come into view. A left turn onto Market Street followed by a right turn onto Union Street will keep you on course (mind the shops!) until you spy Aberdeen's Town House at the head of Broad Street leading to your left. The center is a short distance up Broad Street on the left-hand side, opposite Marischal College and its award-winning Museum of Human History.

Since the discovery of oil in the North Sea, Aberdeen has earned the title of "Europe's offshore oil capital." The city, however, has not been spoiled by its industry. Oil does not come ashore in Aberdeen; moreover, only occasionally can an oil rig be seen on the horizon, under tow to a new location or at anchor awaiting a new contract.

The development of North Sea oil plus the gathering strength of northeast Scotland's agriculture, fishing, and manufacturing industries have combined to give Aberdeen the highest growth rate of any city in Great Britain. Therefore, you will find Aberdeen a city of many moods. It is steeped in history. It is an ancient university town and a thriving seaport as well. It has grown very cosmopolitan, yet it remains old in grace. Above all else, the Aberdonians always have time—time to help, time to be interested, and time to talk.

Today, with more than two million roses, eleven million daffodils, and three million crocuses, Aberdeen is the "Flower of Scotland." Parks, gardens, and floral displays please every visitor, with the most popular being the Winter Gardens at the Duthie Park.

Aberdeen lies between the rivers Dee and Don with 2 miles of golden sand connecting them. But don't think of Aberdeen merely as a large city with a beach. Union Street bisects the city and provides a mile-long shopping center lined with excellent stores sure to satisfy every shopper.

Standing like a sentinel, the gleaming white Girdleness Lighthouse guarding Aberdeen's harbor will be the first welcoming sign you'll see in Scotland's third largest city. It becomes visible on the right as the train curves away to the left from Nigg Bay to cross the River Dee, then glides to a halt in Aberdeen's rail station.

The port of Aberdeen is the jumping-off place for adventurers bound for the Orkney Islands and Shetland Islands to the north. Don't be surprised if you see a cruise ship or two in Aberdeen's harbor. Aberdeen has attracted the cruise ships by constructing a passenger landing stage in its Victoria Dock area. It appears that everyone wants to visit Europe's offshore capital, Aberdeen.

Aberdeen maintains tourist information in the form of a well-stocked literature stand alongside the Travel Centre information counter in the rail station. There's also a twenty-four-hour "View Data" service—a very user-friendly computerized inquiry unit.

The Aberdeen information center has a wide variety of booklets, leaflets, and posters of Aberdeen and the surrounding area. Also available are the publications of the Scottish Tourist Board covering the entire country. The center is divided into three operating sections: inquiries, accommodations, and tickets. Walking-tour and bus-tour information is also available here. You may wish to ask them about the Aberdeen Attractions Card before venturing off.

Clustered around the tourist information center on Broad Street, only a short walk away, are many of Aberdeen's places of interest. In the restored Provost Skene's House on Broad Street, the oldest domestic dwelling in Aberdeen, dating from 1545, you will find rooms furnished in styles covering different periods in Aberdeen's history. After exploring the grandeur of the rooms, traverse upward to the top floor, where displays of Scottish social and archaeological history are to be found. The Costume Gallery, newly added in 1998, has a marvelous collection of fascinating costumes from over the ages. Admission is £2.50 for adults; a £6.00 family ticket is available.

The Scottish Museum of the Year, Aberdeen's Maritime Museum is housed in Provost Ross's House overlooking one of Britain's busiest harbors. Here, attractive displays not only depict Aberdeen's maritime heritage of fishing, shipbuilding, and trade, but also its offshore oil industry. Visitors can experience life onboard a working scale model of an oil rig, or see the nineteenth-century lens assembly from the Rattray Head Lighthouse, plus much more. Admission is £3.50 per adult; £10.00 per family ticket; under age five is free.

Provost Ross's House, a restored sixteenth-century dwelling, also houses a visitor's center featuring audiovisual displays of National Trust for Scotland properties, a fascinating collection of more than 100 properties representing a rich variety of castles, gardens, scenic areas, islands, and historic sights.

The new Tolbooth Museum, housed in the seventeenth-century prison at Castlegate, explores the history of crime, punishment, and incarceration of witches, debtors, and other lawbreakers (plus some of their ingenious escapes). Originally the city seat of government, it also shows the evolution of local power, from the sixteenth-century to the present day. Admission is £2.50 for adults; £6.00 for a family ticket. Teacher packs are available for curriculum assistance for ages five to fourteen.

Winston Churchill called the British Army's Gordon Highlanders "the finest regiment in the world." Therefore, an absolute must-see is the Gordon Highlanders Museum on Viewfield Road, which contains treasures spanning more than two centuries. The museum is open March 31

Edinburgh–Aberdeen

DEPART WAVERLEY STATION	ARRIVE ABERDEEN STATION	NOTES
0810	1045	M–Sa
0855	1126	Su (1)
0905	1131	M–Sa
1025	1259	M–Sa
1055	1326	Su
1110	1340	M–Sa
1210	1442	M–Sa
1240	1509	Su

DEPART ABERDEEN STATION	ARRIVE WAVERLEY STATION	NOTES
1420	1648	M–Sa
1455	1722	M–Sa
1510	1741	Su
1525	1809	M–Sa
1615	1849	M–Sa
1700	1926	Su
1715	1952	M–Sa
1815	2046	M–Sa
1900	2128	Su
1955	2228	M–Sa
2014	2300	Sa
2050	2320	Su
2114	2359	M–Sa
2120	2342	Su

through October 31, Tuesday through Saturday from 1030 to 1630 and Sunday from 1330 to 1630, and by appointment only from November 1 through March 30.

Aberdeen is not only a cultural center, but a family-friendly town as well. Those traveling with wee ones may find the award-winning Satrosphere to be phenomenally fascinating. This hands-on discovery place is located at 19 Justice Mill Lane and is the only one like it in Scotland where kids can explore science and technology first-hand. Admission helps fund a registered charity and is £3.00 for adults and £1.50 for children; *Tel:* (0122) 213–232.

The Baxters Visitors Centre is popular with any age. The Baxters have been making quality jams, marmalades, soups, and sauces from the finest ingredients for the upper crust for nearly 130 years. Take a factory tour, then stop by the Spey Restaurant for a famous Fochabers Pancake. Before leaving be sure to shop in the "Best of Scotland" to find wonderful gifts or visit the Cellar to take home some of the famous goodies for which the Baxters are so well known.

Just north of the city center is Old Aberdeen where you will find one of the oldest universities in Britain. Aberdeen University comprises Marischal College and King's College. Both are architecturally attractive yet totally different. Marischal College is one of the largest granite buildings in the world. It was founded in 1593 and united with King's College in 1860 to form the University of Aberdeen. King's College, in Old Aberdeen, was founded in 1495. The ivy-covered building with its distinctive crown tower has stood for centuries as a symbol of Aberdeen. The Zoology Museum offers a diverse look at the animal kingdom, with a special collection of Scottish birds. For quiet and peaceful walks visit the eleven-acre Cruickshank Botanic Garden on campus and the 400-year-old roses. Or take one of the many guided walks offered, such as the one that leads from Seaton Park to the Brig O'Balgownie across the River Don.

Day Excursion to

Ayr

BURNS' TAM O'SHANTER INN

Depart from Edinburgh Waverley Station

Distance by train: 88 miles (142 km)

Average train time: 1 hour, 30 minutes

Train information and InterCity services: (034) 548–4950

Ayr Tourist Information Centre: Burns House, Burns Statue Square, KA7 1UP; *Tel:* (0129) 228–8688; *Fax:* (0129) 226–9555

   Internet: www.ayrshire-arran.com

   E-mail: ayr@ayrshire-arran.com

   Hours: April–June and September, Monday through Saturday 0915–1700, Sunday 1100–1700 (Sunday hours apply over Easter weekend). July–August, Monday through Saturday, 0915–1800; Sunday 1000–1700. October–March, Monday through Saturday 0900–1700, closed Sunday.

   Depart the train station through the main exit and walk directly across the street to Burns Statue Square. The tourist information center is in Burns House directly across from the rail station.

What William Shakespeare is to England, Robert Burns is to Scotland. Ayr is the acknowledged center of the celebrated "Burns Country." The town is rich in the history of Scotland's bard. Many famous landmarks remain in Ayr today to tell the Burnsian stories.

The Tam o' Shanter Inn on High Street is where Tam began his celebrated ride. The Auld Brig (old bridge) that for 500 years was the only bridge in town still offers a delightful passage across the River Ayr. In a conspicuous location outside the Ayr train station, a statue of Robert Burns waits to greet travelers.

In Alloway, a pleasant southern suburb of Ayr, you will find the Burns National Heritage Park, where visual displays introduce you to the life of Robert Burns and acquaint you with locations in and around Ayr that you may later want to visit. A brief walk from the exhibit will bring you to Burns' Cottage, where the poet was born on January 25, 1759. More than 300,000 visitors pass through the park annually. The ruins of the Alloway Auld Kirk (old church) where Tam spied on dancing witches, also close to the center, were the inspiration for Burns's narrative poem "Tam o' Shanter." Visitors may watch an audiovisual reenactment of the epic tale.

It was from the ruins of the Auld Kirk that witches pursued Tam, but he escaped over the Auld Brig o'Doon–the bridge over the River Doon–and

Edinburgh–Ayr

All schedules require a change of station in Glasgow; either from Queen Street to Central or the reverse. Only a 5–10 minute walk; such changes can be accomplished either by taxi, underground rail, or perhaps by bus.

DEPART WAVERLEY STATION	ARRIVE AYR STATION	NOTES
0700	0928	M–Sa
0730	0952	M–Sa
0800	1026	M–Sa
0830	1052 (1057 Su)	Daily
0900	1126	M–Sa
0930	1152 (1157 Su)	Daily

M–Sa service continues after 0930 every half hour until 2200; Su service continues after 0930 at hourly intervals until 1730.

DEPART AYR STATION	ARRIVE WAVERLEY STATION	NOTES
1413	1620	M–Sa
1443	1650 (1702 Su)	Daily
1513	1720	M–Sa
1543	1750 (1802 Su)	Daily
1613	1820	M–Sa

M–Sa service continues after 1613 at half-hour intervals until 2213; Su service continues after 1543 at hourly intervals until 2143.

eluded his pursuers, because according to legend witches were unable to cross running water. Maggie, the mare that Tam rode, was less fortunate: "Ae spring brought off her master hale,/But left behind her ain gray tail/The carlin caught her by the rump,/And left poor Maggie scarce a stump."

Ayr was a seaside resort long before the term was invented. Well-heeled Glasgow merchants came to Ayr for short vacations, liked what they saw, and built houses there. In addition to providing Scottish gentry with suburban abodes, Ayr also is a market center, for good measure. With all these assets, Ayr is assured of retaining its prosperous, bustling atmosphere even after the summer visitors have gone.

Literature on Ayr, the district surrounding it, and Scotland's famous poet, Robert Burns (who traveled extensively around Ayrshire) abounds by the pound in the information center. You will want to collect informative booklets such as the Ayrshire and Arran Tourist Board's free *Essential Guide to Ayrshire and Arran*. You can visit many places that have been developed to tell the story of Burns and his lifetime. If you are interested in exploring or taking a bus around "Burns Country," you should gather all the details associated with the poet from the information center.

With more than 2 miles of golden, sandy beach, Ayr gets more than its fair share of the summer Scottish sun. Golf, bowling, and tennis are among the many sports activities that can be enjoyed there. The town has three golf courses, forming part of the famous 15-mile stretch of "golfing coast" you'll see from the train approaching Ayr. All the traditional seaside amusements can be enjoyed in Ayr, as well as horse racing, held at Scotland's premier Ayr Racecourse throughout the year.

Away from the beaches, there are many beautiful parks and gardens, notably Belleisle, Craigie, and Rozelle. Rozelle is also the home of Ayr's Maclaurin Art Gallery and displays one of the very few Henry Moore sculptures to be seen in Scotland. Ayr's beauty has frequently brought it the coveted titles, "Britain's Floral Town" and "Scotland's Floral Town." Enjoy the Ayr Flower Show and Gardening Festival, second only to Chelsea's, if visiting the area in late August. If you delight in old houses, Ayr has many, including one that was built in 1470–twenty-two years before Columbus sailed to America!

Day Excursion to

Dunbar

"FORT ON THE POINT"

Depart from Edinburgh Waverley Station

Distance by train: 29 miles (46 km)
Average train time: 30 minutes
Train information and InterCity services: (034) 548–4950
Dunbar Tourist Information Centre: The Town House, 143 High Street; *Tel:* (0136) 886–3353
  Hours: Open during the summer 0900–2000 Monday through Saturday, 1100–1800 on Sunday. During the balance of the year, it is open Monday through Saturday 0900–1700, and closed Sunday.

The tourist information center is a short walk from the railway station. Station Road runs from the front of the station to where it crosses Countess Road and becomes Abbey Road. When you reach the general post office on your right, the thoroughfare has another name change to High Street and remains so until you reach the information center. Part of the Town House, incidentally, is a toll gate dating back to the seventeenth century, when a toll road between Edinburgh and Newcastle ran through Dunbar.

Put on your walking shoes—we're going to Dunbar. The town offers two wonderful walking opportunities: one through the historic center of Old Dunbar to appreciate the great and varied wealth of its traditional Scottish buildings, the other along the cliffs brooding over the North Sea in the John Muir Country Park. Those who like a slower pace can take in Dunbar's harbor area and watch fishermen and their customers on the quay buying and selling freshly caught fish as colorful fishing boats bob about on the tide. Further assurance of a pleasant outing for all is the presence of several public houses in the harbor area. Among them is the Volunteer Arms, which houses the Volunteer Bar and the Haven Lounge.

Dunbar is situated amid some of the most beautiful countryside and coastline in Scotland. There are few other places where it is possible to witness the full range of history of a Scottish east-coast fishing port and market center. Dunbar has always played an important part in Scotland's history. Due to its strategic location, the town has been a stronghold down through the centuries. Dunbar, Gaelic for "the fort on the point," had a castle fortress at least as early as A.D. 856. The remains of the castle stand on the promontory overlooking Dunbar's Victoria Harbor.

The Dunbar Castle was where Bothwell brought Mary, Queen of Scots, when he abducted her in 1567. That same year, the Scottish Parliament ordered that Dunbar Castle be demolished. When the Victoria Harbor was constructed in the nineteenth century, the channel leading into the harbor was cut through the rocky palisade where the ruins of the castle lay. The remains that you may inspect during your visit to Dunbar are only a fragment of the original great castle.

There are two harbors: the Old Harbor, extended by Oliver Cromwell, and Victoria Harbor. Construction on the old harbor began in 1655, and it was improved and extended in the eighteenth century. This harbor, now nearly deserted, still retains the old paving stones as well as a fisherman's barometer that was erected in 1856. As part of the redevelopment, the harbor areas have had cottage-type houses built since 1951 to the special

Edinburgh–Dunbar

DEPART WAVERLEY STATION	ARRIVE DUNBAR STATION	NOTES
0700	0720	M–Sa
0900	0922	M–F
0930	0950	Sa
1200	1220	Su
1400	1420	M–Sa
1630	1650	Su

and a few later, very infrequent, services

DEPART DUNBAR STATION	ARRIVE WAVERLEY STATION	NOTES
1304	1331	M–F
1335	1359	Sa
1502	1529	Su
1550	1617	Su
1655	1722	M–F
1717	1741	Sa
1752	1819	Su
2106	2131	Sa
2146	2213	M–F
2232	2259	Su

design of Sir Basil Spence, the architect of the new Coventry Cathedral. Perhaps the best evidence of Dunbar's beauty is the large number of visitors walking about simply admiring the scenery.

An interesting part of Victoria Harbor is the Lifeboat Museum, well worth a visit. Lifeboats out of Dunbar have saved more than 200 lives since beginning operation in 1808.

For the town tour we mentioned, go to the Dunbar Public Library and ask for a copy of *A Walk Around Historic Dunbar* (£2.50). This cliff-top trail is prominently marked on the previously mentioned street plan, plus on the local town map. The map is available at the tourist information office, as is other information on the town, including the two harbors.

If you brought your walking shoes, the place to use them is the John Muir Country Park, which begins at Dunbar harbor and extends to the

Ravensheugh sands to the west, and on the south it approaches the Firth of Forth. The cliff-top trail has controlled public beaches below. Throughout the summer, a park ranger is normally on duty and available to answer your questions and provide directions. You may join the ranger on a ramble along the cliff-top trail, but times and routes may vary; check with the tourist office. There are several horse-riding routes within the park as well.

If you are a golf nut and have not been able to obtain a tee time for the Old Course at St. Andrews, try the par-64 Winterfield Golf Course maintained by the town of Dunbar.

There is a bowling green on the right-hand side of the Station Road as you proceed toward town. We asked an old Scot, "How can such a green be so smooth and flat?" "It's easy," he explained, "you just plant the best of grass seed and then roll it for a few hundred years."

Day Excursion to

Dundee

CITY OF DISCOVERY

Depart from Edinburgh Waverley Station

Distance by train: 60 miles (96 km)
Average train time: 1 hour, 30 minutes
Train information and InterCity services: (034) 548–4950
Dundee Tourist Information Centre: 7–21 Castle Street, DD1 3AA; *Tel:* (0138) 252–7527; *Fax:* (0138) 252–7550
  Internet: http://www.angusanddundee.co.uk
  E-mail: arbicath@sol.co.uk
  Hours: Open Monday through Saturday 0900–1800, Sunday 1000–1600 during May through September. Closes one hour later during July and August. From October through April hours are Monday through Friday 0900–1700 and Saturday 1000–1600.
  Dundee's tourist information center is easy to find. From the rail station proceed across the pedestrian bridge, then follow Whitehall Street to the right until you come to Crichton Street. Turn left up this street until you reach the top. Turn right again and you have reached the City Square. The next street down to the right is Castle Street.

As your train approaches the city of Dundee, you will be able to witness a scene of railroading history—one of disaster and yet one of triumph. Following the station stop at Leuchars, where you detrain for St. Andrews, watch as the train passes through the local station of Wormit and on to the railway bridge crossing the Firth of Tay inbound to Dundee. The bridge, a double-track structure 11,653 feet long, was opened in 1887 and was considered at that time (as it is even now) to be a triumph of railroad engineering. Alongside the present bridge, you will see a series of old bridge piers. These once supported a single-track bridge that was swept away during a violent storm in 1879, along with a train and seventy-five of its passengers.

Turn your gaze to the east during the crossing of the great Firth (estuary) where the Tay River empties into the North Sea, and you will see a two-lane vehicular bridge 7,365 feet in length that was opened by Queen Elizabeth II in 1966. The River Tay and its rail and vehicular bridges are a vital part of Dundee's existence.

Dundee, the capital of Tayside, is Scotland's fourth largest city. It lies in a magnificent setting between the Sidlaw Hills and the banks of Britain's finest salmon river, the Tay.

Dundee was famous for generations as the city of "jute, jam, and journalism." Its prolific writers still abound, but jute is slowly sinking into the shadows of time as synthetic fibers take over in the cordage industry.

Dundee lies in the heart of Scotland, where the game of golf originated. The latest count reveals forty golf courses within one hour's drive of the city. Five actually lie within the city's district. In Dundee, the name of the game is golf, and its citizens have proven to the world that they can construct courses that can confound and confuse but always entertain. In Dundee and throughout the area, you also will note that the hospitality in the nineteenth holes throughout the region is second to none.

By the way, if your original day-excursion plans were for St. Andrews, but you failed to leave the train at Leuchars Station, you can still make it back to the golf capital by bus out of Dundee in less than one hour. Or, you can capitalize on your error and enjoy Dundee instead.

The cultural aspects of Dundee are enhanced by its McManus Galleries as well as the University Botanical Gardens. Camperdown Park and the Wildlife Centre are also stellar attractions for those who prefer outside activities. Among Dundee's many other attractions, one that we think will prove to be of interest to all, is the frigate *Unicorn*, Britain's oldest warship still afloat. The *Unicorn* is one of the world's four remaining frigates, those fast, lightly armed sailing ships of yesteryear now replaced by the destroyer class of naval vessel. Launched in 1824, she remained in naval service until

Edinburgh–Dundee

DEPART EDINBURGH WAVERLEY STATION	ARRIVE DUNDEE STATION	NOTES
0705	0827	M–Sa
0810	0926	M–Sa
0840	1006	M–Sa
0855	1010	Su (1)
0905	1019	M–Sa
0915	1050	Su
1025	1141	M–Sa
1055	1209	Su
1110	1226	M–Sa
1115	1250	Su
1210	1327	M–Sa
1240	1354	Su

DEPART DUNDEE STATION	ARRIVE EDINBURGH WAVERLEY STATION	NOTES
1427	1548	M–Sa
1501	1619	Su
1530 (1525 Su)	1648 (1659 Su)	Daily
1606	1722	M–Sa
1627	1741	Su
1645	1809	M–Sa
1727 (1725 Su)	1849 (1859 Su)	Daily
1812	1926	Su
1830	1952	M–Sa
1927 (1925 Su)	2046 (2059 Su)	Daily
1952	2125	M–Sa
2013	2128	Su
2109	2228	M–Sa
2127 (2125 Su)	2300 (2259 Su)	Daily
2227 (2228 Su)	2359 (2342 Su)	Daily

(1) Reservations required

1968. Ask at the information center for the *Unicorn* and *RRS Discovery* brochures and instructions to reach Victoria Dock and Discovery Quay.

Discovery Point is a state-of-the-art visitor's center portraying the history of Captain Scott's Royal Research Ship *Discovery* and her Antarctic voyages. Built in Dundee, Britain's first scientific research vessel set sail on her voyage to the Antarctic in 1901. You can visit *Discovery* berthed adjacent to the visitor's center.

Verdant Works, the town's newest visitor attraction, is a mill dating back to 1833. It celebrates Dundee's Jute Industry. The Scottish industrial heritage center offers a range of audiovisual displays, computer inter-activities, sound and light effects along with a café and gift shop.

Dundee's other points of interest include its old steeple, its four castles—Dudhope, Mains, Claypotts, and Broughty—and the Mercat Cross, which is moved about as the population center changes. The old steeple, standing at a height of 156 feet above the ground, dates from the fourteenth century. The steeple has withstood many storms, both natural and man-made. It was the site of the siege of 1651, when the town was invaded by Cromwell's army. The old steeple and all of the castle sites can be reached by public transport buses from the city bus station, a three-minute walk from the rail terminal.

The Mercat Cross, a replica of the old structure that was demolished in 1877, is currently located at the end of High Street. The original cross was erected in the Seagate area. About the beginning of the fifteenth century, however, the city's population began to increase, and the town began to spread westward. The Seagate was abandoned as the principal center of the city in favor of a more open space to the west, which is now High Street.

Dundee has a passion for plaques and has erected a number of them on buildings having historical associations. At latest count, twelve such monuments are located throughout the city. Of particular interest to visitors is the plaque marking the Greyfriars Monastery, which was granted to the city as a burial site by Mary, Queen of Scots, in 1564 and is now known as the Howff.

Day Excursion to

Dunfermline   ANDREW CARNEGIE'S BIRTHPLACE

Depart from Edinburgh Waverley Station

Distance by train: 17 miles (27 km)
Average train time: 32 minutes
Train information and InterCity services: (034) 548–4950
Dunfermline Tourist Information Centre: The Abbot House, Abbot Street; *Tel:* (0138)
372–0999
> *Hours:* Open from April through September 0900–1800 Monday through Saturday,
> 1030–1530 on Sundays. In October it is open on Saturday only.
> Cross St. Margaret's Drive in front of the station and walk down Comely Park.
> After crossing New Row, Priory Lane joins St. Margaret's Street. Bear right and
> continue on St. Margaret's to the intersection of Abbot Street, where you'll find the
> center to your left round the corner, beyond the newly opened Heritage Centre, the
> Abbot House.

Dunfermline was once the capital of Scotland and holds an important
position in Scottish history. The triangle of interest is the Dunfermline
Abbey, Pittencrieff Park, and Andrew Carnegie's birthplace. We suggest visiting the park first, due to its close proximity to the information center.
Stop at the abbey next, then the Carnegie cottage as you proceed back to
the rail station.

Arriving in Dunfermline by train, you can go to the center of the city
either by bus or by taxi. The walk is not too distant to the abbey and the
other attractions in town. It is a bit longer, however, than the stationmaster's advice, "Not more than a four-minute walk from here." Allow fifteen
minutes to cover the ground between the train station and the center of
the city. The tourist information center, the abbey, Pittencrieff, and
Carnegie's birthplace lie between these two points. Taxis queue at the front
of the station. About £2.00 will see you to the city center. The bus stop is
close to the station at an underpass on the left.

The tourist information center is located near the historic sixteenth-
century Abbot House, right next to the abbey in the Maygate. Of course,
Dunfermline's tourist information center specializes in the features of the
abbey and Carnegie's cottage, but you'll find that the staff is very helpful in
suggesting other things to do too.

The majestic spires of the Dunfermline Abbey dominate the town's
skyline. Within the abbey are the graves of seven Scottish kings, including

Edinburgh–Dunfermline

DEPART WAVERLEY STATION	ARRIVE DUNFERMLINE STATION	NOTES
0715	0745	M–Sa
0725	0755	M–Sa
0815	0845	M–Sa
0853	0923	M–Sa
0953 (0955 Su)	1023 (1027 Su)	Daily
1053	1123	M–Sa
1153 (1155 Su)	1223 (1227 Su)	Daily

DEPART DUNFERMLINE STATION	ARRIVE WAVERLEY STATION	NOTES
1339	1414	Su
1403	1436	M–Sa
1503	1536	M–Sa
1539	1614	Su
1603	1636	M–Sa
1703	1736	M–Sa
1739	1814	Su
1811	1846	M–Sa
1903	1936	M–Sa
1939	2014	Su
2020	2053	M–Sa
2120	2153	M–Sa
2139	2214	Su
2220	2253	M–Sa
2320	2353	M–Sa

the Tomb of Robert the Bruce. The abbey was founded by Scotland's King David in the twelfth century as a Benedictine monastery. In the course of time, through royal gifts and other extensive endowments, it became one of the most magnificent establishments in Scotland. In its time, the monastery has played host to a wide range of people, from Edward I of England to Oliver Cromwell.

The site of the Dunfermline Abbey has had continual Christian worship for about 1,500 years. In the fifth or sixth century, the first building on the site was the Culdee Church. Later it was rebuilt on a larger scale by Malcolm III, father of King David I, and was dedicated in 1072. Traces of both buildings are visible beneath gratings in the floor of the abbey's Old Nave.

From April through October the abbey church is open 0930–1700 daily and 1400–1700 on Sunday. Between November and March the abbey is closed, except for services. The abbey shop is open during the same hours as the church between April and October.

Another attraction is Pittencrieff Park, a lovely area with its flower gardens, music pavilion, aviary, and museum. Andrew Carnegie, the Scottish-American philanthropist who was born in a humble weaver's cottage in Dunfermline in 1835, generously donated Pittencrieff Park and gave funds for its upkeep. The park has become a popular place for visitors to pause and reflect on his donations of a library, public baths, and a theater in addition to the park. During your stroll through the park, swing aboard Old Pug and marvel at the advances that have been made in railroading since its engine's fires were banked for the last time.

Andrew Carnegie's birthplace is open to the public daily from April through October from 1100 to 1700 (Sunday opening, 1400). From November through March, it's open 1400–1600 daily, and attracts thousands of visitors every year. A statue of the steel millionaire stands in the center of Pittencrieff. It was erected by the citizens of Dunfermline in grateful appreciation of his many gifts to his native city. From his humble beginnings, Carnegie found his fortunes in the new world. Nevertheless, with his philanthropist attitude, he never forgot his hometown. At age thirty-three, with an annual income of $50,000, Carnegie said, "Beyond this never earn, make no effort to increase fortune, but spend the surplus each year for benevolent purposes." This he certainly did. His generosity in Dunfermline is administered today by a trust fund.

When you visit Dunfermline, you will be following in the footsteps of British royalty. Both Queen Victoria and Queen Mary visited there, and in 1972, Queen Elizabeth and Prince Philip were present to dedicate a Royal Pew in celebration of the abbey's 900th anniversary. You'll find, however, that Dunfermline extends a royal welcome to all of its visitors.

An "Out-and-Back" Excursion to

Inverness

HIGHLAND GATEWAY

Depart from Edinburgh Waverley Station

Distance by train: 176 miles (283 km)

Average train time: 3 hours, 40 minutes

Train information and InterCity services: (034) 548–4950

The Highlands of Scotland / Inverness Tourist Information Centre: Castle Wynd IV2 3BJ; Tel: (0146) 323–4353

> *Hours:* In July and August, the tourist information center is open Monday through Saturday 0900–2030 and Sunday 0930–1800. During the off-season, we suggest that you call the center for information and hours of operation.
>
> For the shortest route, turn left when leaving the train station and continue until you see Marks & Spencer. Cross the street and continue up Inglis Street, then turn right onto High Street, walking until you come to McDonald's. Cross the pedestrian walk, past the Town House and across Castle Wynd, where the tourist information center is located at the top of a short flight of stairs.

The position of Inverness at the eastern head of Loch Ness, Scotland's famous inland sea, earns the city its title, "Capital of the Highlands." From Inverness, you can get to more places in the Highlands than you can from any other location in Scotland. For this reason, we have termed the excursion to Inverness an "out-and-back" excursion, for you may want to use Inverness as your "base city" for exploring the Highlands.

There is so much to do in and around the Inverness that not even a series of action-packed days could absorb all of the possible activities. Here are but a few of the sightseeing possibilities in and around Inverness: Visit the castle grounds and walk along the garden paths at the River Ness. Cruise on Loch Ness, as far away as Urquhart Castle if you like, where most of the sightings of the Loch Ness "monster" (or "beastie," as the locals call it) have occurred. Journey on the renowned railway line between Inverness and Kyle of Lochalsh along 82 miles of railroad right-of-way that involved beauty, romance, history, and endurance in its building. Forge northward to Thurso, Scotland's most northerly town, on a dramatic rail route along 162 miles of Scotland's better scenery. If you prefer the solitude of surf breaking on a shore, take a train east to Nairn, 15 miles from Inverness. Or train south a mere 30 miles to Scotland's St. Moritz, where the ski boom has transformed the town of Aviemore into a continental sports village.

Edinburgh–Inverness

DEPART WAVERLEY STATION	ARRIVE INVERNESS STATION	NOTES
0648	1035	M–Sa (1)
0940 (0935 Su)	1312 (1310 Su)	Daily
1128	1515	M–Sa (1)
1340	1733	Su (1)

DEPART INVERNESS STATION	ARRIVE WAVERLEY STATION	NOTES
1437	1814	M–Sa
1610	2018	Su (1)
1648	2027	M–Sa (2)
1830	2208 (2206 Su)	Daily (1)
2002	2357	M–Sa (1)

(1) Change trains in Perth
(2) Reservations required from Inverness to Perth; change trains in Perth

Eons ago, Loch Ness was carved out along a geological fault between two land masses in northern Scotland. The earth's forces formed a long, narrow lake of approximately 24 miles with depths of up to 750 feet, possibly 1,000 feet in some parts. To go to Inverness and not have a look at Loch Ness would be like eating one potato chip and throwing the rest of the bag away. We urge you to dip into the mystery, the history, and the beauty of Loch Ness.

Loch Ness is reportedly the home of "Nessie," the Loch Ness monster, which has often been described as one of the world's greatest mysteries. The first recorded sighting of Nessie was made by an unimpeachable witness (St. Columba, no less) in A.D. 565. According to the report, the monster attacked one of the members of his group. Since then, there have been too many visual and photographic sightings of the monster for it to be easily explained.

Fact or fiction, there is a continuing similarity in the descriptions of Nessie given by most of those who claim to have seen the monster over the years. Photographs also support a common description, that of a small head at the end of a long, thin neck, with an overall body length between 20 to 30 feet. Underwater evidence gathered by every means from space-age technology to yellow submarines suggests that it may have four flippers. Zoologists recognize this description as a plesiosaur, a type of marine dinosaur that existed more than seventy million years ago and should have become extinct.

Scientific data notwithstanding, the fact that malt whiskeys have been produced in large volumes throughout the area since the beginning of recorded time may account for many or all of the sightings!

Inverness also offers the town attractions of the Balnain House, home of Highland music, the Scottish Kiltmaker Visitor Center, Floral Hall, St. Andrew's Cathedral, and the Inverness Museum and Art Gallery. Enjoy the Castle Garrison Encounter and the Aquadome and Sports Centre. *Flipper* fans should not miss the dolphin-watching boat trips.

If your visit to Inverness is limited, you may want to try the excellent British rail sleeper services. For example, you can board a sleeper one night in London and awaken the following morning in Inverness. Spend an entire day sightseeing, then board another sleeper back to London.

It is an ambitious program, but going in and out of Inverness by sleeper could permit you to board the 1045 train from there to the Kyle of Lochalsh, where you arrive at 1315, then ferry to the Isle of Skye, soak in the sights, and leave Lochalsh on the 1705 to be back in Inverness by 1938 with some time to spare before boarding the sleeper again.

Departing from the Inverness Station, the journey to Kyle of Lochalsh takes about three hours and thirty minutes. The railway between Inverness and Kyle of Lochalsh has been accorded the distinction of being the premier scenic rail line in Great Britain. It offers a lovely journey through the Highland towns of Dingwall, Garve, Achnasheen, and Stromeferry before terminating on the western shores of Scotland overlooking the Isle of Skye. The rail line passes through a region of superlative natural beauty loaded with Scottish folklore. This 82 mile journey, which appears rather uninspiring in the cold prosaic type of the timetable, is in reality a rare mixture of beauty, romance, history, and endurance.

Kyle of Lochalsh Tourist Information Centre: Car Park; *Tel:* (0159) 953–4276
  Hours: Monday through Saturday 0930–2130, Sunday 1230–1630.
    The tourist information center is conveniently located midway between the train station and the ferry dock. To reach it, use the stairs to the overpass and then walk downhill.

When the railroad opened in 1870, the western terminal was the town of Stromeferry on the saltwater Loch Carron. Although the original intention was to build right through to Kyle of Lochalsh, construction money ran out and Stromeferry remained the terminus for twenty-seven years. Completing the remaining 26 miles of right-of-way proved to be a formidable task of engineering. Most miles were forged through solid rock, requiring cuts up to 88 feet deep. Even the area of the train terminal at Kyle required blasting and removing rock. When you reach Kyle of Lochalsh, pause to appreciate the backbreaking toil that created the train station and the right-of-way leading to it.

A bridge was built between Kyle of Lochalsh and Kyleakin on the Isle of Skye. The ruins of Castle Moil stand on a promontory close to the Kyleakin ferry dock. During the time of the Vikings, the castle was the home of a Norwegian princess. History relates that the princess made quite a bundle during her stay in the castle by exacting a toll from ships passing through the narrow straits. To ensure prompt payment, she had a heavy chain attached between the castle and the Kyle of Lochalsh, which was drawn taut when a ship approached. The chain was probably depreciated and charged off as a business expense, for there's no evidence of its existence today.

During the summer, the 1045 train from Inverness includes a special observation car, for which a supplement is payable. The special car returns to Inverness in the late afternoon, departing from Kyle of Lochalsh at 1705. A guide aboard the observation car offers interesting commentary en route. If you're unable to obtain a seat in that car, ask at the railway-station magazine stand for the illustrated booklet *Inverness to Kyle of Lochalsh*. It describes much of the scenery en route, along with a sprinkling of Scottish folktales.

Scottish legends leap out at you as the train plies between Inverness and Kyle. The Castle at Dingwall was said to have been ruled by Finlaec, the father of MacBeth. In a graveyard opposite the castle ruins, the ghost of a young girl wanders nightly in search of her faithless lover. Approaching Garve, you'll pass Loch Garve, where even in the dead of winter there is a small part that never freezes—attributed to the water-horse monsters who carry off local girls. The inn at Garve purveys Athole Brose, a libation of whiskey, oats, and honey, several drafts of which could produce a whole herd of water horses.

Edinburgh through Inverness–Kyle of Lochalsh

DEPART WAVERLEY STATION	ARRIVE KYLE STATION	NOTES
0648	1315	M–Sa (1) (2)

DEPART KYLE STATION	ARRIVE WAVERLEY STATION	NOTES
1520	2208	M–Sa (3)
1705	2357	M–Sa (1)

(1) Change trains in Perth and in Inverness.

(2) A day trip from Edinburgh to Kyle of Lochalsh and return to Edinburgh is not possible on Sundays because the only Sunday trip from Inverness to Kyle of Lochalsh arrives in Kyle at 2027 (and only from June 28 to August 30); there is no return trip from Kyle on Sundays later than 1520. A two-day weekend excursion trip is possible, but only with this schedule: Depart Edinburgh on Sa at 0648, arrive Kyle 1315; Depart Kyle on Su at 0952 and arrive Edinburgh at 2018. Train changes are required at both Perth and Inverness on each trip.

(3) Change trains in Inverness.

The right-of-way passes areas that stir the imagination. Departing Achnasheen en route to Stromeferry, passengers may get a fleeting glance at the Torridon Mountains, the oldest mountains on earth. They are so old that geologists have been unable to find any trace of fossils, indicating the mountains were formed long before life of any description began. The range, consisting of peaks such as Liathach (3,456 feet), Beinn Eighe (3,300 feet), and Beinn Alligin (3,021 feet), has sparkling quartzite peaks, often mistaken for snow.

In the seventeenth century, Brahan Seer, the Highland's prophet extraordinaire, said, "The day will come when every stream will have its bridge, balls of fire will pass rapidly up and down the Strath of Peffery and carriages without horses will cross the country from sea to sea." And so it came to pass: On August 10, 1870, the railroad steam engines began operating from sea to sea.

Day Excursion to

Linlithgow BIRTHPLACE OF MARY, QUEEN OF SCOTS

Depart from Edinburgh Waverley Station or Glasgow Queen Street Station

Distance by train: 18 miles (29 km)
Average train time: 20 minutes
Train information and InterCity services: (034) 548–4950
Linlithgow Tourist Information Centre: Burgh Halls, The Cross, West Lothian EH49 7AH;
  Tel: (0150) 684–4600; *Fax:* (0150) 667–1373
  Hours: Monday–Saturday 1000–1600; Sunday 1200–1600.

Linlithgow lies between Edinburgh and Glasgow and stands in the midst of Scotland's history. To its visitors, the town offers a bevy of attractions, so many, in fact, that our advice on going there is to go early and plan to stay late, very late.

Linlithgow Palace, the birthplace of Mary, Queen of Scots, is the town's main attraction; however, a variety of others will vie for your attention. A mere 100 yards from the Linlithgow Station, there's a canal where you may board a replica of a Victorian steam packet boat. A short walk westward from the Palace along High Street, you'll discover "The Linlithgow Story," a fascinating museum telling of life in one of Scotland's most important Royal Burghs. A scant distance from the town you can visit The Binns, one of the most "lived in" mansions in Scotland. A short bus ride will take you to the town of Bo'ness with its unique set of attractions ranging in historical significance from Roman ruins to the Industrial Revolution.

Bo'ness also has a reconstructed Victorian railway station where you may board a steam train for a delightfully romantic 7-mile round-trip, including a stop in Birkhill where you can go down in a mine. Also nearby is Blackness Castle, at one time one of Scotland's most important strongholds, with a prison cell that's under water at high tide! Meanwhile, back at the palace....

Linlithgow Palace lies in what historians would describe as a splendid ruin. Nevertheless, it tells a poignant tale of Scotland's royal history in an intriguing manner. The palace was the successor to a wooden fortress that burned down in 1424. King James V, father of Mary, Queen of Scots, was born in Linlithgow Palace on April 10, 1512. Mary's mother, Mary of Guise-Lorraine, described the palace as equal to the noblest chateaux in France. Defeated by the English at the battle of Solway Moss in November

Edinburgh–Linlithgow

DEPART WAVERLEY STATION	ARRIVE LINLITHGOW STATION	NOTES
0742	0801	M–Sa
0748	0807	M–Sa
0818	0837	M–Sa
0830	0849	Daily
0848	0907	M–Sa
0930	0949	Daily
0948	1007	M–Sa

and continuing service with the same pattern until midafternoon

DEPART LINLITHGOW STATION	ARRIVE WAVERLEY STATION	NOTES
1404	1426	M–Sa
1428	1450	M–Sa
1434	1456	M–Sa
1436	1459	Su (1)
1528	1550	M–Sa
1536	1559	Su (1)

and continuing service after 1536 at frequent intervals until late P.M.

(1) Departure times on Su change beginning July 26 from 36 minutes after the hour to 43 minutes after the hour; same arrival times.

1542, the king died on December 14 of that year, only six days after the birth of his daughter. The infant child became Mary, Queen of Scots, at six days of age.

In the years to follow, Bonnie Prince Charlie and Oliver Cromwell took brief residence in the palace. At the beginning of 1746, troops belonging to the Duke of Cumberland's army were billeted there. As they marched out on February 1, fires were left burning that soon spread throughout the building. Since that time, the palace has remained unroofed and uninhabited. There has been talk from time to time about restoring Linlithgow Palace. In 1906 the fireplace in the great hall was restored; King George V held court there in 1914. As it stands now, let your imagination "restore" it.

The Union Canal runs through the center of Linlithgow. Some 31 miles in length, the canal was once a major thoroughfare for taking coal from the mines in Falkirk to Edinburgh. You can cruise the Union Canal on board the *Victoria* or *Janet Telford*, two diesel-powered replicas of Victorian steam packet boats, every half hour on Saturday and Sunday afternoons from Easter until the end of September. Short trips of about twenty minutes' duration depart from the Canal Basin at Manse Road, located about 100 yards from the rail station. The Canal Museum at the basin has a small restaurant and is open, when the *Victoria* operates, from 1400 until 1700. The last boat trip departs at 1630. Admission to the museum is free; boat trips are £1.50 for adults, 75 pence for children.

The Binns has been occupied by the Dalyell family for three and a half centuries. The house dates from the sixteenth century. General Tam Dalyell (1599–1685) had some hair-raising adventures in his lifetime, including an escape from the Tower of London and military service in Russia. The house reflects the early seventeenth-century transition from the fortified castle to a more comfortable and gracious house. You'll enjoy a visit there.

Bo'ness is a seaport on the Firth of Forth. It has been the site of many activities, including coal mining, iron founding, and maritime trading. You can get the full details from the tourist center in Linlithgow or from the center in Bo'ness. The Bo'ness center is housed in Hamilton's Cottage, a re-creation of a working-class home from the 1920s.

The Bo'ness & Kinneil Railway runs to the Birkhill clay mine where fireclay was mined. Without fireclay, many say there could never have been an Industrial Revolution. While in Kinneil, you can visit the Kinneil Estate, which houses an interesting museum, an ancient mansion, and the remains of the Roman Antonine Wall.

The running dates for the Bo'ness & Kinneil Railway are on Saturdays and Sundays from April through October; daily in July and August. The standard fare, including the stop at Kinneil, is adults £3.60, children £1.80. If you have the whole gang with you, you can take advantage of the £9.00 family rate.

Be certain to call at the Four Marys' Public House on High Street in Linlithgow. Great atmosphere, excellent libations, and superb food will be your reward. Don't miss it!

Accommodations can also be booked through the Edinburgh and Lothians Tourist Board in Linlithgow.

Day Excursion to

Montrose

SEASIDE RESORT

Depart from Edinburgh Waverley Station

Distance by train: 90 miles (145 km)
Average train time: 2 hours, 10 minutes
Train information and InterCity services: (034) 548–4950
Montrose Tourist Information Centre: 2 Bridge Street; *Tel:* (0167) 467–2000
   Hours: Open April-June, and September 1000-1700; July and August 0930-1730.
   From the station, turn right on Western Road until it reaches Hume Street, where a quick left followed by a right turn one block away onto High Street puts you in view of the Town House and its grand piazza. Stay on the right-hand side of High Street and walk a short distance south. Just after reaching the town's public library, you will come to the tourist information center at 2 Bridge Street.

   Travelers who have visited many villages, towns, and cities throughout continental Europe and the British Isles learn to "read" the history of a place in its architecture and street names. Montrose is an outstanding example of this point.
   Even at first glance, Montrose does not look like a typical Scottish town. Its broad High Street has many elegant houses with gabled ends on the street side. There was a time in the city's history when only Edinburgh surpassed it in prosperity and elegance. The Town House of Montrose—Americans would term it the city hall—is fronted by a broad piazza. From its facade, Montrose looks more like a page out of a Flemish picture book rather than a Scottish one. Its great houses are surrounded by garden walls—not ordinary ones, but remarkably high garden walls. It has oddly named streets, such as "America" and "California"—another hint that the history of Montrose is different.
   When Glasgow was still a village, Montrose was one of Scotland's principal ports. For centuries, the merchants of Montrose traded with the Low Countries. It was only natural that they would bring back some of the things they admired on the continent: for example, houses with gabled ends to the street side as they are constructed in Holland. The wide streets? From the promenades of Europe, no doubt. And what about the street names? Almost within living memory, ships sailed from Montrose to America carrying emigrants and returned laden with lumber.
   For many years, Montrose was Scotland's primary port for tobacco, with its fleet sailing regularly to and from Virginia. Today, North Sea oil is virtu-

Edinburgh–Montrose

DEPART WAVERLEY STATION	ARRIVE MONTROSE STATION	NOTES
0705	0859	M–Sa
0810	1002	M–Sa
0855	1043	Su
0905	1051	M–Sa
1025	1214	M–Sa
1055	1241	Su
1110	1258	M–Sa
1210	1402	M–Sa
1240	1426	Su

DEPART MONTROSE STATION	ARRIVE WAVERLEY STATION	NOTES
1350	1548	M–Sa
1429	1619	Su
1500	1648	M–Sa
1534	1722	M–Sa
1552	1741	Su
1605	1809	M–Sa
1652	1849	M–Sa
1740	1926	Su
1757	1952	M–Sa
1854	2046	M–Sa
1940	2128	Su
2036	2228	M–Sa
2051	2300	Sa
2134	2320	Su
2154	2359	M–Sa
2157	2342	Su

ally pumping life back into the city's harbor, where, until the recent past, an air of sleepiness prevailed as trade with America subsided. The first part of the civic motto of Montrose—*Mare ditat* (the sea enriches)—is again coming true.

Baffled by the high garden walls? History relates that more than 300 years ago, the streets of Montrose ran red with blood when a band of

Highlanders raided the town. Its inhabitants were defenseless as they slept without the protection of a city wall and with only low garden walls about their residences. The carnage was swift and horrible. Within months, the majority of the walls within the town were built up to their present height to prevent attacks from intruders.

When you arrive in Montrose from Edinburgh, take a moment at the train station to look west, away from the town. You will see a tidal basin where thousands of wild fowl forage for food, including the pink-footed Arctic goose during the winter. Seasonally, a great gathering of swans in the basin dot the water with their white tufts of plumage, like so many bread crumbs scattered on a watery lawn.

The tourist office has a wealth of information available regarding both Montrose and the area surrounding it. A *Heritage Trail* leaflet provides information on walks through Montrose for a nominal fee. The information office also has a street map for sale that lists many points of interest. Note for shoppers: Many stores have "half-day closing" on Wednesday afternoons.

Montrose is one of Scotland's leading seaside resorts, and it can become crowded during the peak summer season. Four miles of magnificent sandy beaches attract many an inlander to the sea. Beaches also have a way of indicating their latitudes, just as places reflect their history in their names and facades. Beaches in Britain, for example, attract huge crowds in summertime, but note the distribution of the people on the beach. Except for a hardy few, the majority of holiday makers are on the sands and not in the water.

The city's large indoor swimming pool and two eighteen-hole golf courses, plus numerous other sports facilities, make up for the other-than-tepid temperature of the North Sea waters off Montrose. The seaside also offers something rather unusual, something you'd never find at Atlantic City. On the beaches beside Elephant Rock, you can search for semi-precious stone such as agates, amethysts, carnelian, and onyx.

Cultural life is not lacking in Montrose. The name of William Lamb immediately relates to the world of art in fine sculptures and etchings. This well-known artist maintains a studio at 24 Market Street. On Panmure Place, the Montrose Museum houses an excellent collection of art relating to the natural and maritime history of the area.

If you've been waiting for us to drop the other shoe, the second part of the Montrose civic motto is *rosa decorat* (the rose adorns). If you walk in the Mid-Links Park on a summer day, the air is scented with the perfume of roses. Although the city's name has nothing to do with roses—it was originally called "Monros" (the mossy promontory)—there are few towns in Scotland where roses grow more abundantly.

Day Excursion to

Perth

FIRST CAPITAL OF SCOTLAND

Depart from Edinburgh Waverley Station

Distance by train: 58 miles (93 km)

Average train time: 1 hour, 30 minutes

Train information and InterCity services: (034) 548–4950

Perth Tourist Information Centre: 45 High Street PH1 5TJ; *Tel:* (0173) 863–8841; *Fax:* (0173) 844–4863

> *Hours:* Open from March 29 to June 27 and September 5 to October 31 from 0900 to 1800 weekdays and 1100 to 1600 Sunday. From June 28 to September 4, hours are Monday through Saturday 0900–2000 and Sunday 1100–1800. November 1 to March 28, the office is open from Monday through Saturday, 0900–1700.
>
> The Perth Tourist Information Centre is in the pedestrian High Street area, located at the intersection of Kirkgate and Skinnergate.

"Behold a river more mighty than the Tiber!" History relates that these words were uttered by a Roman commander as, approaching what is now the city of Perth, he caught his first glimpse of the River Tay. Beginning as a mountain stream at Ben Laoigh, the Tay trickles down the hillsides, gaining tributaries as it flows on its 120-mile journey to the sea. Perth stands astride the Tay, their history inexorably linked.

Two vehicular bridges, plus a rail bridge (all with pedestrian footpaths), cross the River Tay today, but "Old Man River" Tay kept the locals quite busy in earlier years, when floods swept away the first bridge in 1210 and its successor in 1621, leaving travelers no alternative but ferries for the 150 years to follow.

Perth is often referred to as "the gateway to the Highlands," but this is not its only attraction. Its prominent position in the history of Scotland has left a legacy of distinctive buildings in an area compact enough to be easily examined on foot. Perth's architecture mixes the modern with the ancient. City fathers are justly proud of Perth's sports centers, with an ice rink, swimming pools, tennis courts, and indoor bowling stadium.

Tay Street fronts the river on the city side. Without straying too far from the river, it is possible to enjoy the riverside and visit places of interest such as St. John's Kirk, the Perth Art Gallery and Museum, the Fergusson Gallery, the Lower City Mills, and the Fair Maid's House, as described in Sir Walter Scott's novel *The Fair Maid of Perth*. Turn left off Tay Street at Queen's Bridge and proceed 2 blocks to sight St. John's to your right. One of Perth's most famous landmarks, St. John's Kirk, is where the Protestant reformer John Knox, following his return from exile in Geneva, preached his famous sermon against idolatry in 1559. The congregation was so taken with his sermon that they wrecked the church and then went on to create similar outrages on the monastic houses of the friars. Originally founded in 1126 and revamped over the centuries, St. John's now is an example of Gothic-style architecture from the mid-sixteenth century.

Returning to Tay Street, continue to walk to the Perth Bridge, where you will find the art gallery and museum on George Street close to the bridge approach. In quest of the Fair Maid's House, ask directions when leaving the museum. It is at North Port, a short distance away, but there are several ways to reach it.

Close by the Fair Maid's House is the North Inch, a beautifully situated park bordered by Georgian terraces and the River Tay and overlooked by Balhousie Castle, the historic home of the Black Watch Regimental Museum. Across the river lies the colorful Branklyn Garden, owned by the National Trust for Scotland and said to be "the finest two acres of private garden in the country." It sits on the wooded slopes of Kinnoull Hill and offers an excellent view over the town.

For centuries, Perth has been a prosperous market town, serving a rich agricultural hinterland and profiting from its geographical position in the heart of Scotland. The town's livestock markets flourish, with the famous Perth Bull Sales in February and October attracting buyers from all over the world. Perth's reputation as a trading center, however, rests principally with its excellent shops. Much of Perth's center is traffic-free and bedecked with floral displays thanks to the city-wide "Perth in Bloom" campaign.

An excellent addition to Perth's city center attractions is the Fergusson Gallery in the Round House (Perth's old waterworks) at Marshall Place.

Edinburgh–Perth

DEPART WAVERLEY STATION	ARRIVE PERTH STATION	NOTES
0648	0806	M–Sa
0935	1049	Su
0940	1057	M–Sa
1128	1248	M–Sa
1340	1455 (1458 Su)	Daily

DEPART PERTH STATION	ARRIVE WAVERLEY STATION	NOTES
1449	1610	M–Sa
1525	1637	Su
1655	1814	M–Sa
1828	2018	Su (1)
1910	2027	M–Sa
2051 (2050 Su)	2208 (2206 Su)	Daily
2220	2357	M–Sa (1)

(1) change trains in Stirling

Here you can view the largest and most important collection of the works of the famous Scottish colorist John Duncan Fergusson. Three specially designed galleries display rotating exhibits taken from a total collection of 6,000 items.

Scone Palace, a mile north of Perth, stands close to the historic spot where Scottish kings were crowned through 1651. The Moot Hill, which stands in front of the palace, is an artificial mound that was constructed in the Dark Ages. Traditionally, Scottish chiefs and lairds came to Scone to pledge their allegiance to the king. This they did, filling their boots before they left home with the earth of their own districts. Thus, with the earth still in their boots, they were standing on their own land when they swore allegiance to their king. Afterwards they ceremoniously emptied their boots on the Moot Hill (or Boot Hill, as it is appropriately known today).

The palace is open to the public, and there is an admission charge. You can reach the palace by taking bus No. 58 from the Leonard Street bus station. Check with the information center for details if you plan to go.

By the way, don't plan to heist the Stone of Scone—it rests safely back in Edinburgh Castle.

Day Excursion to

St. Andrews

WORLD'S GOLF CAPITAL

Depart from Edinburgh Waverley Station

Distance by train: 57 miles (92 km)

Average train time: 1 hour

Train information and InterCity services: (034) 548–4950

St. Andrews Tourist Information Centre: No. 70 Market Street, Fife KY16 9NU; *Tel:* (0133) 447–2021; *Fax:* (0133) 447–8422

> *Hours:* Open 0930–2000 Monday–Saturday and 1100–1700 Sunday during July and August. In June and September, hours are 0930–1900 Monday–Saturday and 1100–1700 Sunday. October through March, it's open 0930–1730 Monday–Friday and 1400–1700 Saturday. The hours in April and May are 0930–1730 Monday–Saturday, 1100–1600 on Sunday.
>
> Leuchars is the rail station serving St. Andrews. From the bus station in St. Andrews, cross City Road and continue along Market Street. The tourist information center is at No. 70 Market Street, on the right-hand side after Church Street.

No town in the world is so completely identified with one game as St. Andrews is with golf. No matter where in the world they have played the game, there is nothing as exhilarating to devoted golfers as a round on the Old Course at St. Andrews. Anyone may play the Old Course, provided he or she can produce a current, official handicap certificate, or a letter of introduction from a bona fide golf club, together with proof of identity. This rule applies only to play on the Old Course. Play on the other six courses at St. Andrews is not affected. The links belong to the townspeople and, as such, are open to all.

In summer and autumn, most available tee times on the Old Course are reserved, in many instances a year in advance. To be certain of obtaining a starting time for the Old Course, it is essential to apply well in advance of the date of play. Latecomers still have a chance because some starting times are retained each day for issue by a random ballot procedure. To enter your ballot, it is necessary to apply to the starter by 1400 on the previous day. (The Old Course is closed on Sunday.)

To obtain full details and reservations for golf in St. Andrews, we suggest you telephone the St. Andrews links secretary at (0133) 447–5757 at least one day in advance of your intended visit. In total, St. Andrews and its surrounding area list sixteen courses from which to choose. For information on courses throughout the St. Andrews area, call the Golf Line at (0133) 447–7685.

How old is the game of golf? Apparently, no one knows. Seemingly it originated on the stretches of grassland along Scotland's east coast next to the sandy beaches—the ground known in Scotland for centuries as "links." The sand dunes interspersed throughout the grasslands became the original traps or bunkers. A round of golf consisted of whatever number of holes were possible in the terrain of a particular link. For more on the history of golf, ask at the tourist information center about the British Golf Museum.

At first, the pastime of golf was indulged in predominantly by the Scottish aristocracy. With the advent of the inexpensive golf ball, however, golfing in Scotland soon became a mass sport. Aristocracy again moved to the fore by establishing clubhouses for the leisured gentlemen, where they could attend dinners to observe the end of matches between players.

Such was the case at St. Andrews in 1754 when twenty-two "noblemen and gentlemen, being admirers of the ancient and healthful exercise of the golf," founded the Society of St. Andrews Golfers, which is now known throughout the world as the Royal and Ancient Golf Club.

St. Andrews and history go together hand in hand. Such stellar sights as the St. Andrews Castle, with its bottle dungeon and secret passage, vie for your attention along with the ruins of St. Andrews Cathedral, once the largest in Scotland. Mary, Queen of Scots, had a house in St. Andrews that you can still see. The town is the home of Scotland's oldest university (1412). Long before Columbus arrived in America or Cooke disembarked in Australia, students were attending classes at St. Andrews University. Another attraction is St. Mary's College and its unique quadrangle. Founded in 1537, St. Mary's is a part of the university complex. To visit St. Andrews and to roam its streets and scenes is to establish a tangible link with the past.

St. Andrews Castle may be reached by proceeding along North Street until reaching Castle Street, where you turn left and then proceed one block to the castle. Continuing one block farther on North Street will put you in front of the cathedral ruins.

Edinburgh–St. Andrews

There is no train service to St. Andrews; the nearest station is Leuchars, 10 km from St. Andrews; service from Leuchars to St. Andrews is by bus.

DEPART WAVERLEY STATION	ARRIVE LEUCHARS STATION	NOTES
0705	0811	M–Sa
0810	0912	M–Sa
0840	0951	M–Sa
0855	0956	Su (1)
0905	1005	M–Sa
0915	1032	Su
1025	1127	M–Sa
1055	1155	Su
1110	1212	M–Sa
1115	1232	Su
1210	1315	M–Sa
1240	1340	Su

DEPART LEUCHARS STATION	ARRIVE WAVERLEY STATION	NOTES
1439	1548	M–Sa
1515	1619	Su
1537	1659	Su
1542	1648	M–Sa
1620	1722	M–Sa
1639	1741	Su
1657	1809	M–Sa
1737	1859	Su
1739	1849	M–Sa
1825	1926	Su
1842	1952	M–Sa
1937	2059	Su
1941	2048	M–Sa
2005	2125	M–Sa
2026	2128	Su
2123	2228	M–Sa
2137	2259	Su
2140	2300	M–Sa
2219	2320	Su
2239	2359	M–Sa

(1) Reservations required

Golfer or not, you must see the Royal and Ancient Clubhouse of St. Andrews during your stay. Though founded in 1754, the present clubhouse was built in 1854. The Royal and Ancient Golf Club is now the ruling authority of the game, and its clubhouse is recognized as the world head-quarters for the game of golf. From the castle ruins, walk along The Scores until you come to Gillespie Terrace. From this point, the clubhouse and the eighteenth hole of the Old Course come into view.

Of all the places and views, we give our nod to St. Andrews Castle overlooking St. Andrews Bay. Initially constructed in 1200, the castle was destroyed and rebuilt during a war between Scotland and England, only to be demolished again during the Reformation. The savagery of those times can be noted on a stone outside the castle gate where George Wishart was burned at the stake. The castle has been in ruins since the seventeenth century, when much of its stone was removed for repairing the harbor.

Day Excursion to

Stirling

STIRLING CASTLE

Depart from Edinburgh Waverley Station

Distance by train: 37 miles (59 km)

Average train time: 50 minutes

Train information and InterCity services: (034) 548–4950

Stirling Tourist Information Centre: 41 Dumbarton Road, FK8 1EA; *Tel:* (0178) 647–5019; *Fax:* (0178) 646–0039

Royal Burgh of Stirling Visitor Center: Castle Esplanade; *Tel:* (0178) 647–9901 or (0178) 646–2517; *Fax:* (0178) 646–1881.

> *Hours:* During July and August, Monday through Saturday 0900–1830; Tuesday 0900–2030 and Sunday 0930–1830. The center operates on more restricted hours during winter.
>
> To get there from the train station, make a left turn onto Murray Place, a short distance in front of the station. Walk to the first traffic light and turn right onto Dumbarton Road, immediately opposite the city wall.

All the information you might need for an enjoyable day excursion in Stirling is available at the Royal Stirling Visitor Centre. Several publications describing walks around Stirling are available. One of particular interest is *Stirling Heritage Trail*, published by the Stirling District Council. It covers a course starting and ending at Stirling Castle and includes photographs and drawings as well as colorful text on the history of Stirling Old Town.

Stirling Castle cannot be ignored. Standing on a 250-foot rock overlooking the River Forth Valley, it offers one of the finest panoramic views in Scotland. The area surrounding the crag on which the castle sits has given up relics of early human's presence from the Stone Age down through the Bronze Age. There is no evidence that the Romans occupied the area, but it seems implausible that they didn't "take the high ground."

Stirling Castle has witnessed endless struggles for power. Kings and queens have been crowned in its halls and great battles fought on the plain below it. Originally named Striveling, which may be translated as "a place of strife," Stirling has been the scene of strife within the Scottish nation since before the time of recorded history. The town of Stirling and its castle truly stand at the crossroads of Scotland. Its position overlooking the Forth Valley and the crossing of the River Forth at its tidal limits has contributed to its past and present importance.

The castle, as seen today, began to develop around 1370 with the accession of the Stuart kings. It served as a royal residence from then until the son of Mary, Queen of Scots, James VI of Scotland, departed for London in 1603 to become James I of England. Scotland's tragic queen spent the first five years of her life in and around Stirling Castle. The castle is perhaps the finest example of renaissance architecture in Scotland, most of its buildings dating to the fifteenth and sixteenth centuries. Having been the royal Stuart residence, Scotland's kings and queens held court there, and parliaments met on its premises.

The Royal Burgh of Stirling Visitor and Tourist Information Centre just below the castle combines a multilanguage audiovisual presentation and photographic exhibition with a bookstore and souvenir shop. According to its innovators, it is the first building in Europe to be designed specifically to bring alive the history of a town. The theme is Stirling Castle through seven centuries.

All is bustle and noise as ships from France and Holland unload their cargoes, and farmers drive their cattle to market. Stirling's market, now the city's Broad Street, is lined with shops selling everything from swords to spices. Meanwhile, back at the castle, a roistering banquet is being held in the great hall, packed with honored guests.

Edinburgh–Stirling

DEPART WAVERLEY STATION	ARRIVE STIRLING STATION	NOTES
0718	0806	M–Sa
0748	0837	M–Sa
and continuing every 30 min until late afternoon		
0930	1025	Su (1)
1030	1125	Su (1)
and continuing at hourly intervals until mid afternoon		

DEPART STIRLING STATION	ARRIVE WAVERLEY STATION	NOTES
1403	1456	M–Sa
1433	1526	M–Sa
and continuing at the same interval until 2133, then 2303.		
1358	145	9Su (1)
1458	1602	Su (1)
1553	1645	Su (1)
1626	1718	Su (1)
and continuing at hourly intervals until 2126		

(1) All Su service requires a change of trains at Glasgow Queen Street Station.

Throughout Stirling during the summer months, the presence of flowers is always evident. You will notice this first in the railway station, and it continues all around town. Possibly Stirling developed its love for flowers from the King's Knot, an octagonal, stepped mound that was laid out as the royal gardens in 1627–28 beneath the walls of Stirling Castle by an Englishman, William Watts, who was brought from London to supervise the project. The raised central portion of the Knot is thought to have originated as a Bronze Age burial mound. It was probably used as an outdoor royal court for tournaments before being incorporated into the formal gardens by Mr. Watts.

There are many historic buildings in Stirling. Below the castle stands the imposing Church of the Holy Rood. It has witnessed great moments in history. Here, at its altar, James VI of Scotland, and subsequently James I of England, was crowned at the tender age of eighteen months to succeed his exiled mother. The tower of the church still bears the marks of the 1745 rebellion, when Bonnie Prince Charlie's troops attempted to capture Stirling Castle. In the overture to the Reformation, the strident voice of John Knox boomed from the church pulpit.

Stirling is indeed a historic center that has played a vital role in the making of Scotland. It has an atmosphere that is hard to match in any other part of Scotland. Over the centuries of its involvement in historical events, it has preserved its heritage.

Day Excursion to

Stranraer GATEWAY TO NORTHERN IRELAND

Depart from Edinburgh Waverley Station

Distance by train: 147 miles (237 km)
Average train time: 4 hours, 45 minutes
Train information and InterCity services: (034) 548–4950
Stranraer Tourist Information Centre: Harbour Street; *Tel:* (0177) 670–2595
> *Hours:* Open daily July and August, including Sunday, 0930–1800. Hours vary during the remainder of the year.
> The tourist information center is located on Harbour Street between the Stena Sealink and SeaCat terminals.

Stranraer is primarily the terminal for passenger and car ferry service to Belfast in Northern Ireland. Remember, however, that the BritRail Pass is not accepted for travel on trains operated by the Northern Ireland Railways. Travelers wanting to cross from Stranraer to Belfast must purchase regular rail tickets or a BritRail Pass + Ireland option, which would include the sea crossing on Stena Line plus rail travel in England, Scotland, Wales, Northern Ireland, and the Republic of Ireland.

All arrangements for visiting Northern Ireland should be completed before departure rather than en route. One important requirement is a control ticket each passenger must have prior to boarding the Stranraer–Belfast ferry. These tickets are issued free of charge. Ticketing and reservations are available in the ferry terminal, along with a comfortable passenger lounge with rest rooms and refreshments.

The crossing between Stranraer and Belfast usually takes three hours by conventional ferry, and trains are waiting at the terminals to take travelers to their final destinations. In both ports, the train terminal is directly alongside the ferry dock. Porter service is available. Hoverspeed's SeaCat catamaran crossing from Stranraer to Belfast takes only one and a half hours. Remember that the BritRail Pass + Ireland option is good on the Stena Line, not Hoverspeed.

Stranraer has direct, daytime express-train connections to London. For sleeper services to London, go from Stranraer to Glasgow for departures out of Glasgow Central. The last train leaves Stranraer for Glasgow at 2110. Frequent train service connecting with the ferries to and from Belfast is also available out of Glasgow. Edinburgh passengers should use the Edinburgh–Glasgow train service for the fastest connections to Stranraer.

The old section of Stranraer clusters around its port area and is entwined with interesting streets and small alleyways. The Stranraer Castle, which houses a visitor's center with audiovisual displays, is a relic of the sixteenth century and adds a certain attraction to the area. The information center can provide you with a map of the city and suggest various sights to see on a walking tour. The area is renowned for its golf and fishing, and there are a number of beautiful gardens, which flourish in the mild climate.

The Stranraer Castle, with the formal title of Castle of St. John, is known locally as the "Old Castle." Built in what is now the heart of Stranraer around 1510, it was erected on a site that gave the settlement its original name, Chapel. The name was later changed to Chapel of Stranrawer and finally shortened to Stranraer. Stranrawer was believed to have referred to a row of original houses on the strand, or beach, now buried beneath the town's streets.

An interesting hotel in Stranraer, one that you might mistake as the town's castle when you first see it, is the North West Castle Hotel. Its castle tower cleverly conceals two well-stocked bars. If you are anticipating a long train trip, you may want to bolster your spirits here in the quaint tower. In the lower bar, there are some fossiliferous wooden beams (no, they are not former patrons), while topside in the Explorers Lounge you are treated to a fine view of the harbor.

The hotel was originally the home of Sir John Ross, the famous Arctic explorer. He gave it the name North West Castle as a reminder of his journeys to the northern and western reaches of the Arctic. Although the "castle" has been transformed into the largest hotel in southwest

Edinburgh–Stranraer

DEPART WAVERLEY STATION	ARRIVE STRANRAER STATION	NOTES
0700	1111	M–Sa (1)
0930	1340	Su (1)
1000	1334	M–Sa (1)

DEPART STRANRAER STATION	ARRIVE WAVERLEY STATION	NOTES
1437	1820	M–Sa (1)
1440	1922	Su (1)
1940	2320 (2329 Su)	Daily (1)

(1) All schedules shown require a change of station in Glasgow from Queen Street to Central or the reverse. Schedules shown allow 15–25 minutes for this change.

Scotland, its origins with Sir John have been carefully preserved. An indoor ice rink caters to curling fans, and the hotel proprietor has also added a swimming pool, sauna baths, and several restaurants. A brochure at the hotel desk gives the full history of this most interesting hostelry.

Stranraer lies at the southern end of Loch Ryan, known since Roman times as a safe harbor. At the point where Loch Ryan meets the Irish Sea, the granite bulk of Ailsa Craig stands as a sentinel guarding the enclosed waters of the loch from the ravages of the storms that sweep into the area from the Atlantic across Ireland.

At one time Stranraer was a small fishing community, but it became the main port serving Northern Ireland and a busy shipping center by the middle of the nineteenth century. Involved in the shipment of ammunition from the United States at the end of World War II, the shipping firm of Townsend–Thoresen (now P&O European Ferries) turned the port into a ferry terminal for what is now the shortest sea route to Ireland.

Glasgow

Glasgow has undergone a sweeping renaissance, shaking off its former image of the grim, depressed industrial city to emerge as one of Europe's foremost culture hubs. Emerging from a century or so of accumulated grime, the cleaning-up process has highlighted some of Europe's finest Victorian architecture in gleaming gold and red sandstone. Bustling city streets lined with imposing hand-carved facades pay homage to the optimism of the Victorian city fathers, as do the stunning marble staircases of the opulent City Chambers in central George Square. Glaswegians have reason to be proud of their city and cordially invite you to enjoy it with them.

Glasgow is Scotland's largest metropolis, with a population approaching one million. It is the gateway to bonnie Loch Lomond and the western Highlands. Glasgow's River Clyde flows into the Firth of Clyde, thus opening its western waterways to myriad islands and the Irish Sea. At the height of its shipbuilding boom, Glasgow was launching more than one-third of the world's shipping tonnage. The *Queen Mary*, the *Queen Elizabeth I*, and the *Queen Elizabeth II (QE2)* were built there. With the industry now only a shadow of its former self, the River Clyde has become a scenic waterway where you can cruise aboard luxury riverboats or the paddle-wheel steamer *Waverley*.

Glasgow abounds with sights to see, ranging from its great twelfth-century cathedral to a variety of museums and universities. It is said that Glasgow has more parks than any other European city of its size. George Square, opposite the Queen Street railway station, projects a panorama of Scottish and British history in its statues of those individuals who forged the British Commonwealth through their scientific, leadership, and literary endeavors.

Direct transatlantic flights into the Glasgow Airport, only fifteen minutes from the city center, as well as regular train services from London and the south, make Glasgow an ideal "base city" for Scotland. It is conveniently located, as is Edinburgh, for access to our Scottish day excursions. For this reason, we are introducing the "Glasgow Connection," wherein the choice of base cities—Edinburgh or Glasgow—becomes a matter of individual selection. The excellent train service between the two cities permits visitors to move with ease between them.

Arriving by Air

Along with its excellent weather, the Glasgow airport offers travelers the opportunity of "open jaw" airline ticketing: arriving or departing on one leg of their transatlantic flight in Scotland rather than flying both in and out of the London complex of Gatwick, Stansted, or Heathrow. Currently, transatlantic service is provided by the following air carriers: Air Canada, American Airlines, British Airways, Icelandair, and Northwest Airlines.

The airport information desk also provides information to incoming passengers. The office is open from 0715 to 2230 daily. Currency exchange services are operated by Thomas Cook. The office is open daily in the summer between 0700 and 2300; in the winter (November to April), it is open from 0800 to 2000 Monday–Saturday, and Sunday 0800–1800.

Airport coach service is available between the airport and Glasgow every thirty minutes from 0550 to 2250 weekdays; Sunday service is every thirty minutes from 0720 to 2220. Journey time is approximately twenty-five minutes, the fare is £2.00.

Arriving by Train

Glasgow has two main railway stations. Trains arriving from southwestern Scotland and England terminate in the Glasgow Central Station. For train travel north and east out of Glasgow to Edinburgh, Perth, and Inverness or west to Oban and Fort William, the Glasgow Queen Street Station becomes the departure point. A convenient city bus service links the two rail stations. The ten-minute walk between them, however, runs through some of the city's finer shopping areas, thereby offering the opportunity to walk off a few British "pounds."

If you choose to walk from the Queen Street Station to the Central Station, walk past George Square and the tourist information center to St.

Vincent Street. At this point, turn right and walk one block farther to Buchanan Street, a pedestrian shopping precinct. Turn left onto Buchanan Street and walk until your path intersects with Gordon Street. The intersection is easy to locate because this section of Gordon Street is reserved for pedestrians (and shops). Turning right at this point and continuing along Gordon Street for 2 blocks will bring you to the Glasgow Central Station, on your left.

From the Central Station to the Queen Street Station, merely reverse your line of march. Those who wish to avoid running the shopper's gauntlet on Buchanan Street may proceed between the two stations by traversing Queen and Argyle streets. Consult a map of central Glasgow, which is available at the tourist information center in St. Vincent Place.

The Interstation Bus Link provides passenger transfer service between the Central and Queen Street Stations with no stops en route. Departures are approximately every fifteen minutes.

Don't look for a kiosk or a newsstand where you can purchase tickets; you pay your fare when you get on the bus. BritRail Passes are not accepted for the bus transfer between rail stations. The time en route varies between five and ten minutes, depending on traffic conditions. For those in a hurry or those who are heavily ladened with luggage, taxis are standing by in queues at both stations.

If you are arriving in one of Glasgow's rail stations to transfer to the Glasgow Airport at Abbotsinch, frequent bus service departs from Buchanan Bus Station.

Glasgow Central Station

Glasgow Central Station, transformed radically in the past few years, caters to those needs of the train traveler ranging from rest rooms with bathing facilities to a grand Victorian hostelry, the Central Hotel. The station's old ticket office has been transformed into a delightful array of quality shops, bars, and restaurants.

The Glasgow Central Station provides InterCity electric services for English destinations, including Liverpool, Manchester, Birmingham, and London (Euston Station). Also provided are connections for Wales, the west of England, and destinations in south and west Scotland, which include Ayr and Stranraer (for connections to Northern Ireland via Larne). Commuter-train service to Gourock and Wemyss Bay for connections with steamer services on the River Clyde also operate from Central Station.

Money exchange is available only within the station during times when the banks are closed. An office of the Royal Bank of Scotland is directly across from the main entrance of the station. After banking hours, ticket window No. 9 in Central Station or the ATMs will exchange foreign currency. The American Express office is to the left of the station entrance at 115 Hope Street. The Thomas Cook office is just one block to the right of the station entrance at 15-17 Gordon Street.

Hotel reservations may be arranged at the tourist information center located at 35 St. Vincent Place.

Tourist information is available in Glasgow's information center at 11 George Square, telephone (0141) 204–4400.

Train information is displayed in the Central Station by means of a huge, digital departures-and-arrivals board located between tracks 2 and 5. For expanded train information, visit the Inquiries and Reservations Office (travel center) on the right side of the main hall at the end of platforms 1, 2, and 3.

Train reservations may be arranged in the travel center. For sleeping-car reservations, you will be directed to the InterCity Sleeper Centre at the entrance to platform 1.

Queen Street Station

Queen Street Station is the terminal for trains operating on the scenic West Highland Line to Oban, Fort William, and Mallaig, where steamer connections can be made to the Scottish islands. From the Queen Street Station, InterCity express trains depart for Edinburgh and connect with destinations in England including York, Doncaster, and London (King's Cross Station).

Services for north and east Scotland, including Stirling, Perth, Dundee, Aberdeen, Inverness, and the Kyle of Lochalsh, depart from the Queen Street Station. Electric trains to Dumbarton and Balloch (for Loch Lomond cruises) also operate from this station.

Money exchange services are not available within the Queen Street Station. There are several banks in the general area, including an office of the Royal Bank of Scotland adjacent to the main entrance of the Central Station. After banking hours, however, the only money exchange facility available in the area is ticket window No. 9 in the Central Station.

Hotel reservations for Glasgow and for all of Scotland may be arranged through the "Book-A-Bed-Ahead" service with the Greater Glasgow & Clyde Valley Tourist Board located at 11 George Square, telephone (0141) 204–4400.

Tourist information in Glasgow is also available at the Greater Glasgow and Clyde Valley Tourist Board. Hours of operation June through September are 0900–1900 (2000 in July and August) Monday through Saturday and 1000–1800 on Sunday. From October through May, the center is open Monday through Saturday from 0900 to 1800, closed Sunday until Easter, then open on Sunday through May between 1000 and 1800.

The center has a wealth of Glasgow tourist information on hand. Call there to request a copy of the *Greater Glasgow Quick Guide* booklet. In addition to a listing of city attractions, the booklet contains information on restaurants, pubs, events, and shopping that will be very helpful for getting to know Glasgow. There is a Bureau de Change in operation in the center as well as an office for theater and sporting events tickets.

Train information is available in the British Rail Travel Centre located on the left-hand side of the station as you face the train platforms.

Train reservations can be made in the travel center. For sleeper reservations, however, use the InterCity Sleeper Centre in Central Station.

Glasgow Gazette

Glasgow's modern subway system is a circular line with trains running in both directions beneath the center of the city. It provides a three-minute service from each of its fifteen stations, achieving a circular journey in about twenty-two minutes. A separate subway, the Argyle Line, links the suburban networks. The main link with British rail services, however, is the subway station at Buchanan Street, connecting with the Queen Street Station by a moving pedestrian platform similar to those found in airports.

For readers going on the day excursion to Loch Lomond, the rail route departing Glasgow is an electric-train service that departs from subterranean platform 8 in the Queen Street Station. To reach it, after entering the main hall of the station, turn left and exit the station by the side entrance, where you turn right to follow the well-marked PLATFORM 8 signs.

In the Queen Street Station's Travel Centre, you may obtain full information and tickets for cruising on the Clyde River aboard the *Waverley*. Connecting rail services to the ship's pier originate in the Queen Street Station. The vessel offers a number of interesting cruises on the Clyde River and the Firth of Clyde. On Saturdays during the summer, a special upriver cruise is conducted. Advance bookings for the cruise are recommended.

Throughout the summer, a two-hour bus tour of Glasgow aboard specially converted double-decker buses will take you around some of the best known places—and some of the more out-of-the-way places—in the city. For bus tour schedules and rates, check with the Greater Glasgow Tourist Information Centre.

Every visitor to Glasgow, and model railroad buffs in particular, will not want to miss Glasgow's Museum of Transport in Kelvin Hall on Argyle Street. The museum is located in the west end of Glasgow only ten minutes from the city center by bus or subway. It's open Monday through Saturday from 1000 to 1700 and Sunday between 1100 and 1700. Displays include ship models, Glasgow trams and buses, locomotives of Scottish origin, Scottish-built motorcars, fire engines, and a reconstructed subway station. There is also a section in the museum known as "The Clyde Room," where meticulously detailed models illustrate the story of shipbuilding and shipping on the River Clyde. An operating model railroad is one of the museum's highlights.

St. Mungo Museum of Religious Life and Art, at 2 Castle Street (in front of Glasgow Cathedral), provides an exploration of the different faiths of the world through paintings and religious artifacts. Included in the collection is Salvador Dali's *Christ of St. John of the Cross*. The museum is open Monday through Saturday 1000–1700 and Sunday 1100–1700.

Glasgow's Art Gallery and Museum is immediately opposite Kelvin Hall. Home of Britain's finest civic collection of British and European paintings, the museum also features displays of natural history, archaeology, and collections of silver, pottery, arms, and armor. In the performing arts sector, Glasgow's Mayfest (which, of course, occurs in the merry month of May) is a key international festival for theater, dance, music, and related performing arts in Europe.

Among the many superb galleries and museums throughout Glasgow is the renowned Burrell Collection in the Pollok Country Park, a unique collection of more than 8,000 objets d'art donated to the city by one man, Sir William Burrell.

Previously, we identified the area of the city between the two rail stations as an ideal place to "walk off a few British 'pounds.'" It is. Glasgow is a shopper's paradise, with more than ample opportunity to find that special souvenir or gift for friends back home and pick up something for yourself, too. Department stores line the great pedestrianized shopping districts of Argyle and Buchanan Streets. Adjacent to them, Princes Square provides some of Europe's top specialty shops blended with an exciting array of restaurants and bars. Slightly farther than a stone's throw from the square, St. Enochs indoor shopping mall offers a wide variety of stores beneath the same roof, and Argyll Victorian Arcade is the place to look for jewelry and fine gifts.

Farther out, but well worth it if you are visiting Glasgow over a weekend, is the city's famous "Barras Street Market." It's a bargain collector's delight with goods ranging from Victorian bric-a-brac to high fashion, all flavored by the antics of the stall holders.

The "Glasgow Connection"

All day excursions described that depart from Edinburgh also may be taken from Glasgow. Refer to the rail schedules on pages 241–42 for Ediburgh–Glasgow and Glasgow–Edinburgh. In fact, two of the day excursions—Ayr and Stranraer—require passing through Glasgow. For these excursions, readers residing in Glasgow need only refer to the appropriate day-excursion schedule.

Two of the day excursions—Dunbar and Dunfermline—can be reached conveniently only through Edinburgh. Consequently, readers need only refer to the Glasgow–Edinburgh shuttle-service schedule for these day excursions.

Five day excursions—Aberdeen, Dundee, Montrose, St. Andrews, and Stirling—are so situated on Scotland's rail lines that they may be reached either by direct connection from the Queen Street Station in Glasgow or through Edinburgh.

Two other day excursions—Inverness and Perth—are reached more conveniently from Glasgow by direct train service from the Queen Street Station rather than through Edinburgh. A condensation of the "Glasgow Connections" for direct service appears on page 240.

The "Glasgow Connection" for express trains to London is given on page 243. All services shown are subject to change. Readers are advised to consult with the schedules posted in the train stations or with a British Rail Travel Centre for train information before commencing each journey.

Regardless of which city you select as your base, don't forget that the frequent train service between Glasgow and Edinburgh enables you to make a day excursion to the one you didn't select as your base. For what to see and do in Edinburgh, consult the chapter on Scotland's capital for details.

There are times throughout the year when one of the two cities, either Glasgow or Edinburgh, may be fully booked. This can take place in Glasgow during May when the city hosts a Mayfest, a festival focusing attention on Glasgow's many activities within its cultural sphere. On the other hand, Edinburgh can be filled to overflowing when visitors attend its world-famous Military Tattoo. When this happens, and your reservationist gives up on the city of your choice, try the other. Your chances of finding accommodations there are very good, and the ease of rail travel between Glasgow and Edinburgh will make it an "easy commute," far better than anything that the Long Island Railroad could come up with!

"Glasgow Connections"

EXCURSION DESTINATION	DEPART GLASGOW	DESTINATION ARRIVE	DESTINATION DEPART	RETURN GLASGOW	NOTES
Aberdeen	0725	1009	1525	1814	M–Sa
	0825	1102	1630	1912	M–Sa
	0925	1218	1932	2223	Su
	0925	1205	1826	2110	M–Sa
Dundee	0725	0850	1545	1712	M–Sat
	0825	0948	1745	1912	Mon–Sat
	0925	1100	1645	1824	Su
	0925	1048	1908	2035	M–Sa
Inverness	0710	1035	1648	2010	M–Sa
	1155	1515	2002	2332	M–Sa
Montrose	0725	0922	1710	1912	M–Sa
	0925	1133	2014	2223	Su
	0925	1120	1906	2110	M–Sa
Perth	0710	0813	1435	1541	M–Sa
	1155	1300	1905	2010	M–Sa
	1345	1508	1782	1945	Su
Stirling	0825	0852	1740	1814	M–Sa
	0915	0959	1744	1824	Su
	0925	0951	1840	1912	M–Sa
	1025	1052	2140	2110	M–Sa

St. Andrews: Train from Glasgow Queen Street Station to Dundee. Transfer to St. Andrews bus, departing every hour on the half-hour.

Edinburgh–Glasgow

There are two services between Edinburgh and Glasgow. Frequent commuter trains operate between Edinburgh Waverley Station and Glasgow Queen Street Station, and there is a less frequent service on the mainline between Edinburgh Waverley Station and Glasgow Central Station—service provided on mainline trains that arrive in Edinburgh and Glasgow from stations in England such as Carlisle, London, and York.

COMMUTER SERVICE: Edinburgh Waverley Station to Glasgow Queen Street Station.

M–Sa: Depart Waverley Station every 30 min from 0700 to 2330; journey time 50 min.

Su: Depart Waverley Station every hour from 0830 to 1730; journey time 65 min. Then at 1805 and 1830 and every 30 min until 2030, then at 2105, 2130, 2230, and 2330.

COMMUTER SERVICE: Glasgow Queen Street Station to Edinburgh Waverley Station.

M–Sa: Depart Queen Street Station every 30 min from 0730 to 2330; journey time 50 min.

Su: Depart Queen Street Station hourly from 0800 to 1800, then at 1830, 1900, and hourly until 2100, then at 2130 and hourly until 2330; journey time varies from 52 to 62 min.

MAINLINE SERVICE: Edinburgh to Glasgow (Glasgow to Edinburgh on the next page)

DEPART WAVERLEY STATION	ARRIVE CENTRAL STATION	NOTES
0809	0917	M–F
0916 (0920 Sa)	1024 (1030 Sa)	M–Sa
1135	1240	Sa
1212	1324	Su
1216	1317	M–F
1305	1412	Sa
1339	1449	Su
1359	1514	Sa
1411 (1409 Su)	1517 (1515 Su)	M–F, Su
1518 (1521 Sa)	1628 (1631 Sa)	M–Sa
1600 (1602 Sa)	1711	M–Sa
1647	1750	Su
1657	1805	Sa
1741	1848	Sa
1807	1916	M–F
1849	1950	Su
1859	2005	M–F
1931	2039	Sa
2131 (2141 Su)	2242 (2244 Su)	Sa, Su
2221	2328	M–F

Glasgow–Edinburgh

MAINLINE SERVICE: Glasgow Central Station to Edinburgh Waverley Station.

DEPART CENTRAL STATION	ARRIVE WAVERLEY STATION	NOTES
0700	0800	M–Sa
0800	0900	M–Sa
0900	1000	Sa
1000	1100	M–Sa
1050	1200	Su
1200	1300	M–Sa
1250	1400	Su
1400	1500	M–Sa
1500 (1450 Su)	1600	Sa, Su
1600 (1550 Su)	1700	Daily
1655	1800	Su
1800	1900 (1906 Su)	Daily
2000 (1955 Su)	2100	Daily

Glasgow–London Train Service

Services shown operate from both London Euston and Kings Cross Stations: services from Euston Station are labeled ES and those from Kings Cross are labelled KC. All trains run to Glasgow Central Station.

DEPART GLASGOW CENTRAL	ARRIVE LONDON	
0615	ES 1215 (1225 Sa)	M–Sa
0700	KC 1237 (1242 Sa)	M–Sa
0720	ES 1300 (1310 Sa)	M–Sa
0800	KC 1335 (1343 Sa)	M–Sa
0900	KC 1441	Sa
0938	ES 1500 (1510 Sa)	M–Sa
1000	KC 1543 (1541 Sa)	M–Sa
1040	ES 1625	Sa
1050	KC 1711	Su
1100	ES 1732	Su
1150	ES 1715 (1720 Sa)	M–Sa
1200	KC 1739 (1741 Sa)	M–Sa
1210	ES 1753	Su
1250	KC 1844	Su
1310	ES 1901	Su
1340	ES 1851 (1913 Sa)	M–Sa
1400	KC 1912 (1932 Sa)	M–Sa
1430	ES 2027	Su
1450	KC 2052	Su
1500	KC 2037	Sa
1538	ES 2110 (2145 Sa)	M–Sa
1550	KC 2142	Su
1600	KC 2145	M–Sa
1615	ES 2202	Su
1655	KC 2308	Su
1700	ES 2215 (2240 Sa)	M–Sa
1730	ES 2256	Su
1800	KC 0002	M–F
2000	KC 0310	F

Wales

Our legends of myth and magic have entranced the whole of the world.
—Paul Barrett, Cardiff Marketing Ltd.

Welcome to Wales, the passionate area of Britain. You will readily notice the distinctly romantic spirit of the Welsh through their lilting language and their crooning, mellifluous voices. According to the Wales Tourist Board's brochure, "Something as simple as travel directions can become a lyrical journey, taking in history, folklore and a fair amount of local gossip." You may be dumbfounded by the Welsh language, but don't let it frighten you. Although the language is considered the oldest living language in Europe—it has been around for more than fourteen centuries—everyone in Wales speaks English.

The Welsh are well known for their extraordinary vocal talent, and in the towns and villages you can hear some of the finest male choirs in the world. With their gift for oratory, it is no wonder the Welsh have figured so prominently in British politics.

Wales is about 170 miles (256 kilometers) long and 60 miles (96 kilometers) wide, about the size of Massachusetts. This compact little country, however, has an abundance of scenic natural beauty, including three national parks and beautiful rivers, streams, lakes, and mountains. Add the myth and magic of a king named Arthur, a magician named Merlin, a knight named Lancelot, and a queen named Guinevere, stir in a castle called Caerleon, and you've got Camelot. If you like castles, choose from 840 to visit in Wales—more castles than any other country in Europe!

Wales is the home and inspiration of many performers and poets, including the great brooding actors Sir Anthony Hopkins and the late Richard Burton, the popular singers Tom Jones and Shirley Bassey, and one of the twentieth century's greatest English-language poets, Dylan Thomas.

South and West Wales contain the majority of the country's 2,921,000 people as well as Cardiff, the capital of Wales, and a new Base City in this edition of *Britain by BritRail*. This region also has some of Britain's most outstanding natural beauty: the Gower Peninsula, the sandy beaches of Pembrokeshire Coast National Park, and the resort town of Tenby.

In North Wales, visit the little village with the longest name in Britain and the second longest name in the world—Llanfairpwllgwyngyllgogerychwyrndrobwllllantysiliogogogoch—whew! (And Raymond Mathias, Wales Marketing Director, USA, can actually pronounce it!) It means "Saint Mary's Church in the hollow of the white hazel near a rapid whirlpool and the Church of Saint Tysilio of the red cave." Found on the island of Anglesey, it is the next stop after Bangor on the North Wales Coast Line. Or journey to "the roof of Wales" and view England, Wales, and Ireland from the summit of Snowdon, the highest peak, at 3,560 feet (1,085 meters). As Helaire Belloc wrote: "There is no corner of Europe that I know which so moves me with awe and majesty of great things as does this mass of northern Welsh mountains."

Snowdonia National Park extends southward through Mid Wales which also contains the smallest town in Britain—Llanwrtyd Wells—the mountainous Brecon Beacons National Park, and the spectacular showcaves of Dan-yr-Ogof, Europe's largest showcaves complex.

Wales Tourist Board, Brunel House, 2 Fitzalon Road, Cardiff CF2 1UY;
   Tel: (0122) 249–9909
   Internet: http://www.visitwales.com
   For brochures and travel information in the United States call (800) 462–2748.

Rail Travel in Wales

National Rail Enquiries: (034) 548–4950

The Great Little Trains of Wales, a very special way of seeing some of the best scenery in Britain, are narrow-gauge steam railways, some more than 100 years old. With a Wanderer Ticket, you can travel on any of the following railways for any eight days within a fifteen-day period or any four days within an eight-day period.

Bala Lake Railway, Yr Orsaf, Llanuwchllyn, Bala, Gwyned, Wales LL23 7DD; *Tel:* (0167) 854–0666.

Brecon Mountain Railway, Pant Station, Merthyr Tydfil, Wales CF48 2UP; *Tel:* (0168) 572–2988; *Fax:* (0168) 538–4854.

Ffestiniog Railway–"Steam and Cuisine", Harbour Station, Porthmadog, Gwynedd, Wales LL49 9NF; *Tel:* (0176) 651–2340; *Fax:* (0176) 651–4715. *E-mail:* festrail.demon.co.uk

The Ffestiniog Railway and the country house Hotel Maes-y-Neuadd have joined forces to create "Steam and Cuisine," a unique "dining by rail" experience. The narrow-gauge steam train travels some 13½ miles through delightful scenery from the coast at Porthmadog to the former slate mining town of Blaenau Ffestiniog. Imagine sipping on a glass of champagne while enjoying the haute cuisine of talented Chef Peter Jackson. The complete package includes a stay at the Hotel Maes-y-Neuadd set in eight acres of beautifully landscaped gardens with stunning views across Snowdonia National Park.

Llanberis Lake Railway, Padam Park, Llanberis, Gwynedd, Wales LL55 4TY; *Tel:* (0128) 687–0549.

Talyllyn Railway, Wharf Station, Tywyn, Gwyned, Wales LL36 9EY; *Tel:* (0165) 471–0472; *Fax:* (0165) 471–1755.

Vale of Rheidol Railway, Park Avenue, Aberystwyth, Dyfed, Wales SY23 1PG; *Tel:* (0197) 062–5819; *Fax:* (0197) 062–3769.

Welsh Highland Railway, Gelerts Farm Works, Porthmadog, Gwynedd, Wales LL49 9DY; *Tel:* (176) 651–3402.

Welshpool & Llanfair Railway, The Station, Llanfair Caereinion, Powys, Wales SY21 0SF; *Tel:* (0193) 881–0441; *Fax:* (0193) 881–0861

For a full "Fact Pack" with details of all the Great Little Trains of Wales and the bargain Wanderer Tickets, write to: The Great Little Trains of Wales, The Station, Llanfair Caereinion, Powys SY21 0BR.

Cardiff

"Cardiff is a vibrant, fast-developing city that has attracted people for literally thousands of years. In Welsh we have a proverb that says 'Do not believe news unless it is old.' We think that the news is now sufficiently old enough to be believed."

—Norma Jarboe, Chief Executive, Cardiff Marketing Limited

Want to go from the first to the twenty-first century in short order? By all means go to Cardiff. The spectacular 2000-year-old Cardiff Castle dominates the historic city center, while the futuristic Cardiff Bay waterfront development encompasses Techniquest, the U.K.'s leading hands-on science discovery center.

Since 1991, when the Cardiff marketing campaign was launched by the late Diana, Princess of Wales, and the then 8-year-old Prince William, Cardiff has been recognized as a world-renowned international center for business, tourism, and leisure. Undoubtedly, Cardiff also is one of the friendliest capital cities in the world and is rapidly becoming the U.K.'s fastest-growing visitor destination. Serving as host city for the European Council in 1998, Cardiff is also the 1999 host for the Rugby World Cup Final on November 9 at the new Millennium Stadium, Britain's first (and Europe's largest) stadium with a retractable roof. Cricket fans will want to attend the 1999 Cricket World Cup on May 8, 11, and 20 at Sophia Gardens.

Cardiff was first developed by the Romans and then by the Normans. Both left their marks in the form of formidable fortifications. The Romans found their way into South Wales and reached the area that is now Cardiff about A.D. 76. At first, they erected a wooden fort, but as Cardiff grew in importance as a Roman naval base, a stone fortress was erected. Following the conquest of England in 1066, the Normans arrived in Cardiff in 1091 and established a stronghold on the site of the old Roman fort. By the sixteenth century, Cardiff had established itself as an important port and trading center, complete with pirates and cutthroats who were primarily responsible for Cardiff's decline over the next couple hundred years. With the arrival of the Industrial Revolution, however, Cardiff was to become the world's premier coal-exporting port, thanks to a successful entrepreneur, the second Marquess of Bute, who was known as the "Creator of Modern Cardiff."

Today's city is largely a creation of the nineteenth century. Cardiff cast off its grim mantle of industrialism to reveal a sparkling paradise of shopping arcades, a glistening white array of impressive neoclassical civic buildings, a cast iron and glass indoor market, a most memorable museum, a transformed harbor area, and the restored (or shall we say "reinvented") Cardiff Castle.

Arriving by Air

Visitors to Wales from North America most likely will use either Heathrow or Gatwick Airport. Refer to the London chapter for information regarding these airports and transfers into London. Transatlantic flights also are available into Birmingham and Manchester Airports.

Cardiff International Airport, 19 kilometers from the city center, provides direct flights to and from Amsterdam, Belfast, Brussels, Dublin, Guernsey, Isle of Man, Jersey, and Paris. It is one of the fastest-growing airports in the United Kingdom. A multimillion-pound expansion has provided an international departure lounge and duty-free shopping and catering facilities. The airport's telephone number is (0144) 671–1111.

Arriving by Train

Hourly trains depart from London's Paddington Station and arrive in Cardiff Central Station in only about two hours.

Cardiff Central Train Station: *Tel:* (034) 548–4950

Train Information: *Tel:* (0122) 222–8000

Valleys Lines (Cardiff Railway Company): *Tel:* (0122) 223–1978 or (034) 548–4950

InterCity Services: *Tel:* (0171) 262–6767

All facilities, including ATMs, train information, and left luggage or lockers, are located in the main concourse. Refurbishment of the entire concourse began in the fall of 1998.

Cardiff Tourist Information Office *Tel:* (0122) 222–7281; *Fax:* (0122) 223–9162 is currently located on the ground floor of the rail station, in the main concourse near the main exit. The office will be relocated to another part of the concourse as part of the station's refurbishment.
Summer hours are Monday and Wednesday–Saturday 0900–1830, Tuesday 1000–1830, Sunday 1000–1800. Winter hours (October 1–April 1) are Monday and Wednesday–Saturday 0900–1730, Tuesday 1000–1730, Sunday 1000-1600. The office is open on Bank Holidays 1000–1700.

Hotel and bed-and-breakfast (B&B) accommodations may be made at the tourist information office in Cardiff Central Station. We highly recommend The Townhouse Hotel (0122) 223–9399), a lovely B&B at 70 Cathedral Road, within walking distance of the city center, including Cardiff Castle. The rate for single occupancy starts at £39.50; twin/doubles, from £49.50. Owned by a charming and friendly couple, Bart and Iris Zuzik, The Townhouse is richly appointed with antiques and paintings and also is home to a few friendly felines. Breakfast is always good too. Just the informative, wonderful conversations with Bart (originally from Chicago,IL) are worth the stay. By taking a left at Sophia Close, you can walk through Bute Park and end up on Castle Street. It's beautiful, convenient, and reasonable. What more could one ask for? Readers of *Britain by BritRail* are entitled to a discount. Just show them this book.

If The Townhouse Hotel is fully booked or if you're allergic to cats, try the Lincoln House Hotel (0122) 239–5558), owned by Neil and Kathy Howard, only about one block farther on Cathedral Road. The Lincoln House is another very charming B&B. Rates are £48 single, £59.50 twin/double, £55 single deluxe, £68 twin deluxe. All rooms have private shower and toilet facilities, and stays include breakfast and VAT.

If you prefer to fork out the extra pounds for superior first class, you'll want to stay at the Angel Hotel on Castle Street. Many a beautiful bride has descended the grand staircase to her "knight in shining armor." But the prices are steep, too. A single room ranges from £92 to £108, and a twin/double is £105 to £120.

Getting Around in Cardiff

The newest and hottest bargain for getting around town is the Cardiff Card. This pass comes complete with a guide booklet and map and provides unlimited bus and train travel on more than 150 routes, entrance to three of the most outstanding castles in Wales—Cardiff Castle, Castell Coch and Caerphilly Castle—museums and galleries, Techniquest (Britain's leading science discovery center) in Cardiff Bay Inner Harbor, parks and gardens, and many more sights and attractions. Discounts at restaurants and on entertainment are provided as well.

Put Cardiff in your pocket with the Cardiff Card—available for twenty-four, forty-eight, or seventy-two hours; kids get a 50 percent discount and those under age five get in free. Prices in U.S. dollars were not available at press time. Please telephone Rail Pass Express, Inc. at (800) 722–7151 or visit http://www.railpass.com for prices.

The Cardiff Card is a great way for visitors to tour the city and visit sights and attractions. By providing free transportation on Cardiff's buses, a regular service that covers the entire city and beyond—even to attractions like Llanerch Vineyard and Castell Coch—Cardiff Bus will take you to most of the attractions covered by the Cardiff Card.

The Central Bus Station is immediately in front of Cardiff Central Station. Cardiff Bus, St. David's House, Wood Street, Cardiff CF1 1ER; *Tel:* (0122) 239–6521.

The train service will take you to attractions like Rhondda Heritage Park (near Pontypridd) and to Llandaff and its cathedral, or to a traditional resort like Barry Island.

You can get a great introduction to Cardiff by booking a Guide Friday tour. The ticket is valid all day and you can get on and off the double-decker sightseeing bus when you want. The tours operate daily from May through September. The bus departs from in front of Cardiff Castle every thirty minutes. Tickets cost £6 for adults, £5 for students and senior citizens, and £2.50 for children.

Capitalize on Cardiff

Begin your tour at Cardiff Castle. From Cardiff Central Station, proceed past the bus station in front, turn right onto Wood Street, then left onto St. Mary Street, which becomes High Street. As High Street intersects with Castle Street, you will see the mighty castle right in front of you.

The Cardiff castle is a lavishly restored medieval fortress with 2000-year-old Roman foundations, parts of which still exist today. The castle's extensive Roman walls, which were 10 feet thick, were well preserved by earthen banks until their excavation in the nineteenth century. Visit the Roman Wall exhibition area immediately behind the ticket kiosk just inside the main castle entrance.

The medieval stronghold built by invading Normans fell into ruin after the Civil War in the seventeenth century and was saved by the first Marquess of Bute in the late 1700s. The third Marquess of Bute and his pal, the eccentric architect William Burges, lavishly reconstructed Cardiff Castle to the nineteenth-century splendor we see today. The extravagant, opulent rooms are laden with an eclectic mix of decor and architectural features inspired by medieval England, Arabia, the Old Testament, Islam, even the fairy tales of Hans Christian Andersen. Each room has a different theme.

Today the castle interior provides the setting for medieval "Welsh Nights" and private or public receptions. The castle and its grounds provide a dramatic backdrop for a series of spectacular events throughout the summer, ranging from a hot-air balloon festival to massed military bands and, in case you have the urge to say "I do" in a castle, even enchanted weddings.

The castle is open daily all year except Christmas Day, Boxing Day, and New Year's Day. From March to October hours are 0930–1800 (last tour/entry at 1700), November–February 0930–1630 (last tour at 1515).

Admission cost is £2.40 for adults; £1.20 for children ages five to sixteen; with a Cardiff Card, there is free admission to the grounds (small additional charge for guided tours). For information, telephone (0122) 287–8100.

Cardiff Civic Centre lies beyond the castle, as does the National Museum & Gallery. The Civic Centre is one of the most impressive buildings in Europe. Separated by wide avenues and parks, the presence in the spring of cherry blossoms and tulip beds creates a perfect setting for the white stone buildings.

In the National Museum & Gallery in Cathays Park, you may view, among other art treasures, four tapestry cartoons by Rubens. Rodin's bronze statuary *The Kiss* is also housed there. The museum is unusual in that it contains a variety of exhibits, from priceless works of art to dinosaurs. Hours are 1000–1700 Tuesday–Sunday and Bank Holidays. Entrance fees: £4.25 adults; children ages 5-16, £2.50; free entrance with a

Cardiff Card. For more information telephone (0122) 239–7951 or visit http://www.cf.ac.uk/nmgw.

Ready for shopping? Cardiff is a shopaholic's paradise. According to Cardiff Marketing Limited, Cardiff "offers the best shopping in Britain outside London," with more big-name retailers than any comparable British city. Seven Victorian shopping arcades blend well with three modern shopping areas. Cardiff claims to have had pedestrian shopping areas long before the phrase was invented. The two main shopping streets, Queen Street and Mary Street, form an L-shape that partially encloses Cardiff's largest shopping mall, St. David's Centre. For those with the "shop till you drop" philosophy, this is the place.

A visit to Castle Welsh Crafts at 1 Castle Street is a must. Located across the street from Cardiff Castle, this shop has traditional Welsh crafts, including intricately hand-carved lovespoons. The tradition of the Welsh peasantry to give their loved ones a carved wooden spoon as a token of affection goes back many centuries. In fact, the English-speaking term, to go "spooning," is almost certainly derived from this old Welsh custom.

Some people believe that the presentation and the acceptance of the lovespoon was confirmation that a courtship was about to start; others believed the lovespoon represented an early form of engagement ring. Certain designs have specific meanings. For instance, the giving of a spoon shaped as leaves or trees represents growing love, a horseshoe represents good luck and happiness, and bells indicate marriage. The lovespoon makes a perfect Welsh souvenir or gift. Visit Castle Welsh Crafts on-line at http://www.castle-welsh-co.uk/ewe or *e-mail:* sales@castle-welsh-crafts.co.uk. *Be sure to show them this page of* Britain by BritRail *and receive a discount on your purchases.*

To sample some traditional Welsh dishes served by waitresses in heritage costume, try the Blas ar Gymru (A Taste of Wales) Restaurant at 48 Crwys Road, about a twenty-minute walk from Cardiff Castle. Proceed north through the Civic Centre to Corbett Road, turn right and over the bridge into Cathays Terrace, right onto Woodville Road, and left onto Crwys Road. Reservations are advised; telephone (0122) 238–3132.

We enjoyed lunch at The Hogshead Owain Glyndwr, St. Johns Square (*Tel:* 221–980 or 399–303), near St. John's Church in the pedestrian shopping area. Their menu says it all: "There's ne'er a moment so sweet when the best of friends choose to meet when conversation fills the air with a jug o' ale and hearty fayre. Eat with gusto, drink with cheer good ale, good food, and good atmosphere."

For a unique and delightful dining experience, have a traditional dinner with a Welsh family; you may opt for the stay-over as well. What better way to get to know more about the Welsh people and their culture? If you purchased your BritRail passes from Rail Pass Express, Inc., you are eligible for this special opportunity. European Vacation Tours & Groups will make the arrangements for you. Telephone toll-free (888) TOUR–404.

Techniquest, Britain's leading science discovery center, is located in Cardiff Bay. The area is also home to the Welsh Industrial and Maritime Museum, the Norwegian Church Arts Centre, Lightship 2000, the Point, and, last but not least, the world's most famous fish 'n' chips restaurant, Harry Ramsden's. Since improving the harbor area is an ongoing process, new venues are rapidly being established. The Cardiff Bay area is definitely one of the "hot spots" of Britain. You can telephone the Cardiff Bay Visitor Centre at (0122) 246–3833 or visit http://www.cardiff-bay.co.uk on the Internet. To get to Cardiff Bay Inner Harbor area, take buses 7, 7A, 7E, 8 or CB1. Shuttle trains operate from Queen Street Station.

The Museum of Welsh Life at St. Fagan's is one of Europe's largest open-air folk museums. Here, you can travel through time from the Celtic village of 2000 years ago to a miner's cottage of the 1980s. "Living" buildings depicting daily Welsh life were reconstructed stone by stone. You'll see an ornate timber-framed barn originally built around 1550, a working blacksmith and bakery shop, an Elizabethan manor (St. Fagan's Castle), a medieval farmhouse, and much, much more. To get there, take bus No. 32 from Central Bus Station, Stand B1. The museum is open daily July–September 1000–1800; October–June 1000–1700. Closed Christmas Eve and Christmas Day. Entrance fees are £5.25 for adults; £4.25 for children ages five to sixteen; there is a 10 percent discount with a Cardiff Card.

Waverley and Balmoral Steamer cruises depart from Penarth Pier, 4 miles from Cardiff. Take Valley Line train to Penarth or buses L1, L2, P10, or P20 to Penarth Pier from the Central Bus Station. Cost varies; with a Cardiff Card, one child under 18 travels free with each paying adult.

The *Waverley* is the last seagoing Paddle Steamer in the world. Both the *Waverley* and the *Balmoral* are beautifully restored and each can carry up to 925 passengers. An afternoon cruise affords the spectacular scenery of Bristol Channel; romantics should opt for an evening cruise. The cruises are conducted by Waverly Excursions Ltd., *Tel:* (0144) 672–0656.

Tradegar House is a magnificent country house set in ninety acres of parkland and gardens. It was the home of one of the great Welsh families, the Morgans, for more than five centuries. See the vastly different lifestyles of those of "the manor born" and their servants. Located in Newport, it is a twenty-minute bus ride (No. 30) from Central Bus Station, Stand E2. Hours: Easter-September, Wednesday-Sunday 1115-1615; August: open daily; October, weekends only. Entrance Fees: £3.95 adults; £2.00 children ages six to sixteen; free with Cardiff Card. After the tour, opt for a carriage ride, go boating on the lake, or visit the craft workshops.

Llanerch Vineyard is an international award winning winery in Vale of Glamorgan. It is the largest in Wales, producing estate bottle white, rosé and sparkling wines. Of course, you may sample a bit o' the juice during your tour. Take Bus 32 from Central Bus Station, Stand B1. Entrance fees: £3.00 adults; £1.00 kids five to sixteen; free with a Cardiff Card.

Second in size only to Windsor Castle, Caerphilly Castle is a mere fifteen-minute train ride from Cardiff's Queen Street Station. Covering thirty acres and remarkably well preserved, it's crammed with interesting things, including a tower that even Oliver Cromwell's gunpowder could not topple—at least not completely. Trains depart Queen Street Station thrice hourly, or take bus 26 at Stand B3 from the Central Bus Station. The castle is open daily from March to late October, 0930-1830. From late October to late March, hours are Monday–Saturday 0930–1600, Sunday 1100–1600. Entrance fees are £2.40 for adults; £1.90 for ages five to sixteen; free with a Cardiff Card. *Tel:* (0122) 288–3143 or visit http://www.castlewales.com/caerphil.html on the internet.

Just at the top of the hill past the tourist office is The Philly Diner Co. in the Pavilion shopping complex. A great place to find a meal for meager means, especially if your appetite needs satisfying after shopping.

If you would rather sit and reflect on the day or daydream of days of yore, we suggest visiting one of the oldest restaurants in the area, The Courthouse, *Tel:* (0122) 288–8120. The view of the castle is spectacular; the back patio overlooks the moat, the walkway that encircles the castle grounds, and the antique decor is almost as enticing as the ale. The Courthouse is on your left as you wind down the hill from the rail station toward the castle.

Not satisfied being a one-castle owner, John Marquess of Bute commissioned William Burges to design a little country retreat, Castell Coch, which is perched on a wooded hillside just a few miles north of Cardiff at Tongwynlais. Known as the "fairy tale castle in the woods," Castell Coch appears to have been magically removed from the pages of *Sleeping Beauty*. Unfortunately, Billy Burges died suddenly in 1881 before completing his Victorian dream of the Middle Ages. Castell Coch was completed by colleagues who remained faithful to the rich, detailed decor, grandeur, and allusion of medieval architecture.

To reach Castell Coch, *Tel:* (0122) 281–0101, take bus 26 from Cardiff Central Bus Station, Stand B3. Entrance fees are £2.40 for adults, £1.90 for children ages five to sixteen; free with a Cardiff Card. For more of what to see and do in Cardiff visit http://www.whats-on-line.co.uk/cardiff and http://www.info.crf.ac.uk/ccin/homepage.html.

Day Excursions

After you've seen Cardiff and its nearby attractions, you may want to venture farther afield. Visit Bath to learn more about Roman England, opt for visiting the most western point of England, the pirates' Penzance, or Plymouth, whose historical heritage is closely related to America. Or see the ideal Swansea and the Mumbles in South Wales. And there is always Tenby for the resort lover.

Edinburgh–Cardiff

DEPART WAVERLEY STATION	ARRIVE CENTRAL STATION	NOTES
0714	1450	M–F (1)
0814	1635	M–Sa (2)
1000	1841	M–F (3)
1100	1830	M–F (4)
1150	1909	M–Sa (5)
1200	1959	Sa (6)
1200	2035	M–F (3)
1300	2113	M–Sa (3)
1400	2214	M–F (3)

DEPART CENTRAL STATION	ARRIVE WAVERLEY STATION	NOTES
0900	1629	M–Sa (5)
1110	1956	Su (4)
1215	1956	M–Sa (7)
1255	2247	Su (8)
1400	2209	Sa (3)
1455	2247	M–F (7)

(1) Change at Birmingham New Street *or* at Cheltenham Spa *or* (Sa only) at Gloucester

(2) Change at Bristol Temple-Meads

(3) Change at Newcastle-upon-Tyne *and* at Bristol Temple Meads

(4) Change at Birmingham New Street *or* at Cheltenham Spa *or* at Gloucester

(5) Change at Cheltenham Spa *or* at Gloucester

(6) Change at Newcastle-upon-Tyne

(7) Change at Cheltenham Spa *or* at Birmingham New Street

(8) Change at Gloucester *or* at Cheltenham Spa *or* at Birmingham New Street; time between trains is 1 hour 30 minute or more.

Cardiff–Glasgow

Services shown are on one route between Cardiff and Glasgow that has frequent service; other routes are possible, i.e., via London or via Birmingham New Street.

Note: Some schedules shown require a short connection time in Crewe, 5 to 6 minutes. Passengers should consult the train information staff at Glasgow Central Station before embarking on such a trip.

DEPART CENTRAL STATION	ARRIVE CENTRAL STATION	NOTES
0510	1212	M–Sa (1)
0720	1357	M–Sa (1)
0845	1521	Sa (1)
1045	1735 (1715 Sa)	M–Sa (1)
1135	1936	Su (1)
1245	1935	M–Sa (1)
1302	2001	Su (1)
1445	2134 (2135 Su)	Daily (1)
1545	2204 (2216 Sa)	M–Sa (1) (2)
1605	2324	Su (1)
1645	2253	M–F (1) (3)

DEPART CENTRAL STATION	ARRIVE CENTRAL STATION	NOTES
0615	1345	M–Sa (1)
0820	1445	M–Sa (1)
0840	1545	M–Sa (4)
1100	1841	Su (1)
1110	1745	M–Sa (1)
1150	1801 (1811 Sa)	M–Sa (1)
1310	2028	Su (1)
1340	1952	M–F (1) (5)
1430	2100	Su (1)
1608	2249 (2255 Sa)	M–Sa (1)
1615	2259	Su (1)
1730	0005	Su (1)

(1) Change trains at Crewe
(2) The connection time on M–F is *only* 5 minutes; on Sa the connection time is 12 minutes
(3) Connection time is only 5 minutes
(4) Change trains at Carlisle *or* at Penrith *or* at Oxenholme *or* at Lancaster *or* at Preston *and* at Crewe
(5) Connection time is only 6 minutes

London–Cardiff

DEPART PADDINGTON STATION	ARRIVE CENTRAL STATION	NOTES
0700	0857	M–F
0800	0952 (0956 Sa)	M–Sa
0830	1045	M–F
0900	1058 (1100 Sa)	M–Sa
0930	1114	M–F
0945	1149	Sa
1000	1157 (1204 Sa)	M–Sa

M–F service continues after 1000 at hourly intervals until 1700, then every half-hour to 1900, then hourly until 2200; Sa service continues after 1000 at hourly intervals until 2100; Su service continues after 1000 at hourly intervals until 2300.

DEPART CENTRAL STATION	ARRIVE PADDINGTON STATION	NOTES
1425	1630 (1637 Su)	Daily
1525	1733 (1745 Su)	Daily

M–Sa service continues after 1525 at hourly intervals until 1925 on Sa and until 2125 on weekdays; Su service continues until 2125, and there are other Su departures at 1655 and 1755.

Day Excursion to

Bath

ROMAN ENGLAND—THE ORIGINAL HOT TUB

From Cardiff: Depart from Cardiff Central Station

Distance by train: 53 miles (62 km)

Average train time: 1 hour, 15 minutes

From London: Depart from London's Paddington Station

Distance by train: 107 miles (172 km)

Average train time: 1 hour, 30 minutes

Train Information and InterCity Services: (034) 548–4950

Bath Tourist Information Centre: Abbey Chambers, Abbey Church Yard BA1 1LY

   Tel: (0122) 547–7101

   Internet: http://wwwbath.uk.com

   E-mail: bath_tourism@bathnes.gov.uk

   Hours: The center is open Monday–Saturday 0930–1800 May–September; and
   0930–1700 October–April. Sunday open 1000–1600.

   To reach the centre on foot, proceed up Manvers Street directly in front of the
Bath Spa rail station until you cross North Parade Road at the traffic light. At this
point, you will see the Bath Abbey tower to your left. Looking to your left, enter
York Street and proceed until reaching an open square on the right. The Tourist
Information Center will be in the building on the right of the square on the ground
floor.

The Roman baths are one of Britain's major tourist attractions and
draw visitors from all points of the globe to their waters. The baths rank a
close second to England's number one attraction, the Tower of London,
and are well worth the short train ride from either Cardiff or London to
see them and the "glory that was Rome," transposed to England.

Bath has been in the limelight as the social center "to see and be seen"
during two eras of recorded history—once during the Roman occupation
of Britain and again in the eighteenth century when Bath became the
"gathering place" for royalty and other well-to-do folk. Development of
the only hot springs in Britain is attributed to the Romans soon after
Emperor Claudius invaded the land in A.D. 43.

To the Romans, the city's name was *Aquae Sulis*—literally translated,
"the waters of Sulis." By the end of the first century, the Romans had
established a great bathing facility. The magnificent hot baths were said to
have curative powers. Although modern scientists are doubtful of the
waters' purported healing properties, there is no doubt that the only hot

Cardiff–Bath

DEPART CENTRAL STATION	ARRIVE BATH SPA STATION	NOTES
0730	0835	M–Sa
0745	0921	Su
0755	0901 (0857 Sa)	M–Sa
0830	0935 (0941 Su)	Daily
0930	1035 (1041 Su)	Daily
1030	1135 (1147 Su)	Daily
1100	1218	Sa
1130	1235 (1243 Su)	Daily
1200	1315	M–Sa (1)
1230	1335 (1348 Su)	Daily (2)

(1) Reservations required on Saturday only.
(2) Reservations required M–F only.

DEPART BATH SPA STATION	ARRIVE CENTRAL STATION	NOTES
1429	1537 (1554 Su)	Daily
1527 (1524 Su)	1635 (1633 Su)	Daily
1627 (1621 Su)	1735 (1738 Su)	Daily
1633	1800	Su
1652	1817	Sa
1717	1830	Su
1727	1841 (1835 Sa)	M–Sa
1800	1910	Su
1822	1928	Su
1828	1937 (1942 Sa)	M–Sa
1857	2018	Su
1915	2032	Su
1928	2035	M–Sa
1954	2109	Su
2006	2113	M–Sa
2023 (2022 Su)	2129 (2139 Su)	Sa, Su
2028	2135 (2142 Sa)	M–Sa
2046	2214	M–F
2129 (2123 Su)	2232 (2235 Su)	M–F, Su
2138	2245 (2252 Sa)	M–Sa
2222	2335	Su
2240	0005	M–Sa

London–Bath

Direct trains from London Paddington only; other service is available from London Waterloo station and may require a change of trains.

DEPART PADDINGTON STATION	ARRIVE BATH SPA STATION	NOTES
0715	0837 (0838 Sa)	M–Sa
0800	0932	Su
0815	0937	M–F
0845	1000 (0959 Sa)	M–Sa
0915	1033 (1037 Sa)	M–Sa
0930	1057	Su
0945	1108 (1109 Sa)	M–Sa
1015	1134 (1144 Sa)	M–Sa
1030	1157	Su
1045 (1042 Sa)	1157 (1156 Sa)	M–Sa
1115	1238 (1237 Sa)	M–Sa
1130	1257	Su

DEPART BATH SPA STATION	ARRIVE PADDINGTON STATION	NOTES
1427	1600 (1605 Sa & Su)	Daily
1457	1620	M–F
1527	1700 (1705 Sa)	Daily
1557	1725 (1736 Su)	M–F, Su
1627	1755 (1804 Sa, 1753 Su)	Daily
1657 (1658 Sa)	1825 (1830 Sa)	M–Sa
1727	1859 (1905 Sa)	M–Sa
1742	1914	Sa
1757 (1758 Su)	1925 (1924 Su)	M–F, Su
1827	2000 (2005 Sa, 2007 Su)	Daily
1927	2100 (2105 Sa, 2107 Su)	Daily
1957	2134	Su
2027	2158	M–F
2042	2225	Sa
2057	2230	Su
2100	2229	Sa
2130	2252	Su
2137	2315	M–F
2145	2325	Sa

mineral springs in Britain played a major role in establishing Bath as the "hot spot" for socializing.

The baths made *Aquae Sulis* famous throughout the empire. Its fame lasted 400 years until the rising sea level and the fall of the Roman Empire brought the city's prosperity to an end. By the end of the seventh century, the city was described as "a ghostly ruin with crumbled masonry fallen into dark pools, overgrown and bird haunted, but still a wondrous sight."

The second revitalization of the city, a cultural one, began in 1705 with the arrival of thirty-one-year-old Richard Nash. Like the Romans, he too conquered, but not by force. Nash was Bath's first public-relations expert. It was during his "reign" that Queen Anne visited Bath, and it again became an elegant and stylish resort for the wealthy. When Nash died at the age of eighty-seven, he had created a kingdom of taste and etiquette over which he reigned as Beau Nash, King of Bath.

Although the hot springs were used again from the Middle Ages, the Roman ruins remained buried even during most of Beau Nash's time. Finally, the gilded bronze head of Minerva was uncovered by workmen digging a sewer in 1727. Although the statues and columns of the present-day Roman baths were added by Victorian restorers, the original bath area still has the lead floor and limestone paving installed by the Romans.

The real restoration and melding of Bath's Roman past and of the city's two eras of fame began in 1878 when the city engineer, while investigating a water leak, came upon the Roman reservoir and the huge complex of baths that it fed. Someone finally called a plumber.

Bath abounds in sightseeing opportunities. The tourist information center has a wealth of information about the city and its surroundings. The Tourist Information Centre sells a wide range of publications to help you get the most out of your stay. We recommend the pamphlet *36 Leisure Attractions in and around Bath*. This informative piece contains a city map and lists places of interest.

Those interested in fashion over the last 400 years will want to visit the Museum of Costume and Assembly Rooms (No. 25 on the pamphlet map), located on Bennett Street. Then, turn left on Bennett Street and proceed to nearby No. 1 Royal Crescent (No. 29 on the pamphlet map) to tour the beautifully restored eighteenth-century town house designed by John Wood.

Bath has won many awards for its floral displays, and its natural beauty makes a walking tour through the city a real pleasure.

On the subject of tours, seek out the Mayor's Corps of Honorary Guides. They conduct guided tours at various times throughout the summer season at no charge. These tours, which depart from outside the Pump Room in the abbey churchyard, take approximately one and a half hours. For advance information, ring up (0122) 547–7786 and ask to be put through to extension 7785. By the way, we'd appreciate having you mention *Britain by BritRail* when the Guides' office asks who recommended their services. We've been mutual admirers for years.

If you are on a tight schedule, the best sights in the city are cloistered about the Roman baths. The baths and the abbey practically adjoin each other. Upstairs from the baths, you may visit the Pump Room and sample its water. Take time to touch the worn paving, and in that moment you can recall the glory that was Rome.

Day Excursion to

Penzance
WESTERN END OF THE LINE

From Cardiff: Depart from Cardiff Central Station

Distance by train: 245 miles (394 km)
Average train time: 5 hours, 30 minutes
From London: Depart from Paddington Station
Distance by train: 305 miles (491 km)
Average train time: 5 hours
Train information and InterCity services: (034) 548–4950
Penzance Tourist Information Centre: Station Road TR18 2NF; *Tel:* (0173) 636–2207; *Fax:* (0173) 636–3600.
   Hours: Please call for hours.
   The tourist information center is located immediately outside the rail station. Upon arrival in the center, the first item of information you should collect is a Penzance & District map. This graphic presentation of the peninsula will help you put the area into the proper perspective for your visit. Publications that are available in the information center will be extremely helpful.

When you arrive in Penzance, you are literally at "the end of the line" insofar as rail travel is concerned. Geographically speaking, you are also at the western end of England. A mere 10 miles more would bring you to Land's End, where a road sign pointing to the west cryptically states,

AMERICA 4,000 MILES. It is difficult to find a grander coastline. This is Land's End Peninsula—the sightseeing opportunities are endless.

Once you are fully armed with the publications needed to explore this most interesting area, we are certain that you will be immediately attracted to the harbor area lying to the left just beyond the rail terminal. We suggest that you make it your first "port of call," since it can readily put you in the proper adventurous mood to see the rest of the area.

At harborside you will want to inspect the old warehouse and granary overlooking Battery Rocks. It has been converted to a craft center and art gallery. Next door is the Dolphin Inn, formerly a smugglers' hideaway and said to be haunted by an old sea captain's ghost. From there, a walk up Chapel Street away from the harbor brings you to a part of Old Penzance filled with Georgian town houses, fishermen's cottages, and the Museum of Nautical Art. This unusual museum, which takes the form of an eighteenth-century battleship with gun decks and life-size figures manning muzzleloading guns, is filled with displays of actual navigational gear from former times. The museum is well worth a visit. It is a delight to young and old alike.

For a unique treat, visit the Trinity House National Lighthouse Centre, which holds probably the largest and finest collection of lighthouse equipment in the world. It's located on Wharf Road (0173–636–0077) and is open daily 1100–1700 Easter to October. Admission is £2.50 for adults, £1.50 for senior citizens; children admitted free when accompanied by two adults. Within the center, you can relax in the audiovisual theater and enjoy your trip back in time to the first lighthouses, those lonely citadels that guarded the treacherous waters around England's shores.

Termed the "Capital of the Cornish Riviera," Penzance occupies an unusually well-sheltered position on England's western coast. Because the town faces due south and is protected from all other points of the compass by a ring of hills, its climate is ideal year-round. Winter is mild and virtually without frost, followed by an early spring and a temperate summer. Botanically, Penzance is noted for its early flowers and produce.

You need not confine yourself to the limits of Penzance, although you'll find it almost impossible to get away from its magnetic attractions. Local bus service can take you to Land's End, and, as we have indicated on the schedule, rail connections can be made to other equally interesting points on the peninsula such as Falmouth, Newquay, and St. Ives. The tourist information center can give you the background on these interesting

Cardiff–Penzance

DEPART CENTRAL STATION	ARRIVE PENZANCE STATION	NOTES
0500	1116	M–F (1)
0630	1222	M–F (2)
0715	1355	Su (3)
0800	1325	M–F (2)
0830	1441	M–F (4)
0830	1423	Sa (5)
1000	1534	M–F (6)
1002	1646	Su (2)
1100	1557	Sa (2)
1155	1704	M–F

DEPART PENZANCE STATION	ARRIVE CENTRAL STATION	NOTES
0515	1053	M–F (6)
0722	1235	M–Sa (2)
0922 (0926 Su)	1435 (1445 Su)	M–F, Su (2)
0955	1554	Su (2)
1054	1635	Sa (2)
1139	1633	Su (2)
1145	1654	M-F
1210	1738	Su (2)
1235	1841	M–F (2)
1325	1942	Sa (5)
1333	1910	Su (2)
1440	2018	M–F (6)
1549	2055	Su (2)

(1) Change trains at Plymouth
(2) Change trains at Bristol Temple Meads
(3) Change trains at Bristol Temple Meads *or* at Exeter St. Davids
(4) Change trains at Bristol Temple Meads *and* at Plymouth
(5) Change trains at Bristol Temple Meads *and* at Exeter St. Davids
(6) Change trains at Exeter St. Davids

London–Penzance

Schedules shown are for direct service that departs from London Paddington Station. Other services are possible by changing trains in Plymouth or by departing from London Waterloo and changing at Exeter St. Davids Station.

DEPART PADDINGTON STATION	ARRIVE PENZANCE STATION	NOTES
0735	1255	Sa
0745	1325	M–F
0800	1355	Su
0905	1423	Sa
0915	1457	Su
1030	1530	Sa
1035	1534	M–F
1115	1646	Su
1135	1630	Sa
1235	1800 (1805 Sa)	M–Sa
1315	1842	Su
1335	1900	Sa
1415	1950	Su
1445	2020	M–F
1535	2055 (2115 Sa)	M–Sa
1615	2142	Su
1715	2239	Su
1733	2230	M–F
1815	2330 (2343 Su)	Sa, Su
1835	2350	M–F
2347	0820	M–F, Su (1)

(1) The 2347 train is an overnight train that operates from London Waterloo Station; the train conveys first- and second-class sleepers and second-class chair cars only. Reservations are required for all overnight sleepers. The arrival time shown is the next day in Penzance.

places, and you can ask the Rail Travel Centre in the train station to work out the needed schedules.

From London, Penzance lends itself more to an "out-and-back" excursion than to a day excursion, although with British InterCity 125 trains, it is possible to visit England's westernmost town in the course of a

Penzance–London

DEPART PENZANCE STATION	ARRIVE PADDINGTON STATION	NOTES
0515	0957	M–F
0642	1152	Sa
0700	1221	M–F
0754	1320	Sa
0805	1325	M–F
0832	1359	Su
0900	1422	Sa
0926	1514	Su
0937	1453	Sa
1004	1530	Sa
1005	1505	M–F
1025	1553	Su
1139	1738	Su
1235	1800	Su
1325	1914	Sa
1440	1955	M–F
1444	2018	Su
1508	2030	Sa
1549	2134	Su
1630	2205	M–F
1640	2229	Sa
1720	2252	Su
2200 (2115 Su)	0530	M–F, Su (1)

(1) The last train shown is an overnight sleeper train that arrives at London Waterloo Station. The train conveys first- and second-class sleepers and second-class chair cars. The arrival time shown is the next day.

day and still be back in London that evening. An excellent way to visit Penzance is to board the sleeper that departs from London's Waterloo Station (and sometimes from Paddington Station) just before midnight. You can board about an hour before departure time, have the attendant make a nightcap for you, and be well into dreamland by the time the train rolls out of London's suburbs. At 0820 you arrive in Penzance Station after being awakened by the attendant bringing your morning tea or coffee and biscuits. After a full day's sightseeing in Penzance, you can board either the sleeper for your return to London or the InterCity 125 at 1630 and return to London by 2200 the same evening.

Penzance also offers a diversion. When you feel it's time to move on from London to the north toward Edinburgh, check out of your London accommodations and take the sleeper to Penzance. Go sightseeing in Penzance, then arrive back in London as described above at 2200 and transfer leisurely to London's Euston Station to board the *Night Scotsman* at 2355. You'll arrive in Edinburgh the next morning at 0645. Passengers may remain aboard until 0800.

Sleeper reservations should be made well in advance. Don't wait until the last minute or you may be disappointed, especially during holidays and peak summer travel periods. Don't forget to check the second-class-sleeper availability if first class is filled. Sometimes if you show up on the departure platform about half an hour before the train leaves, you can pick up a berth cancellation, but don't count on it.

Day Excursion to

Plymouth   PILGRIM'S PROGRESS PORT

From Cardiff: Depart from Cardiff Central Station

Distance by train: 166 miles (267 km)
Average train time: 3 hours, 15 minutes
From London: Depart from Paddington Station
Distance by train: 226 miles (363 km)
Average train time: 3 hours
Train information and InterCity services: (034) 548–4950
Plymouth Tourist Information Centre: 9 The Barbican; *Tel:* (0175) 226–4849; *Fax:* (0175) 225–7955
Hours: Monday–Friday 0900–1700; Saturday 0900–1700, Sundays and Bank Holidays, 1000–1600.

Located in Plymouth's Elizabethan quarter, you can reach the tourist information center on foot from the train station in about twenty minutes through short underground passages and a pedestrianized area. Look for the streams, fountains, and gardens, which form part of an outstanding display. You can also take bus No. 25 or board any bus stopping at the shelter to the right of the station entrance. Pay your fare and ask to be "deposited" at the Barbican. Folks who are in a real hurry can hail a taxi. There is a taxi queue just outside of the rail station; the bus stop is a few steps beyond.

Plymouth has one of the finest natural harbors in Europe. From Plymouth Hoe (a Saxon word meaning "high place above the sea"), there are magnificent views over Plymouth Sound and the harbor. Stand on this huge brow of a hill, which is claimed to be one of the world's finest natural promenades, and you stand in the midst of history. It was here that Sir Francis Drake continued his game of bowls before setting out to deal with the *Spanish Armada* in 1588. Earlier, in 1577, he set sail from the same harbor in the *Golden Hind* on a three-year voyage around the world. Here, too, in 1620 the Pilgrims embarked on the *Mayflower* for the New World. Too few remember that the first airplane to cross the Atlantic Ocean, the U.S. Navy seaplane *NC4*, touched down in Plymouth Sound. This spot is indeed steeped in historical heritage, much of it related to America. Stand here proudly!

While at the tourist information office, ask for a copy of the pamphlet *The Attractions of Plymouth*; it contains an easy-to-read map of the attractions within and near Plymouth. For an introduction to Plymouth, visit the city's latest attraction, the National Marine Aquarium or see the Plymouth Dome. Situated on Plymouth's famous Hoe, the Dome is one of the most up-to-date centers of its kind in Britain. Here you can take a journey through time, use high-resolution cameras to zoom the shoreline, and do many other exciting things. We can guarantee that you won't run out of things to do while in Plymouth.

The Plymouth of today is a city of two distinct parts: the original Elizabethan section called the "Barbican" and the modern city center that rose from the devastation and debris of the last world war. If your time in Plymouth is limited, concentrate on visiting the Barbican area of the city.

The Barbican harbor area, where the old town of Plymouth nestled, derived its name from the fact that at the entrance to the harbor stood an outpost of the ancient Plymouth Castle. According to castle phraseology, such outer fortifications were called barbicans. The Barbican was spared much of the damage that Plymouth suffered during the bombardments of World War II. Consequently, there are still many old buildings and narrow streets in this area that recapture the Elizabethan atmosphere.

One Barbican landmark of particular interest to U.S. citizens is a memorial stone marking the place on the harbor pier from which the *Mayflower* sailed. Historic Elizabethan buildings include the Black Friars Distillery, home of Plymouth Gin since 1793. The distillery is still operating in buildings formerly used as a monastery and dating back to

Cardiff–Plymouth

DEPART CENTRAL STATION	ARRIVE PLYMOUTH STATION	NOTES
0800	1123	M–F (1)
0830	1219 (1149 Sa, 1153 Su)	Daily (1)
0930	1256	Su (1)
1000	1334	M–F (2)
1030	1342	M–F (1)
1100	1402	Sa (1)
1130	1447 (1449 Su)	M–F, Su (1)
1155	1507	M–F
1200	1523	Sa (1) (3)

Plymouth–Cardiff

DEPART FROM PLYMOUTH STATION	ARRIVE IN CENTRAL STATION	NOTES
1344	1654	M–F
1410 (1413 Su)	1735 (1738 Su)	M–F, Su (1)
1410	1817	Sa (4)
1440	1841	M–F (1)
1452	1800	Su (1)
1520	1830	Su (1)
1530	1910	Su (1)
1555 (1556 Sa)	1937 (1942 Sa)	M–Sa (1)
1630	2018	M–F (2)
1710 (1711 Su)	2035 (2018 Su)	Daily (1)
1735	2113	M–F (1)
1757	2109	Su (1)
1825	2129	Sa (1)
1856	2214	Sa (1)
1940 (2010 Sa)	0005	M–Sa (1)
2010	2335	Su (1)

(1) Change trains at Bristol Temple Meads
(2) Change trains at Exeter St. Davids
(3) Reservations required on both trains, i.e., Cardiff to Bristol Temple Meads
    and Bristol Temple Meads to Plymouth
(4) Change trains at Exeter St. Davids and at Bristol Temple Meads

1425. Visitors are welcome. The Merchants House on St. Andrews Street is the largest and finest structure remaining from the sixteenth and seventeenth centuries. Restored, it displays Plymouth's history with the theme, "Tinker, Tailor, Soldier, Sailor. . ." It is open daily, except Mondays.

Towering over the Barbican, the Royal Citadel, built in the 1660s by Charles II, was erected as a warning to the citizens of Plymouth. Many of the fortress cannons still point toward the town and not out to sea, as one would normally expect them to do. They are open to the public daily between May 1 and September 30.

If you have ever sung a chorus or two of "The Eddystone Light," you are a likely customer for the engrossing book *The Four Eddystone Lighthouses* by Robert Sanderson. Additional information on the lighthouses may also be found in the booklet *Smeaton's Tower and the Plymouth Breakwater*. The first Eddystone lighthouse was blown down in a storm. The second lighthouse withstood the elements but was destroyed by fire. Smeaton's Tower stood on the Eddystone Reef from 1759 to 1884 and subsequently was reerected on Plymouth Hoe. The tower is open to the public daily, from the end of April to the end of October, from 1030 to 1700.

If your urge "to go down to the sea in ships" overwhelms you, take a boat trip on Plymouth Sound. The information center has the details, including how to view the nearby Royal Naval Base at Devonport. If your call to the sea is more limited, browsing in the Barbican area will suffice if you throw an occasional glance seaward.

Day Excursion to
Swansea
THE "UGLY, LOVELY TOWN"

Depart from Cardiff Central Station

Distance by train: 46 miles (74 km)
Average train time: 50 minutes
Train information and InterCity services: (034) 548–4950
Swansea Tourist Information Centre: Singleton Street, Swansea SA1 3QG; *Tel:* (0179) 246–8321; *Fax:* (0179) 246–4602
  Internet: http://www.swansea.com
  Hours: Monday-Saturday 0930-1730
    Take any bus from the rail station to the bus station. The tourist center is located just opposite the bus station. On foot, it's a ten- to fifteen-minute walk.

Birthplace of poet and playwright Dylan Thomas (1914–1953), who once referred to Swansea as the "ugly, lovely town," Swansea is now Wales's second largest city and boasts one of Europe's most striking and successful waterfront developments. During the eighteenth and nineteenth centuries, Swansea became an important industrial center when the port was developed to export coal and its rapidly growing copper products.

Thanks to heavy destruction in World War II, Swansea's city center was rebuilt to include pedestrianized shopping areas. In 1974, it was expanded to include the scenic sandy beaches and resort area, the Gower Peninsula, which was designated Britain's first area of "Outstanding Natural Beauty."

In Swansea's magnificent Maritime Quarter, you can enjoy a panoramic view of Swansea Bay from the Observatory Tower. There's a footpath that runs from the Maritime Quarter for about 5 miles along the seafront to Mumbles, a charming little resort. The 900-foot Victorian Mumbles Pier is one of Swansea's most famous landmarks. It affords an excellent view of Swansea Bay. Hungry? Along Mumbles Mile, you'll find no shortage of excellent restaurants and pubs.

The world's first Lovespoon Gallery opened in the Mumbles in 1987 and features more than 300 designs of the traditional hand-carved Welsh gift of love. It's open daily from 1000 to 1730. Since the seventeenth century, Welshmen have given hand-carved wooden spoons, known as "lovespoons," to their lady friends as a prelude to courtship and an indication of their serious intentions. Over the years, the carved designs on the spoons became more intricate, and certain symbols took on definitive meanings. For example, intricately carved boxes with balls inside came to mean the number of children desired. Then, carved chains added to the spoon indicated the number of years together. Perhaps over the years, the original "prelude to courtship" lovespoon matured into the "ball and chain" anniversary spoon.

To better understand the interesting story of Swansea's development, visit the Maritime and Industrial Museum in the splendidly rejuvenated Maritime Quarter. Located behind the Leisure Centre beside the Marina Main Basin, the museum contains a tram shed housing the world's first passenger-carrying railway to run along the seafront. The museum is open: 1030–1730 Tuesday-Sunday and Bank Holidays. (079) 230–1301 or (079) 247–0371.

The Abbey Woollen Mill at the museum features the stages of manufacturing woolen products, and you can take home finished traditional Welsh

Cardiff–Swansea

DEPART CENTRAL STATION	ARRIVE SWANSEA STATION	NOTES
0700	0808	M–F
0708	0758	Sa
0730	0840	M–F
0740	0849	Sa
0756	0853	M–F
0810	0937	Su
0815	0917	M–F
0850 (0851 Sa)	0952 (0953 Sa)	M–Sa
0857	0952	M–F
0912	1006	Sa
0939	1041	M–Sa
0952 (0957 Sa)	1050 (1052 Sa)	M–Sa
0955	1116	Su
1037	1141	Sa
1049	1206	Su
1059 (1101 Sa)	1155	M–Sa
1110	1159	M–Sa

DEPART SWANSEA STATION	ARRIVE CENTRAL STATION	NOTES
1432	1523	M–Sa
1445	1552	M–F
1458	1616	Su
1521(1523 Sa)	1612 (1611 Sa)	M–Sa
1527	1617	M–F
1532	1623	Daily
1600	1713	M–Sa
1602	1652	Su
1632	1722 (1723 Sa, Su)	Daily
1651	1756	M–F
1702	1756	Su
1718	1818	M–F
1722	1815	Sa
1732	1822 (1823 Su)	Daily
1745	1853	Su
1832	1922	Su
1832	1935 (1923 Sa)	M–Sa
1850	1954	M–Sa
1907	2015	Su
1922	2016	M–Sa
1932	2023	Su

and a few later trains at about 30 min intervals

London–Swansea

Schedules shown are for direct trains. Additional service is available by changing trains in Cardiff.

DEPART PADDINGTON STATION	ARRIVE SWANSEA STATION	NOTES
0700	1000	M–F
0800	1050 (1052 Sa)	M–Sa
0835	1206	Su
0900	1155	M–Sa
0945	1242	Sa
1000	1255 (1252 Sa, 1324 Su)	Daily

Daily hourly service continues after 1000 until late afternoon on weekdays and until 2000 on Sa and 2300 on Su.

DEPART SWANSEA STATIONS	ARRIVE PADDINGTON STATION	NOTES
1402	1745	Su
1432	1733	M–Sa
1532	1833 (1840 Sa, 1845 Su)	Daily
1602	1924	Su
1632	1935 (1935 Sa, 1945 Su)	Daily
1732	2030 (2035 Sa, 2039 Su)	Daily
1832	2135 (2140 Su)	Daily
1932	2319	Su
2032	2330	M–F, Su (1)

(1) The 2032 train arrives in London Paddington at 2330 on Friday, 2337 on Sunday, and at 2344 on Monday through Thursday.

woolen goods. Admission is free and the finished products are sold at bargain factory prices, so bring your credit card. The Maritime Quarter also houses a leisure center, theater, arts workshops, and, of course, marinas dotted with colorful boats and yachts.

Follow the Dylan Thomas Trail around the Maritime Quarter to Dylan Thomas Square where you will find the Dylan Thomas Theatre and a statue of Swansea's most famous son. Check out the Dylan Thomas Web site http://pcug.org.au/~wwhatman/dylan_thomas.html and visit Swansea's unique Dylan Thomas Centre, open daily 1030–1730.

The heart of Swansea is a square bounded by four streets: Princess Way on the east side, Westway on the west, The Kingsway along the north, and Oystermouth Road on the south side. Within the square, you'll find the tourist information center, the Grand Theatre, St. David's Square, the Quadrant Centre, two shopping districts, and Swansea's famous Covered Market featuring everything from antiques and books to pottery and fresh produce. Try the local delicacy, a spicy meat dish called hot faggots and peas.

Day Excursion to

Tenby
SCENIC SEASIDE RESORT

From Cardiff: Depart from Cardiff Central Station

Distance by train: 168 km (104 miles)
Average train time: 3 hours, 9 minutes
Train information and InterCity services: (034) 548–4950
Tenby Tourist Information Centre: The Croft, SA70 8AP; *Tel:* (0183) 484–2402; *Fax:* (0183) 484–5439
   Hours: Open daily 1000–1730, with extended hours July–August 1000–2100.
   To get to the tourist office, walk straight ahead from the rail station along Warren Street. At the crossroads, continue onwards onto White Lion Street for 100 yards, then turn left on The Norton. Continue for another 150 yards until you see the sea railings across the street from the Pelican cross walk. Turn left onto The Croft. The center is on the left side overlooking the sea.

History buffs, as well as seaside-and-sun-soakers, will enjoy this picturesque walled town and lively resort. Evidence of coins indicates that Tenby probably existed in some form during Roman times, but it was not until about 875 when it was first mentioned in a poem, referred to as *Dynbych-y-Pysgod* (Fortlet of the Fishes).

The tower on top of Castle Hill was first documented in 1153. Although the castle fell into ruins by 1386, Tenby continued to prosper as a port by importing wines and salt and exporting coal, culm, and cloth until the seventeenth century, when the town again suffered decline. During the Victorian era, Tenby was rescued by the opening of the railway and by Sir William Paxton, among others, who developed Tenby as a resort and playground for well-heeled tourists. Paxton's grand bathhouse promoted sea water as a cure for several ailments.

The Tenby Museum & Art Gallery is open daily from Easter through October, 1000–1800; other months, Monday–Friday 1000–1200 and 1400–1600; (0183) 484–2809 for more information. The Tenby Lifeboat is exhibited year round and the museum features rotating art exhibitions, such as the watercolors of Augustus John.

The town's surviving sections of its thirteenth-century walls are about 20 feet high and stretch along the base of the promontory. With a map from the tourist office, you can conduct your own walking tour of this charming little town. From the famous five-arched St. George's Gate, turn right onto St. George's Street and proceed to St. Mary's Church on the left-hand side. Rebuilt in the thirteenth century, most of what we see today was extensively modified in the fifteenth and nineteenth centuries.

On Quay Hill, just east of St. Mary's Church, is a rare example of a successful merchant's home during the late fifteenth century. The house is the three-story Tudor Merchant's House, open April–October, Monday–Friday 1100–1800, Sunday 1400–1800; (0183) 484–2279.

Take Bridge Street down to the harbor, dotted with small, colorful boats and redolent of the scents of the sea. Take a boat trip to Caldey Island where excavations revealed human remains from the Stone Age. Located only 2 miles south of Tenby, Caldey measures about 2 miles wide and less than a mile long. Here you can watch for seabirds and seals. The main attraction on the island is the Cistercian Abbey, built in 1907–11. A sanctuary for the austere Cistercian monks, the island was at one time a refuge for pirates.

Cardiff–Tenby

DEPART CENTRAL STATION	ARRIVE TENBY STATION	NOTES
0708	0922	Sa
0730 (0740 Sa)	1039 (1043 Sa)	M–Sa
0939	1238	Sa
0955	1255	Su
1110	1341	M–F (1)
1151	1421	Sa

DEPART TENBY STATION	ARRIVE CENTRAL STATION	NOTES
1410	1652	Su (1)
1422	1611	Sa
1429	1723	Sa (1)
1441	1722	M–F (1)
1540	1818 (1815 Sa)	M–Sa (2)
1724	2015	Su
1743	2016	M–Sa
1916	2157	Su
2028	2327	M–F

(1) Change trains at Swansea
(2) Change trains at Swansea on Saturdays only

London–Tenby

All service requires a change of trains in Cardiff; for schedules from London to Tenby, see the separate tables for London to Cardiff and Cardiff to Tenby.

Geographic Index

All places that have a main entry appear in bold-face type.

Appendix

CALLING THE UNITED KINGDOM

To telephone or send a fax to the United Kingdom from the United States, you must first use the international dialing code 011. Then dial the United Kingdom country code 44. All of the area codes within Britain start with a "0," but you do not use it when you are dialing from the United States. For example, to telephone the tourist information office in Bath from the United States, dial 011 (122) 547–7101.

BRITISH TOURIST INFORMATION CENTERS

Below is a listing of British tourist information centers applicable to cities appearing in this edition.

Key to Listing:
* ★ Provides summer service only
* † Accommodation services available to personal callers (for same or next night)
* (B) "Book-A-Bed-Ahead" accommodations for personal callers (for same or next night) in any town with a tourist information center also offering this service

ENGLAND

Bath † (B)
Abbey Chambers
Abbey Church Yard BA1 1LY
(0122) 547–7101
Fax: (0122) 547–7221
Internet: http://www.bath.uk.com
E-mail: bath-tourism@bathnes.gov.uk

Birmingham † (B)
2 City Arcade B2 4TX
(0121) 643–2514
Fax: (0121) 616–1038

and
130 Colmore Row
(0121) 693–6300
Fax: (0121) 693–9600
Internet: http://birmingham.org.uk

Brighton † (B)
Bartholomew Square
Brighton BN1 1JS
(0127) 329–2599
Fax: (0127) 329–2564
Internet: http://www.brighton.co.uk
E-mail: brighton-tourism@pavilion.co.uk

Bury St. Edmunds † (B)
6 Angel Hill IP33 1XB
(0128) 476–4667
Fax: (0128) 475–7084
Internet:
http://www.stedmundsbury.gov.uk
E-mail:
eloise.appleby@burybo.stedbc.gov.uk

Cambridge † (B)
Wheeler Street CB2 3QB
(0122) 332–2640
Fax: (0122) 345–7588
Internet: http://www.cambridge.gov.uk
E-mail: tourism@cambridge.gov.uk

Canterbury † (B)
34 St. Margaret's Street
(0122) 776–6567
Accommodations:
(0122) 745–5567
Fax: (0122) 745–9840
Internet: http://www.canterbury.co.uk

Chester † (B)
The Forum CH1 2HS
(0124) 431–7962 or 431–3126
Fax: (0124) 440–0420
Internet: http://www.chester.gov.uk

Coventry † (B)
Bayley Lane CV1 5RN
(0120) 383–2304
Fax: (0120) 383–2370

Dover † (B)
Townwall Street CT16 1JR
(0130) 420–5108
Fax: (0130) 422–5498

Folkestone † (B)
Harbour Street
(0130) 325–8594
Fax: (01303) 259754

Gloucester † (B)
20 Southgate Street
GL1 2DP
(0145) 242–1188
Fax: (0145) 250–4273

Greenwich † (B)
46 Greenwich Church Street SE10 9BL
(0181) 858–6376
Fax: (0181) 853–4607
Internet: http://www.mx2000.co.uk

Hastings † (B)
Queens Square
Priory Meadow
East Sussex
(0142) 478–1111
Fax: (0142) 478–1133

Ipswich † (B)
St. Stephen's Church
St. Stephen's Lane IP1 1DB
(0147) 325–8070
Fax: (0147) 325–8072
Internet: http://www.ipswich.gov.uk

Isle of Wight; Shanklin † (B)
67 High Street
(0198) 386–2942
Accommodations: (0198) 386–7979
Fax: (0198) 386–3047

King's Lynn † (B)
The Old Gaol House
Saturday Market Place
(0155) 376–3044
Accommodations: (0155) 376–7711
Fax: (0155) 377–7281

Lincoln † (B)
9 Castle Hill LN1 3AA
(0152) 252–9828
Fax: (0152) 256–4506

London British Travel Centre † (B)
12 Regent Street
Piccadilly Circus
(0171) 730–3404

London Tourist Board † (B)
26 Grosvenor Gardens SW1W 0DU
(0171) 730–3450
Accommodations: (0171) 824–8844
Fax: (0171) 730–9367

Nottingham † (B)
1–4 Smithy Row NG1 2BY
(0115) 915–5330
Fax: 935–0883

Oxford † (B)
The Old School
Gloucester Green
(0186) 572–6871
Fax: (0186) 524–0045

Penzance † (B)
Station Road TR18 2NF
(0173) 636–2207
Fax: (0173) 636–3600

Plymouth
Plymouth Discovery Centre
(0175) 226–4849
Fax: (0175) 225–7955

Portsmouth † (B)
Terminal Building
Portsmouth Ferryport
(0170) 583–8635
and
The Hard
(0170) 582–6722
Fax: (0170) 582–2693

City of Portsmouth Civil Offices
(0170) 583–4116
Fax: (0170) 583–4975

Ramsgate † (B)
19–21 Harbour Street CT11 8HA
(0184) 358–3333
Fax: (0184) 359–1086

St. Albans † (B)
Town Hall
The Market Place
Herts AL3 5DJ
(0172) 786–4511
Fax: (0172) 786–3533

Salisbury † (B)
Fish Row
Wiltshire SP1 1EJ
(0172) 233–4956
Fax: (0172) 242–2059
and
Stonehenge
(0172) 233–4956
Fax: (0172) 242–2059

Sheffield † (B)
Leader House
Surrey Street S1 2LH
(0114) 273–4671
Fax: (0114) 272–4225
Internet: http://www.sheffieldcity.co.uk

Southampton † (B)
9 Civic Centre Road SO14 7LP
(0170) 322–1106
Fax: (0170) 363–1437

Stratford-upon-Avon † (B)
Bridgefoot
Warwickshire CV37 8GW
(0178) 929–3127
Fax: (0178) 929–5262

Windsor † (B)
24 High Street SL4 1LH
(0175) 385–2010
Fax: (0175) 383–3450

York † (B)
De Grey Rooms
Exhibition Square YO1 2HB
(0190) 462–1756
Fax: (0190) 462–5618

SCOTLAND

Aberdeen † (B)
St. Nicholas House
Broad Street AB1 1RJ
(0122) 463–2727
Fax: (0122) 484–8805
Internet: www.ayrshire.arran.com
E-mail: ayr@ayrshire-arran.com

Ayr † (B)
Burns House
Burns Statue Square KA7 1UP
(0129) 228–8688
Fax: (0129) 226–9555

Dunbar † (B)
Town House
143 High Street
(0136) 886–3353

Dundee † (B)
7-21 Castle Street DD1 3AA
(0138) 252–7527
Fax: (0138) 252–7550
Internet: www.angusanddundee.co.uk
E-mail: arbicath@sol.co.uk

Dunfermline (B)
The Abbot House
Abbot Street
(0138) 372–0999

Edinburgh † (B)
3 Princes Street EH2 2QP
(0131) 557–1700
Fax: (0131) 473–3881

and
Edinburgh Airport
(0131) 333–2167

Glasgow † (B)
35 St. Vincent Place
(0141) 204–4400
and Glasgow Airport
(0141) 848–4440

Inverness † (B)
Castle Wynd IV2 3BJ
(0146) 323–4353

Kyle of Lochalsh ★ † (B)
Car Park
(0159) 953–4276

Linlithgow † (B)
Burgh Halls
The Cross
West Lothian EH49 7AH
(0150) 684–4600
Fax: (0150) 667–1373

Loch Lomond ★ † (B)
Balloch
(0138) 975–3533

Montrose ★ † (B)
Bridge Street
(0167) 467–2000

Perth † (B)
45 High Street PH1 5TJ
(0173) 863–8841
Fax: (0173) 844–4863

St. Andrews † (B)
70 Market Street
Fife KY16 9NU
(0133) 447–2021
Fax: (0133) 447–8422

Stirling † (B)
Dumbarton Road FK8 1EA
(0178) 647–5019
and
The Castle Esplanade
(0178) 647–9901

Stranraer ★ † (B)
Harbour Street
(0177) 670–2595

WALES

Cardiff † (B)
Central Station
(0122) 222–7281
Fax: (0122) 223–9162

Swansea
Singleton Street SA1 3QG
(0179) 246–8321
Fax: (0179) 246–4602

Tenby
The Croft SA70 8AP
(0183) 484–2402
Fax: (0183) 484–5439

RECOMMENDED INFORMATION SOURCES

British Tourist Authority Offices in North America
http://www.visitbritain.com
New York: 551 Fifth Avenue, New York, NY 10176–0799.
    (212) 986–2200 or (800) GO–2–BRIT. *Fax:* (212) 986–1188
Chicago: 625 North Michigan Avenue, Suite 1510, Chicago, IL
    60611–1977. (312) 787–0490. *Fax:* (312) 787–7746

EuropeanVacation Tours & Groups
http://www.europeanvacation.com
(800) TOUR–404

Rail Pass Express, Inc.
http://www.eurail.com
2737 Sawbury Boulevard, Columbus, Ohio 43235–4583
(800) 722–7151. *Fax:* (614) 764–0711

Scottish Tourist Board
http://www.holiday.scotland.net

Thomas Cook European Timetable
The authorized North American Source is Forsythe Travel Library. *Tel:*
(800) 367–7984.

In Britain, the timetable may be purchased at most Thomas Cook travel agencies and bureaux de change. By credit card purchase, it is also available directly from Thomas Cook Publishing to any part of the world: *Tel:* (0173) 350–5821; *Fax:* (0173) 326–7052. (Use code 44 1733 when dialing from outside the U.K.)

UK Rail Schedules: RAILTRACK
http://www.railtrack.co.uk

Wales Tourist Board
http://www.tourism.wales.gov.uk

USEFUL PHONE NUMBERS—LONDON

Accommodations	Telephone No.
British Hotel Reservation Centre	
Victoria Station, outside Platform 8	(0171) 828–1027/828–1849
Victoria Coach Station	(0800) 716–298/(0171) 824–8232
Heathrow Airport Underground, Terminal 1, 2, 3	(0181) 564–8808
Heathrow Airport Underground, Terminal 4	(0181) 564–8211
10 Buckingham Palace Road, London SW1W 0QP	(0171) 828–2425
	(0171) 828–6439
Expotel Hotel Reservations	
Kingsgate House, Kingsgate Place, London NW64HG	(0171) 328–1790
	Fax: (0171) 328–8021
First Option Hotel Reservations	
Europoint, 5–11 Lavington Street, London SEI 0NZ	(0345) 110–011
	Fax: (0171) 945–6016
Victoria Station, by Platform 9	(0171) 828–4646/828–2629
Gatwick Station	(0129) 352–9372
	Fax: (0129) 253–4851
King's Cross Station, adjacent to Platform 8	
Hotel Booking Service, Ltd.	
4 New Burlington Place, London WIX IFBUK	(0171) 734–4594
	Worldwide: (0171) 434–3434
	Fax: (0171) 734–2124
Hotel Finders	(0181) 202–7000/(0181) 202–0988
20a Bell Lane, London NW4 2AD	*Fax:* (0181) 202–3871
Hotelguide	
The Coach House, 235 Upper Richmond Road	(0181) 780–1066
London SW15 6SN	*Fax:* (0181) 780–2352

The London Bed & Breakfast Agency	(0171) 586–2768
71 Fellows Rd., London NW3 3JY	*Fax:* (0171) 586–6567
The London Tourist Board	(0171) 824–8844

Airlines

Aer Lingus (Irish)	(0181) 569–4646
Air Canada	(0990) 247–226
Alitalia	(0345) 222–111
American Airlines	(0181) 572–5555
British Airways	(0345) 222–111
Continental	(0129) 377–6464/(0800) 776–464
Delta Air Lines	(0180) 041–4767
Icelandair	(0171) 388–5599
Trans World Airlines	(0171) 439–0707

Airport Information

Heathrow, general inquiries	(0181) 759–4321
Terminal 1	(0181) 745–7702/4
Terminal 2	(0181) 745–7115/6/7
Terminal 3 check–in	(0181) 745–7412
Arrivals Concourse	(0181) 745–7412/3/4
Terminal 4	(0181) 745–4540
London City Airport	(0171) 474–5555
Gatwick	(0129) 353–5353
Stansted	(0127) 966–2379/966–2520

American Express

6 Haymarket, Piccadilly	(0171) 930–4411

Bike Rentals

On Your Bike, 52 Tooley Street	(0171) 407–1309
22 Duke St. Hill	(0171) 357–6958

British Tourist Authority, British Travel Centre,

12 Regent Street, Piccadilly Circus SW1	(0171) 730–3404

Canadian Embassy

Canada Centre 62–65 Trafalgar Square	(0171) 258–6356

Emergency

Police or Ambulance	999

Eurostar (034) 530–3030

Express Bus Information

National Express	(0171) 730–0202

Hoverspeed Reservations (0130) 424–0241

London Tourist Board (main office)

26 Grosvenor Gardens, SW1W 0DU	(0171) 730–3450
	Fax: (0171) 730–9367

London Regional Transport (bus/underground)   (0171) 222–1234
Medical Help
   Middlesex Hospital, Mortimer Street   (0171) 636–8333
   Medical Express, 117a Harley Street   (0171) 499–1991
Post Office
   Paddington Main Post Office   (0171) 723–0279
Rail Information
   Anglia Railways Train Services   (0147) 369–3333
   Cardiff Railway Co.   (0122) 248–0463
   Central Trains   (0121) 643–4444
   Chiltern Railway Co.   (0129) 633–2100
   Connex South Central   (0181) 667–2780
   Connex South Eastern   (0171) 928–5151
   Eurostar (UK)   (0171 928–5151
   Gatwick Express   (0171) 973–5038
   Great Eastern Railway   (064) 550–5000
   Great North Eastern Railway   (0190) 465–3022
   Great Western Trains Co.   (0179) 349–9400
   Heathrow Express   (0181) 745–0578
   Island Line   (0198) 381–2591
   LTS Rail   (0170) 235–7889
   Merseyrail Electrics   (0151) 709–8292
   Midland Main Line   (034) 522–1125
   National Rail Enquiries and Intercity Services   (034) 548–4950
   North Western Trains   (0161) 228–2141
   Regional Railways North East   (0190) 465– 3022
   ScotRail Railways   (0141) 332–9811
   Silverlink Train Services   (0192) 320–7258
   South West Trains   (0171) 928–5151
   Thameslink Rail   (0171) 620–5760
   Thames Trains   (0118) 908–3678
   Virgin Trains   (0121) 654–7400
   Wales & West   (0122) 243–0400
   West Anglia Great Northern Railway   (034) 581–8919
   West Coast Railway Co.   (0152) 732–2100
Recorded Timetable Announcements for Services to:
   Amsterdam   (0171) 828–4264
   Brussels/Köln   (0171) 828–0167
   Paris   (0171) 828–8747
Special Rail Offers   (0171) 828–6708
Sleeper Reservations
   Euston Station   (0171) 388–6061
   Paddington Station   (0171) 922–4372

River Trips and Canal Cruises
River Boat Information Service	(0171) 730–4812
London Waterbus Co., Camden Lock Place	(0171) 482–2660
RiverBus	(0171) 512–0555
Catamaran Cruisers	(0171) 839–3572
Jenny Wren Canal Cruises	(0171) 485–6210

U.S. Embassy
24 Grosvenor Square	(0171) 499–9000

USA TTA (Travel and Tourism Administration)
P.O. Box 1EN, London W1A 1EN	(0171) 495–4466
	Fax: (0171) 495–4377

Victoria Student Travel Service
Need student I.D. to book accommodations	(0171) 730–8111

USEFUL PHONE NUMBERS—EDINBURGH

Tourist Information
City of Edinburgh Tourist Information and
Accommodations, Waverley Market, Princes Street	(0131) 557–1700
Tattoo Office	(0131) 225–1188

British Rail
Waverley Station	(0131) 556–2451
Sleeper reservations	(0131) 556–5633
Airport Information	(0131) 333–2167

Scheduled Airlines
Aer Lingus (Irish)	(0131) 225–7392
British Airways	(0131) 225–2525
British Caledonian Airways	(0131) 225–5162
City Transport Information	(0131) 556–5656
Student Travel Centre	(0131) 668–2221

American Express
139 Princes Street	(0131) 225–7881

Emergency
Fire, Police, Ambulance	999
Guide Friday Tours	(0131) 556–2244

USEFUL PHONE NUMBERS—GLASGOW

Tourist Information
Tourist Information, 35 St. Vincent Place	(0141) 204–4400
Glasgow Travel Centre	(0141) 226–4826

British Rail

Passenger inquiries	(0141) 204–2844
Sleeper reservations	(0141) 221–2305

Airport (0141) 887–1111, Ext. 4552
or (0141) 848–4440

Scheduled Airlines

Aer Lingus (Irish)	(0171) 734–1212
Air Canada	(0180) 018–1313
Air France	(0134) 558–1393
British Airways	(0141) 332–9666
British Midland	(0133) 281–0552
Northwest Airlines	(0141) 226–4175

American Express

115 Hope Street	(0141) 221–4366

Emergency

Fire, Police, Ambulance	999

USEFUL PHONE NUMBERS—CARDIFF

Tourist Information	(01222) 222–7281
	Fax: (01222) 239–162
Cardiff Bay Visitor Centre	(01222) 463–833
Great Western Trains Passenger Inquiries	
and Sleeper Reservations	(034) 548–4950
Airport Information	(0144) 671–1111

Scheduled Airlines

British Airways	(034) 522–2111
KLM	(099) 075–0900
Manx	(034) 525–6256
RyanAir	(054) 156–9569

American Express

3 Queen Street	(0122) 266–5843

Emergency 999

A SELECTION OF BRITISH RAIL ONE-WAY FARES

Deciding whether or not you should purchase a BritRail Pass becomes a matter of simple arithmetic. Plan your trip to Great Britain, decide what places you want to visit, and use the fares listed below to determine if the cost of the individual rail segments has exceeded the cost of a BritRail Pass. Round-trip fares are slightly less than double the one-way charge. Children five to fifteen years of age, inclusive, pay half fare. All fares are applicable as of press time and subject to change without prior notice. Fares are given in U.S. dollars. To convert to pounds sterling, apply current rate of exchange. For example, at press time, the rate was approximately $1.00 = 59p.

ONE-WAY FARES				ONE-WAY FARES		
	First Class ($)	Standard Class ($)			First Class ($)	Standard Class ($)
From London to:				**From London to:**		
Aberdeen	190.00	133.00		Oxford	32.00	22.00
Aviemore	190.00	133.00		Penzance	133.00	98.00
Ayr	169.00	119.00		Perth	165.00	113.00
Bath Spa	74.00	48.00		Plymouth	117.00	87.00
Birmingham	70.00	50.00		Portsmouth	40.00	28.00
Brighton	37.00	25.00		Salisbury	43.00	29.00
Cambridge	37.00	25.00		Sheffield	88.00	60.00
Canterbury	37.00	25.00		Southampton	40.00	28.00
Cardiff	94.00	63.00		Stratford-upon-Avon	61.00	40.00
Chester	104.00	80.00		Windermere	130.00	96.00
Coventry	56.00	38.00		Windsor	13.00	19.00
Dover	49.00	33.00		York	136.00	87.00
Dundee	175.00	119.00				
Edinburgh	181.00	123.00		**From Glasgow to:**		
Folkestone	19.00	13.00		Aberdeen	60.00	44.00
Glasgow	186.00	129.00		Birmingham	135.00	96.00
Gloucester	61.00	40.00		Dundee (Tay Bridge)	33.00	23.00
Hastings	44.00	30.00		Inverness	60.00	44.00
Inverness	175.00	123.00		Manchester	115.00	83.00
King's Lynn	66.00	48.00		Oxford	147.00	101.00
Leamington Spa	61.00	40.00		Perth	31.00	21.00
Lincoln	81.00	54.00		Sheffield	123.00	85.00
Manchester	121.00	90.00		Stirling	17.00	12.00
Nottingham	96.00	65.00		York	111.00	77.00

To order rail tickets prior to your departure for Britain call the information department at Rail Pass Express at (614) 793–7650.

PASSPORT OFFICES THROUGHOUT AMERICA

You may apply for a passport at any passport agency and at many Clerks of Court Offices or Post Offices designated to accept passport applications. The regional offices are as follows:

Boston: Thomas P. O'Neill Federal Building, 10 Causeway Street, Suite 247, Boston, Massachusetts 02222–1094; (617) 565–6990.

Chicago: Kluczynski Office Building, 230 South Dearborn Street, Room 380, Chicago, Illinois 60604–1564; (312) 353–7155.

Honolulu: First Hawaii Tower, 1132 Bishop Street, Suite 500, Honolulu, Hawaii 96813–2309; (808) 522–8283 or (808) 522–8286.

Houston: Mickey Leland Federal Building, 1919 Smith Street, Suite 1100, Houston, Texas 77002–8049; (713) 209–3153.

Los Angeles: Federal Building, 11000 Wilshire Boulevard, Room 13100, Los Angeles, California 90024–3615; (310) 235–7070.

Miami: Claude Pepper Federal Office Building, 51 Southwest First Avenue, Third Floor, Miami, Florida 33130–1680; (305) 536–4681.

New Orleans: 701 Loyal Avenue, Postal Services Building, T-12005, New Orleans, Louisiana 70113–1931; (504) 589–6728 or (504) 589–6161.

New York: Rockefeller Center, International Building, 630 Fifth Avenue, Room 270, New York, New York 10111–0031; (212) 399–5290.

Philadelphia: U.S. Customs House, 200 Chestnut Street, Room 103, Philadelphia, Pennsylvania 19106–2970; (215) 597–7480.

San Francisco: Tishman Speyer Building, 525 Market Street, Room 200, San Francisco, California 94105–2773; (415) 744–4010 or (415) 744–4444.

Seattle: Federal Building, 915 Second Avenue, Room 992, Seattle, Washington 98174–1091; (206) 220–7788.

Stamford: One Landmark Square, Broad and Atlantic Streets, Stamford, Connecticut 06901–2687; (203) 325–3530.

Washington, D.C.: 1111 19th Street NW, Washington, D.C. 20522–1705; (202) 647–0518.

PASSPORT INFORMATION

The phone numbers of the passport offices listed above provide a recorded message that describes the documents you need and the application process for obtaining a passport as well as reporting the loss or theft of your passport. It also explains how you can obtain a copy of the report of the birth or death of a U.S. citizen abroad. The message will direct you to the proper agencies for information regarding naturalization, travel advisories, customs regulations, and shots required by various countries. The National Passport Information Center at 1–900–CALLNPIC provides telephone operators that will give you a prompt and accurate response to any questions you may have. You can access more passport and travel information via the Internet at: http://travel.state.gov.

TIPS AND TRIVIA

Do not be surprised to see a 17.5 percent value-added tax (VAT) added to your bill for items purchased or services rendered. The VAT appears on just about everything, excluding bus/rail transportation.

Tipping: For luggage, generally tip £1 per bag; taxis, 10–15 percent, with a 50-pence minimum; for service staff in hotels, 10–15 percent if service charge is not included in bill.

Imports: You can import into Britain 200 cigarettes, two liters of table wine along with either two liters of sparkling wine or one liter of liquor, two ounces of perfume and nine ounces of cologne, and photographic film for your own use.

Shops: Most shops are open from 0900 to 1730. Shops in smaller towns may close for one hour at lunchtime. In London, shops in the Knightsbridge area (Harrods, for example) remain open until 1900 on Wednesday, while those in the West End (Oxford Street, Regent Street, and Piccadilly areas) stay open until 1900 on Thursday.

Banks: Banks are usually open Monday through Friday from 0930 to 1530. Some are open on Saturday mornings. Most banks in Scotland are closed for one hour at lunchtime. The banks at London's Heathrow and Gatwick Airports are open twenty-four hours a day.

Holidays: Most banks, shops, and some museums, historic houses, and other places of interest are closed on Sundays and public holidays. Public transport services generally are reduced, especially during Christmas time.

Voltage: The standard voltage is 240v AC, 50 Hz.

1999 HOLIDAYS

January 1	New Year's Day	May 25	Spring Bank Holiday
January 2	Bank Holiday (Scotland)	July 13	Orangeman's Day
March 17	St. Patrick's Day		(Northern Ireland only)
	(Northern Ireland only)	August 3	Bank Holiday (Scotland only)
April 10	Good Friday	August 31	Summer Bank Holiday
April 13	Easter Bank Holiday		(except Scotland)
	(not Scotland)	December 25	Christmas Day
May 4	May Day	December 26	Boxing Day

CLIMATE

	Jan	Feb	Mar	Apr	May	June	July	Aug	Sept	Oct	Nov	Dec
Average Low (F)	35°	35°	37°	40°	45°	51°	55°	54°	51°	44°	39°	36°
Average High (F)	44°	45°	51°	56°	63°	69°	73°	72°	67°	58°	49°	45°
Average Rainfall (in inches)	2	2	1	2	2	2	2	2	2	2	3	2

TOLL-FREE AIRLINE NUMBERS
(Dialing from U.S.)

Air Canada (AC) 800-766-3000
Air France(AF) 800-237-2747
American Airlines, Inc. (AA) 800-433-7300
Austrian Airlines (OS)............ 800-AIRWAYS
Continental Airlines (CO) 800-525-0280
Delta Air Lines, Inc. (DL) 800-221-1212
Finnair(AY) 800-950-5000
Icelandair 800-223-5500
KLM Royal Dutch Airlines 800-374-7747
Lufthansa German
   Airlines (LH) 800-645-3880
Northwest Airlines,
   Inc. (NW) 800-225-2525
Sabena Belgan World
   Airlines (SN) 800-955-2000
Scandinavian Airlines
   System (SK) 800-221-2350
Swissair (SR) 800-221-4750
TAP Air Portugal (TO) 800-221-7370
Trans World Airlines, Inc.
   (TWA)................................... 800-221-2000
United Air Lines, Inc. (UA) 800-538-2929
US Air (US) 800-943-5436
Virgin Atlantic Airways
   Ltd. (US) 800-862-8621

TOLL-FREE HOTEL RESERVATIONS NUMBERS
(Dialing from U.S.)

B&B My Guest 800-906-4232
Best Western International 800-528-1234
Choice Hotels International,
   Inc...................................... 800-4-CHOICE
Consort Hotels Ltd. 800-55-CONSORT
Forte & Meridian Hotels 800-225-5843
Golden Tulip International........ 800-344-1212
Hilton Reservations
   Worldwide 800-HILTONS
Hyatt Worldwide Reservation
   Centres.................................. 800-233-1234
Inter-Continental Hotels
   Corp....................................... 800-327-0200
Inter-Europe Hotels 800-221-6509
ITT Sheraton Corporation 800-325-3535
International B&B 800-722-3679
Kempinski International 800-426-3135
Leading Hotels of the World 800-223-6800
Loews Representation Int'l........ 800-223-0888
Marriott Corporation 800-228-9290
MinOtels Int'l............................ 800-336-4668
Movenpick Hotels Int'l 800-34-HOTEL
Nikko Hotels International........ 800-645-5687
Preferred Hotels & Resorts
   Worldwide.............................. 800-323-7500
Radisson Hotels, Int'l 800-333-3333
Ramada International Hotels
   & Resorts 800-854-7854
SRS Steinberger Reservation
   Service 800-223-5652
Swissotel 800-63-SWISS
Thistle Mount Charlotte 800-847-4358

FERRY INFORMATION
(Dialing from U.S.)

Bergen Line 800-323–7436
Scandinavian Seaways 800–533-3755
Silja Lines 800–323–7436

TOLL-FREE THEATRE/EVENTS
(Dialing from U.S.)

Edwards & Edwards (Tattoo,
   Festival, Evans Day
   Tours) 800-328-2150
Keith Prowse
   (Apartments) 800-669-8687
London Showline (Air,
   Rock 'n' Pop Concerts) 800-962-9246
London Theatre & More
   TX (Frames Day Tours,
   Hotelink, Soccer Tkts 800-683-0799

BRITRAIL PASSES

A BritRail consecutive-day or flexipass allows unlimited travel on the entire British rail network spanning England, Scotland, and Wales.

Airport Transfers

	FIRST	STANDARD
Gatwick Express	$24	$16

Travel by train from Gatwick Airport to London Victoria Station. Children 5-15 half price.

	ADULT	CHILD
Heathrow Airbus	$12	$8

Transfer from Heathrow Airport to one of many Central London hotels.

Britrail Classic Pass

Valid for consecutive days of rail travel throughout Britain (England, Wales, and Scotland).

	ADULT		SENIOR		YOUTH
	1ST CLASS	2ND CLASS	1ST CLASS	2ND CLASS	2ND CLASS
8 days	$375	$259	$319	NA	$205
15 days	$575	$395	$489	NA	$318
22 days	$740	$510	$630	NA	$410
1 month	$860	$590	$730	NA	$475

Senior age 60+. Youth age 16-25. Children 5-15 half fare. Children under 5 free.

BritRail Family Pass

Buy one adult or senior pass and get a free pass of the same type for one child. Available for the BritRail Classic Pass, BritRail Flexipass, BritRail + Ireland and BritRail + Car. Children under 5 travel free.

Britrail Flexipass

Valid for unlimited rail travel for the days chosen.

	ADULT		SENIOR		YOUTH
	1ST CLASS	2ND CLASS	1ST CLASS	2ND CLASS	2ND CLASS
4 days in 1 month	$315	$219	$269	NA	$175
8 days in 1 month	$459	$315	$390	NA	$253
15 days in 1 month	$699	$480	$590	NA	—
15 days in 2 months	—	—	—	—	$385

Senior age 60+. Youth age 16-25. Children 5-15 half fare. Children under 5 free.

British Heritage Pass

	ADULT
7 days	$45
15 days	$69
1 month	$90

There is a $10 handling fee on all Heritage passes. No discounts for children. The pass is nonrefundable/nonreturnable.

BritRail Party Pass

For parties of 3 or 4 passengers traveling together, a discount of 50 percent will be offered on the 3rd and 4th person's pass. Applies to Classic and Flexipass; first and second class. Passengers must be traveling together to qualify.

BritRail Pass + Ireland

Valid for travel in England, Scotland, Wales, Northern Ireland and the Republic of Ireland.

	1ST CLASS	2ND CLASS
5 days within 1 month	$473	$359
10 days within 1 month	$698	$511

Children 5-15, half fare; under 5 free.
Round-trip Stena Sealink service is included between Holyhead and Dun Laoghaire, Fishguard and Rosslare or Stranraer and Larne via ship, HSS or SeaLynx. Reservations are essential for Irish Sea services. No refund on dated or partially used passes; sea coupons are not refundable if unused.

BritainShrinker Escorted Tours

Tel: (888) TOUR–404; *Fax:* (812) 339–1513; for brochure or visit http://www.europeanvacation.com.

BritRail SouthEast Pass

A Flexipass for a large section of southern England.

	ADULT		CHILD	
	1ST CLASS	STANDARD CLASS	1ST CLASS	STANDARD CLASS
3 days within 15	$94	$69	$27	$18
4 days within 8	$126	$94	$27	$18
7 days within 15	$166	$126	$27	$18

Children: age 5-15.

Freedom of Scotland Travelpass

	STANDARD CLASS
4 days within 8	$110
8 days within 15	$160
12 days within 15	$210

No discounts for children. Includes transportation on most Caledonian MacBrayne ferries to the islands of Scotland. Discounts on several ferry operators and on selected bus companies in Scotland, plus covers Glasgow Underground. 20 percent discount on Stena Sealink to Northern Ireland.

London Day Tour

ADULT	CHILD
$80	$75

Includes: an experienced guide, a luxury air-conditioned touring coach, pub lunch, cruise of the river Thames with afternoon tea, and all entrance fees. Tour operates daily. Children 5–15.

London Visitor Travel Card
Valid for unlimited consecutive day travel in the six zones of the London Underground and on the red double-decker buses.

	ADULT	CHILD
3 days	$29	$12
4 days	$39	$15
7 days	$59	$22

Children 5-15.

EURAIL PASSES

Eurail Passes entitle you to unlimited travel on Europe's extensive 100,000-mile rail network in the 17 western countries of Europe (England, Scotland, and Wales not included) as follows:

Austria • Belgium • Denmark • Finland • France • Germany • Greece Hungary • Ireland (Rep.) • Italy • Luxembourg • Netherlands • Norway Portugal • Spain • Sweden • Switzerland

To order, call (800) 722-7151 or (614) 793-7651 or visit the Rail Pass Express website at http://www.railpass.com.

Eurail Pass
Travel on any or all days for the duration of the pass.
1ST CLASS

Eurail Saverpass
Rail travel for 2-5 people traveling together at all times.

	Eurail Pass	Saverpass
15 days	$554	$470
21 days	$718	$610
1 month	$890	$756
2 months	$1260	$1072
3 months	$1558	$1324

Children 4-11, half adult fare. Under 4 free.

Eurail Flexipass
Choose your travel days and use them within 2 months.
1ST CLASS

Eurail Saver Flexipass
Rail travel for 2-5 people traveling together at all times.

	Flexipass	Saver Flexipass
10 days in 2 months	$654	$556
15 days in 2 months	$862	$732

Children 4-11, half adult fare. Under 4 free.

Eurail Youth Pass*
2ND CLASS

15 days	$388
21 days	$499
1 month	$623
2 months	$882
3 months	$1089

*Available for passengers 12–25 on their first date of travel.

Eurail Youth Flexipass*
2ND CLASS
10 days in 2 months $458
15 days in 2 months $599
*Available for passengers 12–25 on their first date of travel.

EUROPASS

The Europass features unlimited flexible travel in the 5 most frequently visited countries of Europe: France, Germany, Italy, Spain, and Switzerland.

You determine the number of travel days from 5, 6, 8, 10, or 15 travel days in a 2-month period, making the Europass the most flexible rail pass available. In addition you may add up to 2 of the following zones:

Benelux	Belgium, Luxembourg, & the Netherlands
Danube	Austria & Hungary
Greece Plus	Greece & Ferry
Portugal	

Europass

Unlimited rail travel in: France, Germany, Italy, Spain, and Switzerland. May add up to 2 Associate Zones to extend the geographic area of the pass.

	ADULT 1ST CLASS	YOUTH* 2ND CLASS
5 days in 2 months	$348	$233
6 days in 2 months	$368	$253
8 days in 2 months	$448	$313
10 days in 2 months	$528	$363
15 days in 2 months	$728	$513

*Youth price available for passengers age 12–25. Children 5-11, half adult fare; under 4 free.

Associate Zones

May add up to 2 of the following zones to the Europass: Benelux, Danube, Greece, and Portugal.

	ADULT 1ST CLASS	YOUTH* 2ND CLASS
1 Add-on Zone	$60	$45
2 Add-on Zones	$40	$33

Associate Zones extend the geographic area of the pass; they do not extend the pass's length in days. Greece add-on allows ferry crossing from Italy to Greece. Children 5–11, half adult fare; under 4 free.

Europass SaverPass

Unlimited First Class rail travel for 2–5 people traveling together at all times in the countries of: France, Germany, Italy, Spain, and Switzerland. Prices are per person. May add up to 2 Associate Zones to extend the geographic area of the pass.

	ADULT 1ST CLASS
5 days in 2 months	$296
6 days in 2 months	$314
8 days in 2 months	$382
10 days in 2 months	$450
15 days in 2 months	$620

Children 5-11, half adult fare; under 4 free.

Europass SaverPass Associate Zones

May add up to 2 of the following zones: Benelux, Danube, Greece, and Portugal.

	ADULT 1ST CLASS	YOUTH*
1 Add-on Zone	$52	
2 Add-on Zones	$34	

Associate Zones extend the geographic area of the pass; they do not extend the pass's length in days. Greece add-on allows ferry crossing from Italy to Greece. Children 5–11, half adult fare; under 4 free.

COUNTRY AND REGIONAL PASSES

Arctic Fjord Pass

Valid for rail travel in Belguim, Luxembourg and the Netherlands.

	1ST CLASS
7 days	$99

Valid from June through September. Covers Northern Sweden above the Arctic Circle with 24-hour Midnight Sun exposure, from Gallivare, Sweden to Narvik and the Northern Fjord country in Norway. Possible excursions to Lofoten, Norway.

Austrian Railpass

	ADULT		CHILD	
	1ST CLASS	2ND CLASS	1ST CLASS	2ND CLASS
3 days in 15	$151	$102	$76	$51
Additional Days	$22	$16	$11	$8

Children 4–11; 3 and under are free. 5 day maximum additional rail days. Bonuses include discounts on steamers, local trains, and bicycle rentals.

Balkan Flexipass

Unlimited rail travel in Bulgaria, Greece, Former Yugoslav Republic of Macedonia, Montenegro, Romania, Serbia, and Turkey.

	1ST CLASS	
	ADULT	YOUTH
5 days in 1 month	$152	$90
10 days in 1 month	$264	$156
15 days in 1 month	$317	$190

Children 4-12 half of the adult fare. Youth ages 13–25.

Benelux to Tourrail Pass

Valid for rail travel in Belguim, Luxembourg and the Netherlands.

	1ST CLASS	2ND CLASS
5 days in 1 month	$217	$155
Youth 5 days in 1 month	—	$104

Benelux to Tourrail Pass For Two

Prices are for two people traveling together.

	1ST CLASS		2ND CLASS	
	1ST PERSON	2ND PERSON	1ST PERSON	2ND PERSON
5 days in 1 month	$217	$109	$155	$78

Valid for rail travel in Belgium, Luxembourg and the Netherlands. Youth for persons 4-25; under 4 free.

Bulgarian FlexiPass

	1ST CLASS
3 days in 1 month	$70

Children 4–11, half adult fare; under 4 free.

Copenhagen Sightseeing Pass

Valid for trail travel from any German/Danish border crossing to Copenhagen and return within seven days for holders of a Europass or German Railpass.

	1ST CLASS	2ND CLASS
Adult	$100	$70
Youth	$75	$50
Child	$50	$35

Free Canal Sightseeing Tour is included from April 15-October 15. Youth 12-25. Child 4-11. Stop overs are permitted.

Czech FlexiPass

	1ST CLASS
5 days in 15 days	$69

Children 4–11, half adult fare; under 4 free.

European East Pass

Austria, Czech Republic, Hungary, Poland, and Slovakia

	1ST CLASS
5 days in 1 month	$195
Additional Days	$21

Up to 5 additional days can be added. Children 4–11, half adult fare; under 4 free.

FestPass

$25 per person

Your passport to over 150 jazz, classical, ethnic, art and other festivals across Europe and Britain ranging from the vast and famous to the intimate and eclectic.

FinnRail Pass

	1ST CLASS	2ND CLASS
3 days in 1 month	$185	$123

Children 6–16, half adult fare; under 6 free..

France Pass

	2 ADULTS*		ADULT	
	1ST CLASS	2ND CLASS	1ST CLASS	2ND CLASS
3 days in 15	$156	$132	$195	$165
Additional Days	$30	$30	$30	$30

	YOUTH
4 days in 2 months	$150
Additional Days	$25

Maximum of 6 extra days. Youth 12–26; children 4–11, half adult fare; under 4 free.
*Price per person based on 2 people traveling together, includes 40% companion discount.

German Railpass

	ADULT		YOUTH
	1ST CLASS	2ND CLASS	2ND CLASS
4 days in 1 month	$189	$130.50	$138
Additional rail days up to a maximum of 10 days $24		$16.50	$18

German Twinpass–For 2 Adults Traveling Together

	ADULT	
	1ST CLASS	2ND CLASS
4 days in 1 month	$189	$130.50
Additional rail days up to a maximum of 10 days $24		$16.50

*Youth ages under 26. Children 4-11 half adult fare.

Bonuses for passholders include free travel on KD River Steamers on certain Rhine, Main, and Moselle River sections and free travel on selected bus lines operated by Deutsche Touring/Europabus.

Greek Flexipass

Valid for 1st class rail travel in Greece.

	ADULT	YOUTH	CHILD
3 days in 1 month	$86	$62	$58
4 days in 1 month	$110	—	$74
5 days in 1 month	$120	$89	$85
6 days in 1 month	$144	—	$101

Valid for first class travel in Greece. Youth 12–25; children 2–11; under 2 free.

Holland Railpass

	ADULT		YOUTH
	1ST CLASS	2ND CLASS	2ND CLASS
3 days in 1 month	$98	$65	$52
5 days in 1 month	$147	$98	$79

	SENIOR		CHILD	
	1ST CLASS	2ND CLASS	1ST CLASS	2ND CLASS
3 days in 1 month	$78	$52	$50	$33
5 days in 1 month	$119	$79	$74	$49

*Youth 12–25; seniors 60+; children 4–11; under 4 free.

Holland Railpass Plus

	ADULT		YOUTH
	1ST CLASS	2ND CLASS	2ND CLASS
3 days in 1 month	$101	$81	$69
5 days in 1 month	$161	$125	$94

*Youth 12–25. Entitles the holder to travel free on all buses, metro trains, and trams throughout the Netherlands.

Holland Rail TwinPass

| | ADULT | | YOUTH |
	1ST CLASS	2ND CLASS	2ND CLASS
3 days in 1 month	$147	$98	$78
5 days in 1 month	$221	$147	$119

| | SENIOR | | CHILD | |
	1ST CLASS	2ND CLASS	1ST CLASS	2ND CLASS
3 days in 1 month	$117	$78	$75	$50
5 days in 1 month	$179	$119	$111	$74

Valid for rail travel in Belgium, Luxembourg and the Netherlands. Youth 4–25; under 4 free.

Hungarian Flexipass

	1ST CLASS
5 days in 15 days	$64
10 days in 1 month	$80

Children 5–14, half adult fare; under 5 free.

Italian Kilometric Ticket

The Kilometric Ticket is good for 20 trips on the entire Rail Network—limited to 3,000 kilometers (1,875 miles) within 60 days and used by as many as five persons traveling together. When used by more than one person, each trip is calculated by multiplying the distance by the number of persons. Travel on the Intercity, Eurocity, Rapido, and TR450 trains is possible provided that corresponding supplement fares are paid at the railway stations when reservations are made.

1ST CLASS	2ND CLASS
$264	$156

Italian State Railways imposes an administration fee of $15 on each pass ordered. This fee is included in the price above. Fee is nonrefundable.

Italy Railcard
Consecutive days

	1ST CLASS	2ND CLASS
8 days	$269	$187
15 days	$335	$228
21 days	$386	$263
30 days	$462	$312
Flexi RailCard		
4 days in 30	$214	$150
8 days in 30	$306	$204
12 days in 30	$380	$259

Valid for unlimited travel on the entire Italian Rail network including InterCity, EuroCity and Rapido trains with no surcharge. A supplement is required for ETR Pendolino trains. Children 4–11, half fare; under 4 free. Price includes a $15 nonrefundable issuing fee.

Norway Rail Flexipass

| | ADULT | | SENIOR | | CHILD | |
	1ST CLASS	2ND CLASS	1ST CLASS	2ND CLASS	1ST CLASS	2ND CLASS
3 days in 1 month	$172	$132	$138	$106	$86	$66
4 days in 1 month	$213	$164	$170	$132	$107	$82
5 days in 1 month	$240	$185	$192	$148	$120	$93

Children 4–16, half fare; up to 2 children under 4 travel free with one adult. Few trains in Norway offer first class. No supplement required for the Flam Line.

Le Paris Bus
Consecutive Days

	ADULT
2 days	$34

Bus makes a continuouis loop of the major sights in cnetral Paris. Equipped with English-language commentary. You may get on and off the bus as many times as you wish to see such sights as the Eiffel Tower, Notre Dame, Arc de Triomphe, Louvre Museum, the Opéra, and the Grand Palais.

Paris Plus Pass/Le Paris Visite
Consecutive Days

	ADULT
3 days	$64

Provides unlimited travel on all zones of the entire Paris Métro (subway), Paris bus routes, RER trains to the airports, Versailles, Eurodisney, and the funicular at the Sacré Coeur.

Portuguese Railpass

	1ST CLASS
4 days in 15 days	$99

Children 4–11, half adult fare; under 4 free. Not valid on the Luis de Cameos train.

Prague Excursion
Valid for rail transportation from any Czech border crossing to Prague and return within seven days.

	1ST CLASS
Adult	$49
Youth	$39
Children	$25

Youth 12–25. Children 4–11.

Romanian Railpass

	1ST CLASS
3 days in 15 days	$60

Children 4–11, half adult fare; under 4 free.

Scanrail Pass
Valid for unlimited rail travel in Denmark, Finland, Norway and Sweden.

	ADULT		SENIOR	
	1ST CLASS	2ND CLASS	1ST CLASS	2ND CLASS
5 days in 15 days	$228	$182	$203	$162
10 days in 1 month	$364	$292	$324	$260
21 days	$422	$338	$376	$301
1 month	$532	$426	$473	$379

	YOUTH		CHILD	
	1ST CLASS	2ND CLASS	1ST CLASS	2ND CLASS
5 days in 15 days	$171	$137	$114	$91
10 days in 1 month	$273	$219	$182	$146
21 days	$317	$254	$211	$169
1 month	$399	$320	$266	$213

Senior 60 and over; youth 12–25; children 4–11.

Spain Flexipass
Unlimited rail travel in Spain.

	1ST CLASS	2ND CLASS
3 days in 1 month	$196	$154
Additional Days	$40	$32

Maximum of 10 days. The AVE and Talgo 200 require an additional supplement. Children 4–11 travel half price.

Sweden Railpass
Unlimited rail travel in Sweden. Special: Two children (under 16) travel free together with one adult.

	ADULT		ADD'L CHILDREN	
	1ST CLASS	2ND CLASS	1ST CLASS	2ND CLASS
7 days	$340	$250	$230	$170
14 days	$420	$325	$295	$230
3 days in 7 days	$170	$130	$120	$90
5 days in 14 days	$215	$160	$150	$110

Please call Rail Pass Express at (800) 722-7151 for information on a variety of other country and regional rail passes or visit: http://www.railpass.com.

Swiss Card (Ideal for Skiers)
One round-trip rail journey within 1 month.

	1ST CLASS	2ND CLASS
1 month - 1 round trip	$166	$128

Children under 16 free with parent; children 6–15, half adult fare in 2nd class and 40 percent of adult fare in 1st class.

Swiss Pass
Consecutive days

	2 ADULTS*		1 ADULT	
	1ST CLASS	2ND CLASS	1ST CLASS	2ND CLASS
4 days	$211	$150	$264	$188
8 days	$253	$190	$316	$238
15 days	$294	$230	$368	$288
21 days	$322	$255	$403	$320
1 month	$406	$320	$508	$400

Flexipass

3 days in 15	$2211	$141	$264	$176
Additional Days	$24	$19	$30	$24

Unlimited travel on private railways, lake steamers, and city bus lines with any Swiss pass. Children 6–15, half adult fare; under 6 free.
*Price per person based on 2 people traveling together, includes 40 percent companion discount. Children under 16 free with a parent.

Rail Pass Protection
Entitles traveler to a 100% reimbursement on the unused portion of the rail pass if lost or stolen while traveling in Europe or $15 for the driver on a drive pass.
   $10 per pass
See "Drive/Pass Protection" on last page of Appendix.

DRIVE PASSES

BritRail Pass + Car (Option 1)

Valid for 4 days of unlimited rail travel within 2 months and 2 days of car rental for travel in Britain, Scotland, and Wales.

Car	1ST CLASS		2ND CLASS		ADD'L.
Category	2 ADULTS*	1 ADULT	2 ADULTS*	1 ADULT	CAR DAY
Economy	$358	$408	$264	$314	$58
Compact	$378	$448	$284	$354	$76
Intermediate	$388	$468	$304	$374	$87
Comp. Auto.**	$408	$518	$314	$424	$112

3rd and 4th persons are $299 each in 1st class and $205 each in 2nd class. Children ages 4–11 are $158 per child in 1st class and $110 per child in 2nd class. Additional rail days are not offered.

**Compact automatics are available at limited locations.

BritRail Pass + Car (Option 2)

		3 RAIL & 3 CAR DAYS WITHIN 1 MONTH		6 RAIL & 7 CAR DAYS WITHIN 1 MONTH	
Group	Class	Adult	Senior	Adult	Senior
Manual Transmission					
Economy	1st	$393	$360	$740	$689
2dr/4st	2nd	$325	—	$634	—
Compact	1st	$440	$407	$852	$801
4dr/5st	2nd	$372	—	$746	—
Intermediate	1st	$484	$451	$954	$903
4dr/5st	2nd	$416	—	$848	—
Automatic Transmission					
Intermediate	1st	$564	$531	$1141	$1090
4dr/4st	2nd	$496	—	$1035	—
Full Size	1st	$644	$457	$1327	$1276
2dr/4st	2nd	$576	—	$1221	—
Additional Person Rail Supplement					
	1st	$221	$188	$340	$289
	2nd	$153	—	$234	—

Children 5–15 half the adult rail supplement; under 5 free. Includes unlimited mileage and free drop-off. Minimum rental age is 25. Many local trains in England, Scotland, and Wales have Standard Class accommodations only. This is allowed for in the First-Class price.

Eurail/Drive Pass

Any 7 days (4 rail, 3 car) within 2 months for travel in any of the seventeen Eurail countries. Add up to 5 additional rail days and unlimited number of car days.

Car Category	2 ADULTS* 1ST CLASS	1 ADULT 1ST CLASS	ADD'L CAR DAY
Economy	$348	$428	$58
Compact	$378	$488	$77
Intermediate	$388	$518	$87
Comp. Auto.**	$408	$558	$102
Add'l. Rail Day	$50	$50	

Third and fourth person sharing car $259 per person. *Prices per person based on 2 people traveling together. **Cars with automatic shift are available at limited Hertz rental locations. Children ages 4–11 = $130 basic package. Extra days = $26.

Europass Drive

Any 6 days (3 rail, 3 car) within 2 months for travel in France, Germany, Italy, Spain, and Switzerland. No zones may be added.

Car Category	2 ADULTS* 1ST CLASS	1 ADULT 1STCLASS	ADD'L CAR DAY
Economy	$288	$368	$56
Compact	$308	$418	$74
Intermediate	$328	$448	$84
Comp. Auto.**	$348	$488	$98
Add'l. Rail Day	$41	$41	

*Prices per person based on 2 people traveling together. third and fourth person are $199 each. No discounts for children. **Cars with automatic shift available at selected rental locations.

France Rail 'N' Drive

Any 5 days (3 rail, 2 car) within 1 month for travel in France. Add up to 6 additional rail days and car days. 3rd and 4th persons may buy regular rail passes.

Car Category	1ST CLASS 2 ADULTS*	1 ADULT	2ND CLASS 2 ADULTS*	1 ADULT	ADD'L. CAR DAY
Economy	$189	$259	$174	$234	$45
Small	$209	$309	$194	$274	$65
Medium	$229	$349	$214	$314	$85
Small Auto.	$239	$359	$224	$324	$95
Add'l. Rail Day	$30	$30	$30	$30	

German Rail/Drive

Valid for 4 days of unlimited rail travel in Germany and 3 days of car rental. Up to 1 additional rail day may be added.

Car Category	1ST CLASS 2 ADULTS*	1 ADULT	2ND CLASS 2 ADULTS*	1 ADULT	ADD'L. CAR DAY
Economy	$278	$358	$218	$298	$52
Compact	$298	$408	$238	$348	$70
Intermed.	$308	$438	$248	$378	$79
Comp. Auto.**	$338	$488	$278	$428	$96

Additional rail day $40 First Class, $30 Second Class.
*Price per person.
Extra person $189 1st Class; $129 2nd Class.
**Cars with automatic transmission are available at limited locations.

Spanish Rail/Drive

Valid for 3 days of unlimited rail travel in Spain and 3 days of car rental. Up to 6 additional rail days and unlimited car days available.

Car Category	1ST CLASS 2 ADULTS*	1 ADULT	ADD'L. CAR DAY
Economy	$258	$338	$55
Compact	$288	$388	$74
Intermed.	$298	$418	$84
Comp. Auto.**	$328	$478	$102

Extra Person	1ST CLASS
Adult	$180
Child	$90
Add'l. Rail Day Adult	$43
Add'l. Rail Day Child	$21.50

Scanrail/Drive

Valid for 5 days of unlimited rail travel and 3 days of car rental to be used within 15 days.

Car Category	1ST CLASS 2 ADULTS*	1 ADULT	2ND CLASS 2 ADULTS*	1 ADULT	ADD'L. CAR DAY
Economy	$304	$394	$264	$344	$57
Compact	$334	$444	$284	$404	$75
Intermed.	$344	$474	$304	$434	$85

Car rental not available in Finland. Able to add unlimited number of car days. *Price per person.

Drive/Pass Protection

This program entitles you to a 100 percent reimbursement on the unused portion of combination Rail Pass/Drive programs if lost or stolen while traveling in Europe.

> $15 for the driver
> $10 for each additional person

Upon discovery of the loss or theft, please follow these instructions:
1. Report the loss or theft to the local police in Europe within 24 hours and obtain a police report.
2. Mail the following to Rail Pass Express within 30 days of returning home.
   - Notarized written report of the circumstances of loss or theft.
   - Official police report.
   - Receipt for replacement ticket.

Rail Pass Express will reimburse you in full for the unused portion of your pass.

Rail Pass Express, Inc.   Ph: 800.722.7151
2737 Sawbury Blvd.   Ph: 614.889.9100
Columbus, OH 43235-4583 Fx: 614.764.0711
USA   http://www.railpass.com

ORDER FORM

Pass you would like to purchase: _____

Days: _____ Cost: _____

Estimated First Day of Travel: _____

Birthdate: _____

Please indicate whether the pass is 1st or 2nd class, Youth, Adult, Senior, or Child.

Would you like Pass Protection*: Yes No
* *Covers unused portion of pass if the pass is lost or stolen in Europe. $10 per pass.*

● COPIES OF ORDER FORM ACCEPTED FOR LARGER ORDERS / OTHER PRODUCTS ●

NAME AS IT APPEARS ON PASSPORT:

Mr. / Ms. First: _____ Last: _____

Country of Permanent Residence: _____

Mr. / Ms. First: _____ Last: _____

Country of Permanent Residence: _____

DELIVERY ADDRESS (NO PO BOXES): _____

_____

City: _____ State/Country: _____ Zip/Postal code: _____

Phone: _____

PLEASE CHECK ONE:

❏ Visa ❏ Mastercard ❏ American Express

Card Number: _____ Expiration Date: _____

Cardholder Name: _____

Signature (Required): _____

BILLING ADDRESS: _____

_____

City: _____ State/Country: _____ Zip/Postal code: _____

Phone:_____ Fax: :_____

TYPE OF SHIPPING (ALL ORDERS REQUIRE SIGNATURE UPON DELIVERY):

❏ 2-Business Day FedEx – $10.00

❏ Standard Overnight FedEx (8-5 next business day) – $15.00

❏ Priority Overnight FedEx (by noon next business day) – $25.00

❏ Certified Mail (8-10 days) – $8.50

❏ 2-Business Day FedEx (Canada, Hawaii, & Puerto Rico) – $18.00

❏ International FedEx – $38.00